JUDAS WAS A BISHOP

AN OLD MAN IN HIS REFORMING CATHOLIC CHURCH

WILLIAM M. SHEA

ANAPHORA LITERARY PRESS

AUGUSTA, GEORGIA

ANAPHORA LITERARY PRESS
2419 Southdale Drive
Hephzibah, GA 30815
http://anaphoraliterary.com

Book design by Anna Faktorovich, Ph.D.

Cover Image: "The Fight Between Carnival and Lent" by Pieter Bruegel, 1559.

The author welcomes comments on the book either on Amazon.com or at wmshea53@gmail.com.

Published in 2015 by Anaphora Literary Press

Judas Was a Bishop: An Old Man in His Reforming Catholic Church
William M. Shea—1st edition.

Print ISBN-13: 978-1-68114-211-1
ISBN-10: 1-681142-11-2
EBook ISBN-13: 978-1-68114-212-8
ISBN-10: 1-681142-12-0

Library of Congress Control Number: 2015916077

JUDAS WAS A BISHOP

AN OLD MAN IN HIS REFORMING CATHOLIC CHURCH

_____

WILLIAM M. SHEA

CONTENTS

Dedication

To Nathanael and Christopher who have kept a filial eye on the
old man and to my grandchildren whenever they appear.
To William Kremmell of the Presbytery of the Archdiocese of
Boston, at the top of my list of the many priests with whom I
worked and whom I admire unreservedly.
To Charles Curran, Margaret Farley, Elizabeth Johnson, Hans
Kung, and Garry Wills who opened doors that cannot be shut.
To Bernard Lonergan, S.J., whose mind and spirit live on
in the minds and spirits of tens of thousands of students and
readers and who delivered far more than even he thought.
And to Jacob Neusner, the Rabbi and scholar who talks good
Catholic and whose hand Pope Benedict held.

And to Jonathan Swift who wrote these prescient lines in 1731.

Judas
As ancient Judas by transgression fell,
And burst asunder ere he went to hell;
So could we see a set of new Iscariots
Come headlong tumbling from their mitered chariots;
Each modern Judas perish like the first,
Drop from the tree with all his bowels burst;
Who could forbear, that view'd each guilty face,

To cry,
"Lo! Judas gone to his own place.
His habitation let all men forsake,
And let his bishopric another take."

Introduction

For you were once darkness, but now you are light in the
Lord. Live as children of light, for light produces every kind
of goodness and righteousness and truth. Try to learn what
is pleasing to the Lord. Take no part in the fruitless works
of darkness; rather expose them, for it is shameful even to
mention the things done by them in secret; but everything
exposed by the light becomes visible, for everything that be-
comes visible is light. Therefore, it says: "Awake, O sleeper,
and arise from the dead, and Christ will give you light."
                          —Ephesians 5

A playground stands on west side of Castle Hill Avenue in the Bronx, a hundred yards short of East Tremont Avenue. I stood in that playground in a double line in the fall of 1941 with my first grade classmates and about three hundred kids in other grades. We all had our eyes on a Sister of Charity dressed in voluminous layers of black, including a black bonnet with a bow tied under her chin, holding a hand bell. My mother stood in that same playground in 1910, and now she stands pressed against the fence watching me. The yard adjoined red-bricked St. Raymond's School ("the old school") to the south. The rectory of cream brick, three stories high, bordered the schoolyard to the north, where at least four priests lived in the old days. The church, which dominates the neighborhood still, stands on the other side of the rectory. It faces East Tremont Avenue and overlooks the graves of four of its 19th and 20th century pastors, each one a giant in his days, all of them teachers of the ancient faith.

In that church on a Friday afternoon during Lent at the Stations of the Cross, my heart first broke at the sight of Jesus falling under the weight of the cross, and it never got repaired. It was there, too, on Trinity Sunday in 1961 that I kissed the altar stone for the first time. The last time I kissed an altar stone was at the Church of St. Rose of Lima in Gaithersburg, Maryland in December 1979 on the third Sunday in Advent.[1]

---

1   A priest kisses the center of the altar when he begins Mass. There is a relic of the patron saint of the parish, in this case St. Raymond of Penyafort, placed in the altar stone or wood, and by kissing it he honors the

My parents were married in St. Raymond's Church in August of 1934. My mother had been baptized there in 1905, and my brother Tim and I were baptized in 1935 and in 1939, and attended grammar school there. My father was baptized in the parish church in Piltown in County Kilkenny in 1910. I once prayed at my Irish grandparents' grave but never knew them. In St. Raymond's Church in the east Bronx I celebrated my father's funeral Mass in 1977 and attended my mother's Memorial Mass in 1994. They are both buried in St. Raymond's cemetery (not the one where the illustrious pastors are planted) off Tremont Avenue about four miles to the west in a middling sized plot filled with Powers, McClearys and Drohans, my mother's family. I never knew my Power grandparents either. Now I visit the grave and church in the Bronx a couple of times a year to pray for them all and to remember all the ones I knew. My sister died as a two-day old infant and was buried there. I don't shed tears now, in my last years in this vale of tears, but I know whom I have lost. The names are all cut into granite.

After each visit to the grave I drive east on Tremont Avenue, pass through Westchester Square and under the El, and turn left onto Frisby Avenue where I grew until I entered the seminary. From there, I turn right onto St. Peter's Avenue where I walked to and from St. Raymond's School every day for eight years, and on Sunday to and from the church. It is also where the Frisby Tavern stood. Climbing the steps and entering the church I genuflect and kneel and gaze prayerfully around the center of the world where heaven and earth touch. It has always been beautiful in my eyes and it is even more beautiful now, this "Cathedral of the Bronx."

In July 1982 I watched a cone head emerge from the womb of Helene Lutz, the woman I married two years earlier, and in 1984 a second, a roundhead. The sight of the two births joined me to my wife as baptism and the Eucharist joined me to the Catholic Church. I telegrammed my in-laws that first birthday, saying "They used to call me Father but they'll call me daddy now." By then I knew, for the first time in my life, where I belonged. They had become my home.

On Memorial Day 2012 my second son married an unusual young woman—no altar, no priest, no church, no marble statues of Our Lady and St. Joseph. Instead they married on a lawn sloping toward a Maine lake. They made up their own vows, nobody said the old prayers, and the un-ordained minister (a bishop, really, though he would never call himself that) of the bride's housechurch family said no Mass. He wore a striped vest, purple shirt

---

patron. In this case the patron was a Dominican priest and canonist of the twelfth century.

and a creamy white tie with white slacks, no alb and no stole, no mitre and no crosier, and preached and blessed the couple. Though my wife was allowed to offer a prayer for the spouses I was not permitted to participate in any way because I had been a Catholic priest and still am a Catholic (this was a no-no to the ex-Catholics in the house church of the bride founded as it was by a former Catholic priest).

The groom (and his chef friend Matthis Stitt) oversaw the cooking of a hundred pound pig and the groom served three ales of his own making (he's a professional brew master). My first son Nathanael (he's now chief of staff to Senator Sonia Chang-Diaz in the Massachusetts Senate) helped me down the undulating lawn to the lakeside to save me from tripping. Arthritis and age have taken their toll. There were photos to be taken of my wife and myself, my newly married son Christopher and his wife Nichole, my unmarried son and his friend Deborah Opar, and Bridget our greyhound. But no Catholic church, no St. Raymond's, no priest, no Eucharist. The bride and groom are, at this writing, divorced after a year of marriage for reasons having to do with differences in their religions. Nathanael, my elder son, married Deborah on April 18th 2015 at Camp Bournedale in Plymouth MA, by the lakeside, with a Disciples of Christ minister presiding whom we had known since 1991 as a next-door neighbor and friend. Nathanael might as well be called her nephew. But no priest, no church, no Mass. Of course, according to church law neither of the marriages is valid. The second one seems valid to me, but who am I to judge? These two weddings are among the happiest days of my life, but tinged with sadness because the link to the Catholic church was severed.

Something has happened, something so thick with meaning that it is beyond my understanding. I changed from a child to an old man in these eighty years, during which even the elites of the Catholic Church changed in a few small ways, but none of those changes match the enormous and mysterious change in the Catholic people. St. Raymond's Church has remained the same, but the people of the church have not. The Catholic people are darker hued now and they speak different languages. Many Catholics even speak in strange tongues, and the great cloud of priests has dissipated. Young people are leaving the practice in droves. Many Catholics no longer believe that Jesus handed over the leadership of his church to bishops and popes. Neither do I. The marriages of my sons brought home to me the effects of some of these changes. How could my sons, educated as they were in Catholic schools, living their lives in a Catholic home, decide to go another way?

I used to be an academic but this is not an academic book. It's a book about a broken heart and an overtaxed mind (my own). My heart is broken because the church is suffering, and my mind is overtaxed because I can't understand the church anymore. The Church (the leadership that is) revealed itself to me, as one decade ran into another, to be an impossible and distressing melding of holiness and corruption. I am a man who has had a seventy year romance with the Roman Catholic Church, and now I find myself wondering if the corruption outweighs the holiness, a man who knows, whatever the case may be, he can do nothing about it except pray.

I never believed, from the time I was a child, that I could trust the rich and the powerful of the earth, for my father told me stories of the scary carnivores that roamed his land of business. I have avoided them ever since. Between 1968 and 1974 I found out that I couldn't trust American presidents: they turned out to be liars, Democrats and Republicans alike. They were killers of men, women and children, pure and simple, and all in the name of national interest and the preservation of "our way of life." A distressing discovery may I say. It took me nearly half a century of adult life to find out that I must not trust the popes and bishops whom I was taught to revere even more highly than presidents. The institution that I trusted above all others as a child and a young man has failed my trust and hope just as I failed my trust and hope in myself. The Church now seems no better morally than I am.

The circumstances of my life have changed over these decades. For one thing I'm much rounder and two inches shorter than I was fifty years ago. In 1994, when I was fifty-nine years old, I made a Jesuit retreat called "the Nineteenth Annotation."[2] In the notebook I was instructed to use, I wrote this description of myself:

> Qualities: dogged Catholicism, persistence, intelligence, loyalty, anxiety, suspicion of feelings, suspicion of outsiders, suspicion of my own motives and dreams, social unease, humor, simple tastes, easily satisfied, honest, respect for truth... excitement over truth and ideas, willingness to take risks but fear of responsibility, tribalism yet vitally interested in others, overactive emotional system, a dialectical imagination and psyche but a Catholic synthetic mind, a short fuse, high sexual interest, reserved judgments of others, large appetite, love of writing, rhetorical sense and gifts,

---

2   It was given this name after St. Ignatius of Loyola added a note to his *Spiritual Exercises* to let people know that they could spread the famous thirty-day retreat over nine months if they were unable to get time off for the thirty full days.

self-depreciating humor, negative self-image, high moral sense, constructive mind and attitude most of the time, and an ever growing suspicion of authorities.

I wish now that I had found a way over the years to unify all of this and bring peace to my soul, but there doesn't seem to be one at least within my own grasp. Perhaps I needed an exorcism. The peace I now know is not an achievement but a gift given with the grace of the sacrament of marriage. I wish my path had been smooth but I lurched through life.

You may note tension in this self-description, sounding as it does like an astrological reading, and this will be verified in what follows. Much has changed in the past twenty years, yet the description still fits. It fit twenty years before it was written. The big change in me over these seven decades is this: for forty-five years, I was sad and unhappy, but for the past thirty years, I have had more than enough happiness and satisfaction to cover the first forty-five. The sacrament of ordination to the Catholic priesthood did not bring peace of soul; paradoxically, marriage and lay life in the church has brought stability.

The Roman Catholic Church was and has remained my obsession, along with my own inner life and experience. You will see that, too. Surely, I should have paid far less attention to the Church and my throbbing innards and far more attention to Christ and to the rest of the world. I have been, and am, parochial. Neither obsession was I able to break. There has been so much psychic fusion of the mother church of Western Christianity and myself that often I cannot distinguish the two. What hurts "it" hurts me; what is good for "it" brings me joy. Pope Francis brings me joy; the American episcopate makes me sick.

I am part of a story, then, that is far larger and more important than mine, and my living and dying are inconsequential compared with the life of the church. I will die, and all I love will die, but the church will not. The church will never die. A lover once told me that my sense of the church is mythical and not historical. I have tried hard to get that mythic sense under control through reading and thinking. I managed to do so partially but I failed to do so for the most part, thank heaven. Like a magnet pulling iron filings to itself, the church (the people) pulls on my affections and my mind. Compared with being in the assembly of the Catholic saints, living and dead, being an American citizen is a matter of indifference. I would just as happily be a citizen of Mexico or Israel, but I would never choose to join another Christian church.

For all my satisfaction in being a Catholic, I am profoundly sad about the leadership of the Catholic Church. I agree (in their terminology I give "religious assent") to what they teach about God, Christ and the world, but I disagree ferociously with what they teach about themselves. I am aghast at what they have done to the church over the centuries. They think the doctrines about Christ and about the Church are of a piece, and I do not. Their history proves that they are blatantly and tragically wrong about themselves and that they have deceived the Catholic people. When they denominate themselves the Successors of the Apostles, when the pope calls himself the Successor of Peter, then they must be reminded constantly that Judas was an apostle and a bishop according to their own reading of the founding of the church. Thus the title of the book: Judas, fresh in his consecration as an apostle and bishop, walked out of the Upper Room and betrayed Him. The popes and bishops have misinformed and misled the church over the past centuries in their nearly insane struggle against the Protestant reform and later by what they are still pleased to call "the modern world." The culture wars of these centuries may have been Catholic and Protestant but they surely have not been Christian.

In this war against Protestantism and Modernism, they have proved themselves without wisdom and holiness. The ongoing, worldwide clergy sex abuse scandal and their disgraceful handling of it are the final straws in my "awakening." Their misuse of leadership and delusions about themselves are not new, even to an obtuse person like me. Had it been at all possible for them over the centuries, they would have dammed up the grace of God and controlled the divine sluices. God knows they tried. Think of what might have been accomplished in the past five hundred years had they not been so self-centered and so blinded by their own 'humble service'! "If the blind lead the blind, beware lest they stumble into a ditch." (Mt. 15:14) The Roman Catholic Church is in a ditch, a ditch they are responsible for digging.

I may be a heretic but I am not a schismatic. I have no interest in joining another religious community at this point. I am not Martin Luther who started one, nor Jimmy Breslin who imagined one, nor Garry Wills who wants to rid the church of the priesthood. The question for me is, if things are as bad as I think they are, why go on? Why not forget about their Eucharistic table and have dinner with Richard Dawkins and Sam Harris? Two reasons: (1) Richard Dawkins and the latter day atheists are even more wrong-headed about God and religion than the Catholic bishops are about themselves; and (2) I have been, and am, a Catholic because of the Catholic people with whom I have shared life and bread over eighty years, because of the gospel of Jesus, because of the common worship and sacraments, because of my parents in whom I saw the value of Catholic life, and many nuns and priests, and because of the members of the churches I have preached in as a priest and attended as a layman. Their light blinds me!

I have had long and vital experience of Catholic Church life, inside and outside the sanctuary. The church, this 'real church' and not the Vatican, is my spiritual home. I have never been seriously tempted to visit the Vatican and I never will. My home is St. Raymond's Church in the east Bronx and St. Columba's Church in Paxton MA, and all the churches in between. I do not deny that the popes and bishops have borne, and still bear, an indispensable witness to the truth of Jesus and His gospel at the very same time as they play supernatural games with themselves protecting their calling with cultural and legal barbed-wire fences. Catholicism is one way of Christian life, my way of life, and the bishops have a big symbolic, as well as practical, part in it. Nothing is going to change this for me—except excommunication, and that would be nothing but another incident in my Catholic life.[3] Frankly, I don't have much to worry about on this score. The bishops don't care what an ex-priest, or a layman, says or does. To them I am a nonentity. Besides, I don't have enough money to earn their attention even if I were their obedient servant.

I have some proposals to make here and there throughout the first two sections, and especially in the third, that may help in a decent reform of the church.[4] I won't live to see any of it realized, of course. I say here, at the outset, that the general principles of reform have to do with communication and cooperation in the church as well as ending the curse of clericalism and hierarchism and their attendant corruptions, the primary blocks to a decent Christian community life. The narratives have to do with these themes overall: why the church holds my heart still, how the hierarchy has screwed

---

3   I was excommunicated in 1980-1983 because I married without Vatican approval. I was restored to communion when the Congregation of the Doctrine of the Faith allowed me to marry in a Catholic ceremony just after Christmas, 1983. See appendix 9 below.

4   Archbishop John Quinn, *Reform of the Papacy* (NY: Herder and Herder, 1999) and *Ever Ancient, Ever New: Structures of Communion in the Church* (New Jersey: Paulist Press, 2013). His suggestions for reform are mild and strictly in accord with the doctrines about the hierarchy which I reject. Perhaps Pope Francis will take Quinn's suggestions seriously. The pope could do worse. For example, the pope might take advice from my archbishops, Rigali and Burke, formerly of St. Louis and now cardinals of the Catholic Church who were driving the Church when it went into the ditch.

up, how I myself messed up my own Christian life, how I was saved by a woman and two sons (they broke the dam of sin and sadness), and how the church could be saved from The Church now in the present crisis. The book is meant to be a thoughtful reflection on my life in the church. It isn't meant to cover all the bases, just some of the important ones, admittedly with an occasional sprig of well-deserved vitriol.

My usage of the term 'church' may be a cause of confusion. I have tried to be consistent but I may in places have failed. By "The Church" and 'Church,' I mean the hierarchy and their attendant clergy. By "the church" and "the churches," I mean the assemblies of Christians all over the world that are in basic communion of baptism, faith and hope in Christ. Of course the hierarchy are members of the church, too, when they are not exercising their magisterial powers and lording themselves over the church. They, too, even if it is harder for them, can be Christians. The 'church' I consider to be the church catholic designated in the creeds, and it includes the assemblies of Catholics, but is not restricted to Catholic Christians alone. I do not intend to argue over the usage of these terms but simply adopt it in accord with my own thought and experience. The distinction fits the traditional and contemporary usage of hierarchical figures, including the second Vatican Council. It also articulates my state of mind and soul, my moral and doctrinal judgment of the hierarchy, and my solution to the problem confronting the church now.

To keynote the theme of the book, let me quote words from an editorial in the *National Catholic Reporter* on the removal of Bishop Robert Finn from the Diocese of Kansas City, MO.

> It may seem unfair that Finn had to take this role. Bishops and cardinals who should have faced criminal prosecution for covering up crimes more extensive and horrible by many degrees than those ignored by Finn have avoided, via legal technicalities, such scrutiny and gone quietly to either retirement or the grave.
>
> Bishops overseeing the crisis dismissed themselves for decades from any responsibility in the scandal. It was a brazen attempt to sidestep the mountains of evidence revealing that they had long ignored the plight of child victims while engaging in elaborate schemes to hide the heinous behavior of thousands of priests. Any lack of fairness is the result of nothing more or less than the clerical culture that looked first to protect itself and its privi-

leges. Only when forced by legal processes and public pressure did bishops deign to consider the deep wounds inflicted on the most vulnerable in the Catholic family.

Finn's example shows how easily those in authority can ignore even the most basic steps in prevention. The church has made tremendous strides in such areas as requiring background checks, educating both adult ministers and children appropriately regarding proper boundaries, and creating safe environments for children. However, the recently released annual Report on the Implementation of the Charter for the Protection of Children and Young People makes clear that continued diligence is essential—but is in some places lacking. [5]

Yes, "diligence is essential" in all cases where children are at risk but diligence in the case of the Catholic Church is far from a solution. The editorial is quite correct in pointing to the irresponsibility of bishops (and popes!), and in its claim that "clericalism" is at the root of episcopal and papal failure. But the crisis is so severe and coheres so well with Catholic clerical culture that only a thoroughgoing reform of the what is universally regarded as the "Catholic system" (that is, hierarchy) itself will prove adequate. If you and I want to set in motion a reformation of the many evils of clerical culture, then clerical culture must be eviscerated, and we won't get that with otherwise indispensable "due diligence." In my view, we will only reform the system by changing the system and eliminating the clerical culture of which I was a willing part for almost thirty years. This is the view I wish to press in the last two sections of the book. The first section, serving to introduce the rest, is on my part in the clerical mess.

Notwithstanding my apparent anti-clericalism, I remember with gratitude and affection all (or almost all!) the priests I have known. I love and respect them from Fr. Daniel Shea who married my parents in 1934 and baptized me, to Monsignor Myles Bourke who taught me the Bible in my seminary years, and to Fr. William Kremmell who is my model of a parish priest. They don't make the church—Christ makes it—but they make the church catholic. The hierarchy, on the other hand, has made it by their exclusions just another denomination. It should be impossible for a pope to be a sectarian but ordinarily they have been such. The more powerful the hierarchy, the less an assembly of God and Christ the church becomes. They like to proclaim themselves our servants but they are not servants, they are masters and they mean to be such. They suppose themselves to provide the church with unity yet they divide it into cliques. Not because of them but in spite of them there is hope, the second of the cardinal virtues, which carries us on to things unseen. In the long run, it is these three, faith, hope and love, which continue to make me Catholic.

Finally, I would like to thank those who read parts of the manuscript and tried to save me from myself, among them Frs. Bill Kremmell and Ken Brown, Professors Darrell Fasching and Francis Nichols, and for the comments of Professor Margaret Mary Kelleher, O.S.U. and Dr. Michael Lacey. I am proud to have known them all and grateful for their honesty.

And so, on to the story.

Section 1.

The Priesthood

Coming and Going

1. Apologia

A *New York Times* reporter visited with Fr. Hans Kung, a highly regarded (by many outside the Vatican) Swiss Catholic theologian, in his office at Union Theological Seminary in New York. Kung held a visiting professorship at the time (c. 1970). The reporter told Kung that a vesicle had been discovered by an Israeli archeologist that contained bones that may be the bones of Jesus. He asked Kung what he would make of that. Kung responded that his faith would not be at all shaken if Jesus' bones were recovered since the Resurrection of Jesus was a spiritual, not a material phenomenon. The reporter continued down the long hall until he came to the office of Fr. Raymond Brown, S.S., perhaps the leading Catholic biblical scholar in America at the time (one must always make room for Joseph Fitzmyer, S.J.). The reporter repeated the story of the vesicle and the bones, and added that Fr. Kung said he would not be at all discombobulated by the discovery of the material remains of Jesus. Fr. Brown said that the issue is not whether Fr. Kung would be surprised but whether Peter, James, Andrew, John, Philip, Bartholomew, and the other six Apostles would be surprised. In this possibly apocryphal story, I join Fr. Brown. I certainly would be surprised and more. After all, what is the point of a "spiritual" resurrection of a human being? Are we Gnostics? Are we spirits waiting to be liberated from the flesh? No, we *are* our flesh. If the flesh is not saved, we are not saved. This is the original and ancient Christian doctrine: if Jesus is still in the grave, we Christians are the most unfortunate of people. (1 Cor. 15:13-19) With this, Paul drew the line between Christians and Gnostics.

Again, let us suppose that Jesus were found to be a child molester. Would that tell on our belief that he is the Messiah and Son of God? Would our faith be challenged? Well, of course it would! Suppose we found out that the Apostles, once they realized the cost of discipleship and that a rainy day was sure to come, banked all those collection funds meant for the poor in Jerusalem and prepared for a comfortable retirement. What would be our grading of their witness to the Risen One? Certainly an "F." Who's going to believe an embezzler? Suppose the self-proclaimed successors of the Apostles, the bishops of the Catholic Church, were found to be hiding child-molesting priests from public exposure. Essentially, they would be passing them on to new victims, and thereby deliberately thwarting even the minimal legal processes and moral standards of protection of children and the administration of justice. Suppose that bishops and popes were found to be among the molesters, the fornicators, the adulterers, receivers of bribes. What would their witness to Jesus's resurrection be worth? Not much, I'd say. The North African Catholics of the fourth century known as Donatist heretics did have a point after all: the Christian witness of the morally reprobate is very difficult, if not impossible, to take seriously. After all, Jesus himself was a righteous man and his own contemporaries didn't believe him. Shall we take seriously priests and bishops who toy with children? I think not. In fact, we might be tempted to conclude that they were not successors of the Apostles at all and that priests were not "other Christs."[6]

Simply put, if you betray the church you shouldn't be leading the church. When Benedict XVI told us that the evil confronting the church these days is not outside the church but within it, I agree. However, it is still hard to know exactly what evil he refers to and where precisely it is "within." He surely didn't mean his brother bishops—else he would have had to act to clean up the moral mess. Yet that is precisely where the mess is and he did next to nothing about it except talk, accept a few resignations, and approve changes in some procedural rules and policies that his bishops in America too often ignored even though they wrote and voted on them.

Oh, true enough, a bishop or an archbishop here and a cardinal there have resigned when their own sexual behavior was so egregious that the public wouldn't stand for it. But as for those who cover up the crimes, few if any have been removed. The pope might fire an Australian bishop for merely suggesting that the Church might consider the ordination of women but he couldn't bring himself to correct cardinals and archbishops who lied in their teeth to grand juries in sworn depositions. The same men sit upon the same thrones (only the faces and names change—a Rigali retires and is replaced by a Chaput, an Egan by a Dolan), wearing the same silly hats, the same sacred gloves, rings, vestments, the same slippers, carrying the same shepherds' staffs, and looking and acting like not one of the Twelve ever looked and acted. Surely, everyone knows that Benedict's successor(s) are unlikely to dethrone any of them, never mind some or many or all of them.[7] In fact, the popes

---

6   "Other Christ" (*alter Christus*) is a designation of a Catholic priest. It carries the same message as "successor of the Apostles" and "successor of Peter." But every Christian is another Christ.

7   We must wait upon the workings of the office announced by Pope Francis (June 2015) to review the actions of bishops during the abuse crisis to see if it will produce genuine reform of the episcopacy in this matter.

seem to be doing with the offending bishops just what the bishops did with the sexual abusers—covering for them and moving them hither and yon, and above all forgiving them in brotherly sentiment. Think of Cardinal Bernard Law. The Catholic Church that I have grown old and sad in is morally as moldy as it has so often been in the past. The mold is not quickly or easily removed, and it has immense powers of regeneration.

Of course, Catholics, especially bishops and popes, have the ready answer they've been hawking without a blush for fifteen hundred years: sins, they say, are the sins of individual Christians, not of the sinless church we all reverence as the Body of Christ. Double-speak, if you ask me. There is, according to them, no such thing as Sin in the church but only the sins of individual leaders, but for them the Bride of Christ remains as sinless as her Groom. Even though they are self-proclaimed successors of the Apostles their sin is theirs and not the church's! No one, it appears, can say that the "church" is responsible for the moral collapse of its leaders any more than Germany killed Jews, or America tolerated and promoted slavery "from sea to shinning sea"! The mythic and mystical Church remains pure while children are raped by her servants. This is a stunning case of dissociation. It has to be self-deception, for the True Church smells of mold again. We shall take this issue up later on again and again, but I must now take a step further into the mystery of evil, and for this meandering there is a theological point as well. For it seems to me that as the church is responsible for the sins of Churchmen and Churchwomen, God is responsible, both as creator and sustainer, for the immense suffering involved in human and animal existing, for every fire ant bite, every pound of road kill, every victim of a serial killer as well as the serial killer, and the dead and wounded of every war, for your death and mine, even for the terrifying violence that exists across the material universe. For the sake of a higher good, some tell us, God watched Jesus suffer and die—as God watches every son and daughter suffer and die. The witnesses tell us that the Resurrection of the Son and promise of resurrection for us all overmaster suffering and death as God recreates the cosmos but they don't tell us how God gets off the moral hook for all the suffering and death, as they have no explanation how the church gets off the moral hook for the sins of its ministers.

However, I don't believe that resurrection erases suffering and death any more than forgiveness erases sin. Nor will a new creation on the Last Day, when a new Jerusalem comes down from heaven as a bride adorned for her husband, replace the old world that groans under the burden of sin, suffering and death. (Rev 21:

9ff) If everyone, and most of all the Jews, forgive the Nazis, there remains the Shoah. No forgiveness can erase that, not even God's. Even if *God* forgives them, still there remains the Shoah. When God raised Jesus from the dead, there still remains the cross with the broken corpse on it. Here is the reason for atheism: God never explains evil or the part He/She plays in it. True, God tells us how to face up to it, but never does God reveal its origin except by way of the story of the talking snake.

I'm trying now to distinguish Christian fact from Christian fiction. Christ didn't die *in the past* for our sins and rise for our justification as St. Paul wrote to the Romans; he *is* dying and he *is* rising. How come? God's "past" cannot be erased any more than ours can. We have a past but God has no past just as God has no future. Many philosophers, almost all of them long dead white males, have suggested that the God who is out of time (infinite) is thereby present in every moment of time. This makes a great deal of sense to me, especially since I would approve of holding God responsible for the bad times as well as the good. For if God is eternally present in every moment, then every moment is eternally present to God. These moments, their moral content, and their every pain (and every joy!), are eternally a content of God's eternal present. The scholastic philosophers called that present the *nunc aeternum*, the Eternal Now. We, in our time-bound state that forever passes and never stands still, ARE. Please try to put yourself in this perhaps fanciful but logical frame of mind: there is no "was" and will be with God as there is with us. What was and will be for us, IS for God.

There are attractions to this line of thinking but there is a problem as well: Jesus IS forever on the cross and the sins of the forgiven are forever in the mind of God. God doesn't forget because God doesn't have to remember. God is *there*—or *here* as you will. The Resurrection, which is eternal as well as temporal, does not cancel out what God confronts. The lash is being laid, the Blood still spurts, the prayer for our forgiveness is being gasped. According to the letter to the Hebrews in the New Testament, when the risen Jesus entered the heavenly temple to offer the sacrifice, it, he (and we!) were already *there/here* in the presence of God. Given the divine presence to every moment and the presence of every moment to God, we'd have to say that God has no memory just as God has no foresight. God doesn't need to remember or foresee, for everything that was, IS, everything that will be, IS.[8] Our suffering, our

---

8   The ancient toy of theologians, Catholic and Protestant, the divine fore-knowledge, is thereby a moot question. God doesn't fore-see anything; God "sees" everything. Why God permits pain and evil, though, is

pain *is*—just as God *is*. And so with sin: the sin that I did before the eyes of the Almighty, I *am* doing before the eyes of the Almighty. Papal sins, episcopal sins, my sins may be forgiven, but they are not forgotten. I expect that in heaven I will see it all as God does, but I do not now see it as such. Forever in the mind of God there is every act of child molestation by priests and bishops. Thank God that I can forget!

Pardon me for searching for a way to hold God close to pain, suffering, and even sin and evil. I have not entirely bought the tale that the Serpent, Adam, and Eve alone are responsible for the mess. (Gen. 2:15ff) That's a great story and there is some truth to it, but I want to lay the mess on the doorstep of heaven. I want, like Job, to interrogate God knowing that God is even more dangerous for me than God was for Job (Job, after all, was a righteous man and I am not). Perhaps, like Job, I will learn that God is innocent, comprehends all, but mysteriously wills only good to be. This is one tough project, though. I do interrogate and have gotten no response. I get only eternal silence on one side and theological platitudes on the other. I am unable to get God off the hook for the world that *is*.

I must suppose that this problem, then, is part of the *Mystery of faith*, and perhaps the heart of it. I must say this, otherwise I will go mad and perhaps become Richard Dawkins or Christopher Hitchens, the "Ditchkins" as Terry Eagleton calls them, our century's village atheists.[9] The *Mysterium fidei*, as far as I am concerned, is exactly what it was for me at age ten when God did not answer my plea for relief from pain: the Man is innocent and yet dies in pain, and this is what God wants (or does He?). The Man falls, he rises, and he falls again. Again, the evil overwhelms him, and again he falls. For what? We are supposed to live this way ourselves? Suck it up, as they say.

What follows are tales about sinful men in a sinful church and a guilt that no one can escape, not God, not the Bride of Christ, and most of all not me. Unlike popes and bishops, we Catholics live in a church that fails and is broken daily as we are. We Catholics have no ideal sinless church as bishops and popes do. We have only the real one, one that is not innocent and surely belongs in the dust, on its face, under the weight of the wood, and on the wood and in the air.

There are, as I mentioned, three parts to this book. The first part tells about the struggle of an unrighteous man for some semblance of righteousness in a church that, he is told, is righteous. The sec-

---

still a mystery.

9   Terry Eagleton, *Reason, Faith, and Revolution: Reflections on the God Debate* (New Haven: Yale University Press, 2009), *passim*.

ond tells about the man's various encounters with the hierarchy of the church and his internal wrestling over what to do. The third lays out my view of a (unlikely) reform of a Church still dominated by dreams of the Constantinian era. In addition, three chapters follow on related church issues that have mesmerized me for half a century. I do hope you will find the book interesting and valuable, even if things do not turn out well. Nothing does. We all die, and good doesn't always triumph in our time, but that is no excuse for keeping our eyes closed and our mouths shut.

2. Memories of the Priesthood

While living with my parents and my younger brother Timothy in a three-room apartment in the east Bronx and attending a Catholic high school, I contracted a vocation to the priesthood. Let's get one thing straight at the outset: I liked being a Catholic priest. I celebrated the Eucharist with joy, I heard thousands of confessions, and I preached happily. I was at home with thousands of Catholics who made up the parish communities I ministered to, and whom I counseled and taught. I have never regretted being ordained or doing parish work. However, I write with much sorrow (but with little regret) about chastity and me. I chose to be a celibate priest and then married civilly, and, therefore, I was excommunicated. Later, as it is called in Catholic parlance, I was "laicized" or "reduced to the lay state." I became what over half a century ago one author called a "Shepherd in the Mist."[10]

Both of those choices are still mysteries to me, the first a good deal psychologically thicker than the second. Not that I don't know a lot *about* both choices but I haven't reached the roots of either. Some might suggest that they remain mysteries simply because both were free. Freedom is always mysterious. If so, I think that the decision to leave and marry was free and the decision to be ordained was not completely free. Bernard Lonergan, in a lucid analysis of freedom in *Insight: A Study of Human Understanding* (1957), distinguished between essential freedom and effective freedom.[11] To adopt his terminology, I was essentially free when ordained and effectively free when I married. This is how I see it now.

The first mystery was my vocation, my training (1953-1961), and its culmination in my ordination to the priesthood — something that shouldn't have happened but did — plus the nineteen years of priesthood that followed. What I'd like to do here is comment on

---

10   E. Boyd Barrett, *Shepherds in the Mist* (New York: McMullen Company, 1949), a taste of pre-Vatican Council Catholics' appreciation of the priesthood and what was thought of "fallen priests." Barrett was a fallen priest who later in life was restored to communion but not to the active priesthood. He was allowed to be an altar boy. I am not allowed even that honor.

11   *Insight, A Study of Human Understanding* (New York: Philosophical Library, 1957): 619-633.

two aspects (celibacy and psychology), of the twenty-seven years (1953-1979) in which I trained for and practiced the priesthood. My point is that (a) I was afraid of becoming a priest but even more afraid of not becoming a priest; and that (b) celibacy was not an active part of the decision to be ordained. In fact, I turned as blind an eye to it as I could manage even in training, the worst mistake a man could make who decides to be a priest in the western Catholic church.

Over seven years following my ordination, I served in three New York parishes under three pastors, living in rectories with a total of eight other priests, including the three pastors. Later I lived and taught at the College of New Rochelle (1968-1971) while I attended graduate school at Columbia University, living with two priest-chaplains of CNR in succession, both of whom married before I did by some years. To isolate myself in order to write my doctoral dissertation I moved from the college to a fourth parish (1971-72). Here, I lived with two priests, one a pastor and the other an associate pastor, the latter a seminary classmate and friend. The duties were light and I came close to completing the dissertation in a year. Then, in the summer of 1972, I took a job teaching theology and religion to undergraduate and graduate students at The Catholic University of America (CUA) in August 1972. It lasted until May 1980. While at CUA, I regularly said Mass on weekends at a Maryland parish (St. Rose of Lima in Gaithersburg MD) for five years. There I preached my last sermon in December 1979 (see appendix #6). I left CUA in December, moved to Yale Divinity School as a visiting scholar, and there, in February, married my fiancée Helene Lutz who had been studying at the Divinity School for the previous year and a half. That was the second and considerably lighter mystery. As far as I am concerned, it is a marriage made in heaven; Helene more than occasionally has her doubts about this.

What follows is not fiction, nor is it *creative* non-fiction. It is a summary statement of an experience that ran on and off from my second year in the priesthood (1962) to the last (1979). I tell of it with much sorrow but little regret, remember. The reader can easily imagine the spiritual agony that enveloped me and perhaps the others involved. By 1962, one year after ordination with its "sacred" promise of celibacy, I became emotionally attached to a female parishioner in my first parish. This upset me so much that I had to ask Bishop Terrence Cooke for a transfer to another parish to get away from the situation. I was already fantasizing about leaving the priesthood and marrying the woman. I was in a complete muddle of mind and emotion, and above all, scared stiff. The attachment was not so much profound as profoundly distressing. At my request, a priest-friend and another woman parishioner helped defuse the situation in the months before the transfer of assignments took place. At this time, unlike the post-Vatican II church, leaving the priesthood was nearly unthinkable. The Great Exodus from the Catholic priesthood was just beginning.[12]

Shortly after the transfer in 1963, I visited a highly touted spiritual director to put before him what had happened and get his advice. He told me I should have stayed in the parish and dealt with the problem. He also said that since I was not a particularly handsome and attractive man, it would be unlikely for me to run into another difficulty of the sort. He didn't understand the most basic thing about women or about me. I didn't visit him again. The woman to whom I was so confusedly attached called me a coward for securing a transfer. She was right. I never contacted her again, nor she me.

In the second parish, I behaved myself quite well, if "quite well" can be taken to mean I formed no overt emotional attachments with women in the parish. However, I was constantly warning myself not to, for the emotional flow from me toward a number of them was powerful. To keep cool was a struggle. Those years were the last in which I even approached the proper practice of chastity. I was about to enter a decade's long hormonal explosion at age thirty.

The pastor of the second parish was so obnoxious and self-satisfied, so clerical, so defensive of his own authority that I couldn't live with him any more than three years. The parish itself was most interesting and a pleasure to work in, but I had begun to think of a way out of parish ministry and considered the possibility of college teaching. Residence and teaching part time at the College of New Rochelle (CNR) to support myself as a graduate student later convinced me that college teaching was at that point something in the neighborhood of a secondary vocation (an avocation). To reach that goal I would need a doctorate, and so while still in the Pelham Manor parish I enrolled in a joint program of Columbia University's School of Philosophy and Union Theological Seminary (liberal Presbyterian) that was housed in a Columbia department for the study of religion. The department was located in a brownstone on 116th Street east of Broadway. I began there in 1965, taking a course a semester in comparative religions, philosophy and theology. By 1968 I realized that I had to get serious about study and so needed to take the required two years of residency (full time course work, nine credit hours a semester), a year of examinations, and

12   Estimated at ten thousand in the USA and a hundred thousand worldwide. See Andrew Greeley, *Priests: A Calling in Crisis* (Chicago: University of Chicago Press, 2004).

then write the dissertation for the doctorate (at least another year), for a total of four years. In 1968 I left my third parish assignment in Bedford Village and spent the summer at Harvard Divinity School trying to learn enough German to pass a required exam, and in the fall moved into the chaplain's residence at the College of New Rochelle as a part time chaplain and instructor and a full time student at Columbia, all of this with the reluctant permission of the Vicar General of the Archdiocese of New York, John Maguire.

Over the next three years I formed a relationship with a divorced woman with children, a relationship lasting until I moved to CUA in the fall of 1972. During the same period of time, another relationship came to a head with a woman I had known for over a decade, a married woman with children. I was so horrified and frightened by the sudden, passionate explosion of this second attachment that I felt forced to break the relationship off immediately and entirely, for fear that my attraction for her and hers for me would lead to the dissolution of her marriage, a possibility I couldn't face morally. Now I must correct myself, for this was the one regret I had over those nineteen years. When I lost her I lost the best friend I had ever had, and I hurt her deeply. I regret both. Desire and clerical self-protectiveness trumped genuine love, and I proved myself a coward once again.

In the seven years at Catholic University of America (CUA), I had perhaps four or five close women friends, to two of whom I was deeply attached and one of whom I came close to marrying. Finally, I found myself in love with the woman I married, a woman whom I had known for a decade and loved for two years before I left CUA at Christmas 1979. We married three times, in fact: once in front of a justice of the peace in New Haven (February 1980), once again in front of a crowd of friends and relatives at her parents' home in Greenwich CT (March 1980), and a third time two and a half years later when I received permission from Rome to marry in the Catholic Church. (See appendix #9) I was intensely happy at all three, far more so than I had been at my ordination twenty years before. I would marry her a fourth time if I could come up with an excuse. In the thirty-odd years since then my spirit quieted a bit and I came out of the teenage tunnel of love.

About this mystery, I have not even a twinge of regret. I needed a woman to love and I found one who loved me and would stick with me. And I needed a strongly Catholic woman, for I had no intention of breaking from the church, communion with which meant the salvation of my soul as we used to say. I still think Divine Providence was and is involved. It took fifteen years, but my prayers were answered in a 1978 graced release from the psychological bond to the priesthood, which held me for twenty-eight years.

My sorrow is that the decision to leave the priesthood took so long to execute, hurting many people in its wake. So much was the priesthood a defining factor in my "identity" that leaving it was even scarier than marrying. Coming to a decision took two years of intense spiritual direction (1976-1978) by a revered Jesuit director, in the course of which he said the decision would come when I was free enough to make it. When I told him that I was coarse and dense spiritually and emotionally, a fact attested to by the rest of this book, he did not disagree. A third year of very effective spiritual direction was given to me by a sister on the ministry team at Georgetown University. The decision was made in 1978 and I spent the next year at CUA looking for a job in a college or university. My avocation was about to become my vocation. Over the year, I sent out ninety applications to colleges and universities and finally found a job in the University of South Florida (USF). I began teaching there in the fall of 1980. It was the one application out of ninety that got a response—those were nerve-wracking months! Before I closed on the job at USF, I even considered studying law or business, work that was far more ill-fitting than the priesthood. Thank God for the university system of the state of Florida!

I am not much of a prayer but I prayed long and hard over that decade. However, my mind was more on my own problem and not as much on God's will, I admit, and the struggle was about me and not so much about God. There was still a spiritual ambiguity that I have not escaped. I have never been well-tuned to the tiny whispering sound of God (1 Kings, 19:12). Like a donkey, I need a mallet to move me (Numbers 22: 22ff).

During this time the spiritual director, imitating St. Ignatius method, would assign me New Testament readings to meditate upon, asking me to watch and listen in imagination to the dialogue, and would ask me at our next meeting "what did Jesus say to you?" Without exception, my response was "nothing." I couldn't figure out what the director's question meant. Several years earlier, after undergoing the spiritual exercises of St. Ignatius for nine months with its concentrated daily prayer, I did the same and concluded that there was No One on the other end of the celestial phone and stopped calling altogether. The God who was always present was also always silent, or, better, I was unable to hear. But this, too, is another story. Right now I want to go on about celibacy and the priesthood.

The second aspect of these long, confused years was psychological, as you may well imagine. A year after starting the major seminary education, I fell into a depression from which pleas to heaven and spiritual direction did not extract me. The philosophy courses in the seminary alone were boring enough to bring on depression. It lasted, on and off, for most of the academic year (1956-57) and, because of it, the seminary spiritual director sent me to a priest-psychologist at a suburban psychiatric branch of St. Vincent's Hospital. I do not recall meeting him more than once, and I don't know what he told my spiritual director, but the director proposed that I take the next year off.

I was still deeply depressed enough to inform my father and mother during summer vacation that I had decided to leave the seminary. My father refused to accept the decision. He told me to return to the seminary and if I need to quit, quit from there. I agreed, mistakenly but perhaps providentially, to stay. The decision was more my father's than my own. I was caught, a coward if I quit and a coward if I did not, and either way searching for agreement and support of the high command. I needed someone to tell me what to do, and my father obliged. My praying, too, had been an attempt to get God to tell me what to do; only God did not oblige. What I did not want was to decide for myself and take full responsibility for an unambiguous life.

The depression vanished as soon as I became fascinated by the study of the Scriptures and theology in my third seminary year. Odd that my introduction to historical study of the sacred text should so grip me! Depression did not return till three and a half years later, in the three months leading to ordination. I was so perturbed at the prospect of ordination that I lost twenty-five pounds in one of the very few times my appetite failed me. During the final retreat, six days of silence before the day of ordination, I called a priest friend and ask him to come to the seminary. I told him I wanted out of ordination and asked him to help me. I was sure I was making a mistake being ordained. He told me that this "butterfly effect" was common and not to worry about it. I don't think he understood the swirl of spirit I was in. It was not the butterfly effect! But I took his advice and went ahead with the ordination on the eve of the feast of the Holy Trinity in 1961 and celebrated my first Mass the next day in St. Raymond's Church. This did not promote a psychological release, and I suffered the two days in a state of high tension with a sense of distance from the people around me, as if I were witnessing the celebratory gathering of family and friends rather than participating in it. My parents were ecstatic.

My first parish assignment to Our Lady of Mt. Carmel church in Yonkers was an exciting total immersion into the work of a priest in a parish of working class Italian-Americans of the first and second generation. The pastor, Joseph P. Caramanno, was one of the most genial, kind, and pastoral men I have ever met. He was also leery of the diocesan authorities, and was overworked and over-burdened with responsibility. He gave me my head and I flourished, in a short time becoming like him overworked, over-burdened and strongly wary of diocesan authorities.

In Pelham Manor, my second parish assignment (1963-67), I ran chest-to-chest into a pastor who had earned a diocesan-wide reputation as impossible to live and work with. There had been various assistant priests, one after another, who chose to leave the parish rather than work with him. He was a dedicated, domineering, snippy pack-leader without out a pack. I believe he was a frustrated bishop-in-waiting. I watched him several times a year preening himself is his pseudo-episcopal garb. He got to dress as a bishop on those occasions. He occupied a minor hierarchical slot referred to by the lowest rung clerics as "mule bishops," i.e., they dressed like bishops on occasion but couldn't reproduce. Desiring to be a Successor to the Apostles, the most he was able to squeeze out of the system was the costume. He was an alpha male, the ultimate clerical alpha being Saint John Paul II. He tried to civilize and socialize me into the clerical state but I quickly fell into my usual patterned response to authority figures, resentful silence and minimal contact. I hated sharing meals with him, something I had to do five times a week, three times a day. After a year or so of this tension I blinked (he never did) and tried to make nice. He at one point proclaimed himself worried (presciently!) about the validity of my vocation to the priesthood, but in the end we had become chummy enough that he drove me to my next assignment to introduce me to my new boss as a fine assistant priest. Perhaps he thought he had tamed me, but he was too shrewd a judge of the ecclesiastical scene to be fooled by the likes of me. I think he knew that I had sought another assignment.

I fell into a second acute depression in those years in Pelham Manor, suffered stomach cramps, made the acquaintance of *Tums,* and began a three-year monthly visit to a psychiatrist, a specialist in family therapy. This was an extraordinary educational experience on human emotion in close relationships—and distant ones, for that matter. He remarked that a celibate ought to have a close personal relationship with Christ, and that I didn't seem to have one. That was a genuine insight. I had thought my apperception of Christ was quite lively, but in fact, it was a sliding amalgam of distance and fusion. He said this at the time I had moved out of parish work to the College of New Rochelle (1968), and had begun an intense affair.

Thinking that I should close some of the gap between my parents and myself, at least in their knowledge of me and of my fear of disappointing them, the psychiatrist, Doctor Thomas Fogarty, asked my parents to attend some sessions with me. It didn't work. They broke it off after the first session. The discussion that day was about affection in the family, and about what family therapists call distance and closeness. They were distressed by the discussion and refused any part in it. I recall that he asked my parents to hold hands, something I cannot remember them ever doing. Months later Fogarty asked me to tell them of the affair I was having. I did, but it didn't help at all in the short run. I was a thirty three year old priest announcing to his devout Catholic parents that he was regularly having sex with a divorced mother of three. Imagine the impact of that if you can. Add three more years of spiritual counseling by experts, between 1976 and 1979, and you get the picture of a man in a moral and emotional fog trying to find a way out of the fog, but unable to do so except by quitting the priesthood. Did I have a problem with the priesthood or with celibacy? Both, alas, and I shall try to speak to both.

First, I must address the priesthood. I am not a communal person in practice. I very much liked the people I met and loved helping them whenever that was possible, but it seemed most often impossible. I worked hard, felt privileged to hear the confessions of my fellow Catholics, found much happiness, even exultation, saying Mass and preaching. I liked counseling though I didn't know what I was doing. I liked the day-to-day work of the priest, some of it bureaucratic, and loved the teaching often involved in parish life. The school children and altar boys were a frequent source of joy. I didn't like visiting hospitals and conducting funerals—I felt an inability to help the suffering and dying and felt very uneasy in sharing the burden of bereavement. I couldn't in conscience, preach the Roman Church's obsessive sexual ethic (pre-marital and extra-marital sex, birth control, abortion, divorce and remarriage, etc.). I could talk about them in the confessional or the counseling sessions but never from the pulpit.

I stopped the required daily reading of the Latin Divine Office (an hour's worth of psalms and prayers) within a year or two after ordination, though I did read it in English for a while rather than the required Latin. I did have several good friends within the priesthood and I enjoyed most of the priests with whom I worked, always joining gleefully in the barracks humor and camaraderie that infest the daily life of men in the absence of women. However, I avoided the requisite clerical gatherings, including the annual ordination ceremony in St. Patrick's Cathedral and my class annual reunion dinners where clerical fellowship was to be cultivated. I didn't like the clerical street garb and dumped it as early as I could coincident with my move to the College of New Rochelle in 1968. Clerical garb and clerical gatherings were a bother from the outset. I could drown in that sea of black! Where I didn't have to be identified as a priest, I didn't want to be identified as a priest. I didn't enjoy the social life that parish priests must engage in (e.g. marriage receptions and parish social functions, etc.). I found myself uncomfortable in crowds when acting as an official—except when celebrating Mass. I enjoyed the people whom I got to know on a family by family basis, I enjoyed being with those three or four priest friends whom I found sympathetic and admirable. I also liked to eat and drink. I put on those twenty- five pounds I had lost prior to ordination in my first year in the parish where I began, an Italian parish with mothers who thought that it was an obligation of faith to fatten up the skinny Irish priest, and cooked what couldn't be refused. So the life of a priest was a peculiar combination of happiness mixed with sadness and distance.

There was also something else that remains hard to state simply: an elation that overcame me often when I celebrated the Eucharist. It was an unbidden joy that was, ironically, deeply troubling. The joy seemed not to come from me but it ran through me; it felt like a spirit of unknown origin had taken up residence in me for a short time, minutes really. The trouble was I couldn't tell what that spirit was or where it was summoning me. The same spirit also entered my personal prayer. I couldn't tell whether it was my own soul, the Holy Spirit, or the evil spirit, and so I ended up paying little attention to it. The same elation happens to this day when I am alone and trying to sit with God. Now, I take it as a small, indescribable happiness, a gift to a man who suspects affection. These days I quietly accept the Presence that always seems to be "there," and I know it is not my own spirit or an evil one; it is the presence of the Holy One. But in those days, it felt like a beckoning to a place where I would be lost, swallowed up in something I could in no way control. It might have been a door but I closed it.

And then celibacy: it was never a *religious* fact for me; at best, it was a morally neutral legal obligation. I could make no sense of it religiously as a way to be with God. In the Christian faith, it is a gift of the Holy Spirit surely, but She sailed over me like the angel of death over the houses of the Israelites in Egypt (Exodus 12:23ff). I didn't get it. I wasn't against it, certainly, as an institution of the Western church. I never regarded myself in a position to determine what was or is best for the entire church. I certainly wasn't longing for the ultimate commune, marriage, until I was forty. I thought I could live with celibacy but it became increasingly obvious that

I couldn't and didn't want to. My affections were flying all over the place. I needed to live with a woman, and then with children if I was to live decently. To say that this repulsion from the celibate life and from rectory living was due to sexual desire would be true but took second place to the desire for intimacy and stability which life in the priesthood did not afford me.[13] I didn't want to live alone and certainly didn't want to live with men. I had had enough of that (1955-1979). I needed to be with a woman. I needed a life of privacy and regularity of the sort that is incompatible with the parish priesthood. People come at priests unpredictably. The priesthood was cluttered with ideals and obligations while I was driven by a desire for quiet and a large dollop of order. After thirty years of intimacy in marriage, I can say unequivocally that living with a woman and two sons was exactly what was missing in my thirty incomprehensible years of the struggle with chastity and celibacy. I needed faces, bodies, souls who were mine and me theirs'. I needed a woman and a family. My love of God, of Christ, and of the church couldn't (all three it seems to me genuine), or at least didn't, fill that void. Helene, Nathanael and Christopher did. They put an end to my loneliness. In the seminary, I was offered a clerical bromide: "A priest belongs to all families but is a member of none." I agree if this is taken as a description; as the prescription it was meant to be, it left me cold.

I didn't fit the life of constant love of neighbor and the sacrifices involved in the priesthood, and instead wore the priesthood like a life jacket in a sea of the ordinary life that I feared. It turned out to be something quite different than I expected. I expected to be safe and good. I had long thought ordinary married life to be chaotic and painful, and I was repelled by "making a living" as my mother and father and brother had. I had to grow up fast to make it in the priesthood and I didn't. For a long time I grew down. I knew little about married life but I knew a lot about celibacy, and when the time came, I chose what I didn't understand over what I did. Married life is complicated, often painful, and rich; the celibate life is simple and thin. To this day I can't figure out why The Church wants it for priests aside from the obvious reason that celibacy saves bishops an awful lot of trouble (and money).

---

13   A. Greeley, *Priests*, 60.

3. Dropping Out

I had worked in three New York Catholic parishes over eight years. The first was in the gritty section of Yonkers. Another was in Pelham Manor, a suburban bedroom community for New York executives. The third was in a horsey northern Westchester County town (Bedford Village) where, as usual, Catholics didn't own the horses yet shared modestly in the American dream by living near them. The place actually had a village green, something I had never seen. For a month or so, I wondered why they didn't build on it. During those eight years of parish work, I didn't like rectory living and kept falling in and out of love with women who lived in the parishes. The strains were intense. I gradually edged my way out of parish work and toward something that at the outset I did not understand. But I knew that I had to change direction. I needed something to do that I liked, while finding a way of life that provided order in the midst of the unexpected chaos of a priest's life. In the 1960's I decided that my aim was clear enough, and it was headed for college teaching. In the longer, far more clouded, run was the flight from the priesthood itself. Toward the priesthood my attitude was ambiguous, constantly shifting and conflicted. No one could solve it but myself and I didn't want the responsibility of solving it. Becoming a priest was a difficult enough identity project; even contemplating leaving the priesthood cost a decade's worth of psychic strain.

After three years of part time classes at Columbia University and Union Theological Seminary, I needed to put in full-time class work (residency) for a couple of years. In order to do that, I had to see someone in authority in the archdiocese of New York to get permission. I didn't like bishops. I had only met half a dozen of them in a dozen years and held conversations with none of them. To me, bishops were similar to the two percent of Americans who take up eighty percent of the economic product. Like archangels, they were much rumored but rarely seen. In the official statistics there are currently over one billion Catholics and about five thousand bishops. Not one of the dozen of them in New York, I'm sure, could have picked me out in a lineup—except Terrence Cooke. While I was in training, the future Cardinal Cooke was procurator, that is, administer of the non-academic side of seminary life. He was a warm and respectful superior, with a sense of humor. When the class president, Thomas Farrelly, and I dared tell Cooke that the margarine in the seminary dining room was rancid, he replied that far from being margarine and rancid, the yellow stuff was "the finest whipped butter, whipped so well that it may have taken on a slight cheese tang." He said this with a straight face and then broke into a broad smile. We smiled back. The margarine improved. My only other discussion with him until the last one took place during a priests' retreat in June of 1963 when I asked him to arrange a transfer from my first church assignment because I had become emotionally confused and psychologically stressed over my relationship with a female parishioner. He arranged it. While I had begun to flounder, he was on the ecclesiastical escalator.

Francis Cardinal Spellman, at that time an old man and soon to die (December 1967), was the ruling archbishop of New York. Over the years I saw him only a few times in formal circumstances, and I may even have genuflected to kiss his ring. I never spoke with him. He was a chubby little man who seemed to walk on his toes, nodding side to side with what he must have taken to be a cherubic smile. He scared the lower clergy. He was a real big shot and I wanted nothing to do with him. By dint of Spellman's pull in the Vatican, his vicar general was also an archbishop. Generally for an archdiocese to have two archbishops is an anomaly, but then again Spellman himself was an anomaly of sorts. Archbishop John Maguire, oversaw the day-to-day life of the Catholic churches from Staten Island to Kingston, from the Catskill Mountains to Long Island Sound, so he was in charge of priests. He had a head like an intercontinental missile and a neck like the Minotaur. He scared me, too. These sacred men were charged with even more of that fearsome divine authority that possessed my father. For my kind of business (a release from parish work for fulltime study) I had to see Archbishop Maguire. While Spellman's reputation among priests was that of a sacred version of the Godfather, Maguire's was that of a cold fish, a *consiglieri*. Unlike George W. Bush or Barak Obama, these are not men with whom you'd like to have a beer.

Maguire sat behind an impressive leather-accented desk in a huge wood paneled room with a twelve foot ceiling (maybe even more than twelve) in the old Random House building on the northeast corner of Madison Avenue and 50th Street. It was just across from 452 Madison, the "Powerhouse" where Cardinal Spellman lived. Maguire and the other archdiocesan clerical notables lived in a penthouse atop Random House. I was ushered in by his priest-secretary and seated opposite His Grace at the desk, slightly to his right. I noticed Spellman's episcopal crest on the wall behind Maguire and the unobtrusive crucifix on his desk, and very little else, so nervous was I. The priest-secretary sat at a desk several feet behind me. We ordinary parish priests didn't get to see, or even want to see, Maguire. I had learned a lesson in the seminary: "Flee from bishops as you would from the plague unless you pine for the plague yourself." I met only a few priests whom I was sure were infected with episcopal ambition. One was the pastor of my second parish, a man whom I genuinely detested, a second died an alcoholic, and the third became the cardinal archbishop of Washington D.C.

I told Maguire that I wanted to study theological German at Harvard Divinity School in the summer of 1968 and then spend two years at Columbia to finish my course work and take doctoral exams. When the Archbishop had listened long enough to understand what I wanted (he knew what I wanted beforehand), he took his eyes off me and lowered them to the desk and then, for a split second, across the desk to the crucifix. He raised his eyes again, breathed deeply and slowly, looked at me squarely and said: "You are on the cross. He didn't come down from the cross." I got his point but I said nothing. He stared at me, waiting. He said: "Alright, go. I'll put you on a leave of absence." "Thank you," I said. A line was drawn and I stepped over it. Maguire stayed at his desk while the secretary led me out.

My guess now is that he understood better than I what was going on with me, a conflict that would take me another decade to resolve. If he did realize that I was taking the first step toward leaving the priesthood, he didn't show it. Maguire ordained me to the priesthood in 1961 when Cardinal Spellman was temporarily blinded and so I had a certain sentimental, not to say sacramental, bond to him. Those few moments were the only time I ever spoke with him. He seemed to me far from relaxed and I didn't like being around people, lay or clerical, who had money or power, who could force me to make a decision I was not anxious to make. Maguire could have said no, and then what? Crisis and resignation, perhaps. I was determined in the spring of 1968 to find my own way in the priesthood. I have often wondered what would have happened had he said, "Let's have lunch and talk about it." As it was, autonomy and authority bumped heads at 451 Madison, and autonomy won. I felt it but didn't know what it meant for the long run.

As I came out of the marble tiled Chancery and down the granite steps into the courtyard, I was elated. My joy surprised me. It would be, from the point of view of a good priest, an impure joy over the wrong kind of freedom. I looked across Madison at Spellman's residence and thought, "At least I didn't have to face him." With Maguire behind me in Random House and Spellman across the avenue in The Powerhouse, I recognized that the joy was a release from people who had authority over me. How could a man with such a spirit have become a priest in the Roman Catholic Church and expect to be happy? The priesthood was a bad fit from the start, a mistake that I still do not regret.

A year later, as instructed, I was back in the same building, sitting across a smaller desk in a smaller room opposite a larger priest, one of Archbishop Maguire's administrative underlings, a shotgun really, who breathed quickly and didn't take his eyes off me for a second. He sat back, his manicured fingertips on the edge of the desk. He didn't look angry, just intent; his puffy Irish face utterly still, no trace of a smile, just a stare. I had never met this man though I knew him by reputation, and in three minutes, I detested him. He didn't gaze, even momentarily, at the crucifix. As I sat he asked, "What are you doing at Columbia?" "Working hard," I said. I told him about a year's course work, ten courses in history of religion, Greek philosophy, medieval philosophy, and all sorts of stuff that had bored me in the seminary. I told him I had done pretty well. He tried again: "What are you up to?" I said, "I'm just starting a second year of course work, and then..." "You know damn well what I mean. Just what the hell do you expect us to do with you when you're done?" "I don't know...maybe I could teach." "There's nothing for you to do in this archdiocese," he said. Quick breath. "We're not going to pay the tuition anymore." "OK, I'll borrow the money." "See me in another year." He was one of the people with power over me, and a mean one at that. There was plenty for me to do in the archdiocese and he knew it. He was telling me that a decision had been reached that I was wasting my time and their money. I never saw him—or Maguire—again.

A lot of men were leaving the priesthood in the late 1960's. The archbishop and his shotgun didn't want to push me out the door but they didn't want me working my way out of the priesthood on their dime. As for me, I was still telling myself a story that combined a Roman collar with the degree of autonomy I could live with. But my church leaders didn't put much stock in autonomy. They expected obedience and, though they had no intention of talking about it, they knew exactly what I was "up to," and they were making decisions based on a shrewd guess. The ties were breaking.

By the spring of 1972, I had finished most of my doctoral dissertation on American philosophical naturalists. They held that the cosmos needs no explanation. By then I was living and writing the dissertation in St. John the Evangelist parish in Beacon NY (1971-72). Terrence Cooke had succeeded to the archbishop's chair held so long by Spellman (1939-1967). I had written to the Dean of the School of Theology at the Catholic University of America about a teaching job there.[14] There happened to be a job open and, apparently as a result of my letter, the Dean asked Cardinal Cooke to give his permission for me to take it.

The rector of the major seminary in Yonkers, a former philosophy teacher of mine, called to tell me that Cardinal Cooke wanted me to think about teaching in the college seminary on Long Island. I told the rector I wanted to go to Catholic University to teach. It was a far better academic situation. He told me that the Cardinal would like it if I stayed in the diocese. I said, "Of course I'll do whatever the Cardinal wants. But if he leaves it to me, I'll go to CUA." He said he'd tell the Cardinal that.

When a few days later I got the rector of the Long Island college seminary on the phone and asked him just what job was open in his seminary, he was mystified. "There's no job open here. I wonder where Ed got that idea?" I said to myself, "I've known Ed for fifteen years. Why would he mislead me?" The answer was obvious. The offer amounted to a last stab at keeping me in the diocesan service. The Cardinal might have been willing to create a position there for me, and that was the carrot. But he finally released me to teach at CUA. I had gotten past an archdiocesan trap. At this point, it was clear that I wanted to escape not only from the parishes but from

---

14   Walter Schmitz was dean at the time. I mistakenly assumed that Charles Curran was dean and wrote the letter to him. He passed it on to Schmitz. Curran later told me how amused he was at that assumption. He had been refused tenure at the university just a few years before and only a threatened faculty strike forced the Board of Trustees to offer him tenure. The guillotine fell on Curran in 1987 when Cardinal Ratzinger insisted that he leave the university, no longer to be recognized as a Catholic theologian. Ratzinger might as well have told Stan Musial that he was no longer a St. Louis Cardinal. Cf. Charles Curran, *Loyal Dissent: Memoir of a Catholic Theologian* (District of Columbia: Georgetown University Press, 2006).

the service of the archdiocese as well. This is the message you send when you tell a cardinal you'd do what he wants but, left to yourself, you'd do what you want. The demon of autonomy again! It was supposed to have been driven out of me in seminary training, but like the seven demons in the gospel accounts it was back. (Luke 8:2)

In the seven years that followed, the cloud of ambiguity about the priesthood had dissipated slightly by practical necessity. I had a lot of work to do measuring up academically to the standards of Catholic University, I was very pleased to be there, and I had found a parish that I liked and a pastor that I admired. I could do week-end ministry. I had worked my way up the academic ladder and applied for tenure as an associate professor of religious studies at CUA. Additionally, I had had half a dozen affairs, and had decided to leave the priesthood. Sitting in his sunny and spacious office in Caldwell Hall (another high ceiling), the new Dean interviewed me about my application for tenure. He looked very nervous. He kept shifting buttock to buttock the whole time and toying with the letter opener. He hardly looked at me. "I have to ask every priest up for tenure the same question, Bill. Do you have any intention of marrying?" I didn't think he asked it of everyone. "If I did, it would be between myself, God, and my confessor, Carl. But you can be sure of this: if I did, I wouldn't hurt the university in the process." He was not happy with my response. He had heard via the clerical-academic grape vine that I was applying for jobs elsewhere and now he had from my own lips an indirect confirmation of his suspicion but hadn't gotten the answer he could act on. Since CUA had a unique and legally enforceable statute that forbad a married priest to teach or hold tenure, he would be in a tough spot if one of his priest faculty members was to marry openly and fight legally to remain on the faculty, or even attempt to trade a resignation for a cash settlement. It would have been a losing battle for me and another embarrassment for the university. This had happened once, before the statute was passed, and resulted in an unwelcome cash settlement. At Charles Curran's advice I immediately retained (*pro bono*) a civil lawyer.

A few months later, after tenure was granted to me in the spring of 1979, the Dean had me in again. "Bill, if Cardinal Baum hears about this from anyone but me, he'll be very upset. What are your plans?" "Carl," I said, "keep your hands off me. I'll take care of it, and the university won't get hurt. I'll be here till I get a job. When I get a job I'll leave." "Bill, I'll be forced to go to Cardinal Baum soon." Shit, I said to myself, I'm caught. I've got no job lined up, and Carl is doing his job protecting the university (and himself, it must be said) and, at the same time, warning me. It was time to go to The Residence at 452 Madison.

Helene drove into New York City with me on a cloudy day from her parents' home in Greenwich. This time in the fall of 1979— the only time—I sat in The Powerhouse in a tiny office next to the front door, dark and convent clean, waiting for Cardinal Cooke. I had heard rumors that he had terminal cancer. He came in with my letter in his hand. He sat with his knees nearly touching mine, and talked quietly, without rush. I knew it would not be a long talk. He told me not to worry; my job at Catholic University was safe for the spring semester and for that time I would still be on the CUA payroll. I would not be fired precipitously. I had worked hard for the university, he said, and he was grateful. He would speak with Cardinal Baum, the Chancellor of the university, and tell him that everything is taken care of. He said, "You can start a leave of absence in January and take your academic sabbatical. I'll ask the University to give you five thousand in moving expenses. But please remember, if you receive a special grace, a renewed call to the priesthood, let me know immediately and I'll find a position for you somewhere else in the country." As we stood facing one another I asked him a favor. Would he write to my mother telling her what he just told me, about the fine job I had done at the university? He said he would and he did. My mother got his note months later and it lifted for a moment the worry that enveloped her. I came out relieved. I never saw him again.

Ten minutes in and out, with everything said that needed saying, and nothing left out. None of the conversations with the high priests took more than ten minutes. Not one of them asked how I was doing, what had happened, what price I paid, or what it all meant to me. I had volunteered nothing. We had gotten done what had to be done. They didn't want to know any more about me and my troubles than was needed for a Roman administrative decision and I certainly knew enough about them not to want to know them any better. Anyway, the line had been drawn ten years before in Maguire's office when I decided to come down from the cross. Not one of us stepped over that line. How could this be in the kingdom of love and forgiveness where trust should be at a premium and where the black sheep count, too? Not even an exit interview!

It wasn't till I stood on the pavement, looking across Madison at the Chancery, that I realized that Cooke meant he'd take care of me if I wanted to get away from Helene and continue in the priesthood, just as he had done for me in 1963. I turned onto 50th Street, entered the Cathedral by the side door, and found her sitting immediately inside, in front of the altar dedicated to the Virgin. I sat and said to her: "He told me that if a special grace of renewed vocation were to be bestowed upon me he will arrange for me to teach somewhere else." She said with a smile: "You should have told him that your special grace is sitting in the Cathedral." I wish now that I had.

Cooke also asked me to see the archdiocesan spiritual director and then to file a formal request for laicization. I did speak with the Franciscan spiritual director, Fr. Benedict Groeschel, within a week or so after visiting Cooke. It seemed to me that Cooke wanted to file Groeschel's opinion of my mental balance or lack of it, but he also wanted Groeschel to deliver a message that Cooke could not, namely, that the new pope's ban on release from the promise of celibacy made it impossible for me to marry in the Church.[15] Much to my surprise, Groeschel suggested that I go ahead and marry civilly. While that suggestion was both wise and humane, still it was peculiar that I was advised by an official holy man, with Cooke's apparent agreement, to ignore canon law, go through a marriage ceremony that would not be recognized by the Church, and so be excommunicated for marrying without the pope's permission.[16] Had we moved in together it would have been a simple case of serial fornication rather than a case of sacrilegious pretense of marriage by a clerical celibate, an excommunicable offence.

As far as the application for a dispensation from celibacy was concerned, a year later (December 1981) I visited the Tribunal of the Archdiocese (1011 First Avenue) and gave an extensive testimony of my unfitness for and unwillingness to continue in the priesthood. This was to clarify and provide back-up to my letter of request to Pope John Paul (appendices #7 and 8.). It added some data on my ministry and my failures to live a celibate life and so might have proved embarrassing and even humiliating had it not been for the extraordinary sensitivity and professionalism of the interviewer, a vice-chancellor of the Tribunal, Msgr. Desmond Vella. He drew out of me the connection between my increasing detachment from the practice of the priesthood and my un-chaste life. I'm sure that the papal dispensation that arrived two years later (1983) hung to a

---

15   The new pope was John Paul II and the ban lasted from 1978 to 1982.

16   See *The Code of Canon Law* (cf. Canon 1394. #1 & 2; 1395, #1 & 2; 194, #3).

considerable extent on Vella's expert questioning and Cooke's rec-
ommendation. For his sympathetic handling of a difficult situation
I remain, forty years later, deeply grateful. The Church is sometimes represented by human beings and Christians.

4. From the Sacred to the Profane

Exiting the priesthood can be bitter and, like divorce, writing about it should be left to experts. There are serious and responsible social science studies of the priesthood, among them illuminating recent volumes by Andrew Greeley and Dean Hoge.[17] There are a few models for a former priest to follow if he decides to contribute to public understanding. The subject is difficult to talk and write about because, whether for priests, former priests, or Catholic laity, it touches on the deepest wellsprings of Catholic and personal identity. Most of us, and myself certainly, do not know a concrete Catholicism without priests, though there are plenty of examples of Christian churches without them. For me, imagining a priestless Catholicism is near impossible.[18] Without priests, Catholic Christianity is a huge set of communities without heads. Christianity can get along without priests but I believe that Catholic Christianity cannot.

Some scholars would argue that the Catholic Church came into existence not with the Resurrection and Pentecost (the Christian movement did so) but with the rise and spread of the episcopacy and the priesthood during the second and third centuries. Surely, in the absence of priests (I include bishops here), we would have the church and churches but we would have no *Catholic* Church.[19] The Roman Catholic Church is what it has come to be, and the chief agents in its coming to be have been priests and bishops and, for a millennium and a half in the west, the bishop of Rome.

---

17   Greeley, *Priests*; Dean Hoge, *Pastors in Transition: Why Clergy Leave Local Church Ministry* (Grand Rapids: Wm. Eerdmans, 2005). A particularly good example of ex-priest literature is Paul Dinter, *The Other Side of the Altar: One Man's Life in the Catholic Priesthood* (NY: Farrar, Straus and Giroux, 2003).

18   One shot at that is Garry Wills, *Priests: A Failed Tradition* (NY: Penguin, 2013). I disagree just a bit. The priesthood, even a demythologized version, is central to the "Catholic experience." Without the priesthood, you have a "Protestant experience." The priest, even by another name, is not a minister only.

19   The doctrine of priesthood and episcopacy is another matter. Bishops and priests have made all too much of themselves. I don't object to them or their tasks but to what they have made of themselves.

In the face of the few models, then, I assume that my story is much like the stories of other former priests: I found the priesthood a source of constant and various tensions. I tired of the tensions of celibacy, decided I shouldn't live with them, and fell in love, left the priesthood and married. I worked my way out of the priesthood in small steps, over two decades, during which the internal argument involved a complex of personal elements. These elements included loyalty to the church and my promise to it, faith and its meaning for my life, the realization that I didn't like the practical circumstances of the priest's life, the discovery that my becoming a priest had been a way to avoid marriage and family life, my growing resentment of a church leadership that has power and no ears, and the convictions of my parents who thought, as I do, that there is no profane vocation that can match the priesthood both in service and honor. No one else in the Catholic community can say Mass and preach, absolve sinners, comfort the sick and dying with the last sacraments and, as long tradition has it, stand in for Christ (i.e., for the church).

Perhaps social science and historical research in the future will show that there are similarities in the tens of thousands of individual cases, but the resources for such research are meager indeed. Thousands of the priests who exited in the 1960's and 1970's have passed on, and many of the living are hard to find, and so survey work is chancy. There are dozens of memoirs written by ex-priests offered at Amazon.com. There is one vital source that will probably remain untapped: each priest seeking permission to marry is obliged to write to the pope explaining in detail why he thinks he should be released from his ordination promise of perpetual celibacy.[20] These letters might bring the researcher closer to the truth about the struggles men have had in the priesthood and leaving the priesthood. The letter is akin to one's last confession and requires immersion in one's own soul.[21] It certainly did in my case. I for-

---

20 Celibacy is a promise to one's bishop, not a vow to God. Celibacy is not to be confused with chastity. Celibacy involves a promise not to marry. For one who makes that promise, as I did, cannot sacramentally marry without papal permission. Chastity is a virtue incumbent on all Christians and subject to a vow by members of religious orders in the Roman rite. Franciscans and Dominicans, for example, make vows of poverty, chastity and obedience. Diocesan priests, for their part, promise their bishop obedience and celibacy, i.e., not to marry.

21 Many went ahead and married without the dispensation as I did, and some never requested it and married civilly in the presence of a priest (clandestine). As a consequence there is no record of the latter's personal experience in the Vatican files. The latter are still under formal suspension

mally requested a dispensation from celibacy less than a year after my civil marriage and received it two years later when Pope John Paul II decided to reinstitute the procedure of laicization that he had suspended for several years. (See appendix #9)

In 1967, an exodus began which amounted to more than 10,000 priests in the USA and 100,000 worldwide, for most of them ending their practice of the priesthood. That is a significant social and religious phenomenon by any standards. Why did it happen then and not before? The answer is not only personal but also cultural and ecclesiastical. There were monumental changes in both church and western society in the 1960s. In addition, Vatican II did issue in a form of Catholic sensibility and practice different from that of the Church of the Councils of Trent (1545-1563) and Vatican I (1869-70). The change rocked the church over the following decades. Catholics did begin to show far different attitudes on a host of things such as the priority of individual conscience over authoritative teaching on such issues as contraception and priests leaving the priesthood, and even the centuries long divinization of the authority of bishops and popes.[22] These changes are part of the sociological and cultural background to the exodus.

For example, as a matter of conscience I could not bring myself to preach against birth control nor to apply the received teaching (namely, that birth control is mortally sinful) in the confessional. When I did not carry out the latter, I was guilty of the canonical crime of solicitation to a sin against the sixth commandment and thereby immediately suspended from the exercise of the priest-

---

from the priestly ministry and excommunication (cf. Canon 1394. #1 & 2; 1395, #1 & 2; 194, #3). One can only speculate on the refusal to apply. My suspicion is that, unlike myself, they did not wish to leave the priesthood but only to marry and still consider themselves priests, and regard themselves still as "called." Numbers of former priests joining the ministry of other churches supports this claim. There are indications as well that many former priests continued to act like priests, ministering to small communities of Catholics even though, canonically speaking, they have no right to do so. Their "communions" are out of communion with the bishops of the Catholic Church.

22   William V. D'Antonio, James D. Davidson, Dean R. Hoge, Mary L. Gautier, *American Catholics Today: New Realities of Their Faith and Their Church* (NY: Rowman and Littlefield, 2007). These changes are parallels to the sudden and unexpected change over the past decade (2004-2014) in the American Catholic laity's acceptance of homosexual love and marriage. Catholic Ireland approved homosexual marriage by plebiscite in 2015. The latter is a monumental change. See the bibliography for works by Francis Sullivan, Diarmaid MacCulloch, and Garry Wills.

hood.[23] I paid no positive attention to that part of official church moral doctrine, nor to the imposed penalty. Clearly, I had a "problem with authority." I was as a matter of church law suspended from exercising the priesthood from 1962 on. That problem hovered over my head like a dark cloud, and still does. Admittedly the Catholic Church was not and is not responsible for my problem but it did serve as a petri dish in its development, as did my family.

The flood became a steady trickle as the years passed. I was on the cascade of that exodus when I made the switch from the sacred to the profane in 1980. I'm not trying to provide an explanation of the phenomenon or an adequate description of its context. Such an aim is well beyond my competence. I'm starting with a few insights into one case, the one I know best.

First, as far as I am concerned priests are admirable and generous men who live for the church and the communities they serve. No matter the over-the-top claims of bishops and popes about themselves, it is the parish priest who is the anchor of Roman Catholicism. Priests who minister in parishes are the connecting link between Catholics and The Church. They, and not the bishops, "save souls." I like priests (one at a time) and always have. A couple of them remain my very best friends. I admired my childhood parish priests and my priest high school teachers. Their inspiration brought me to the seminary. My affection for them has not lessened over the decades.

This may be hard to believe after years of shocking publicity, but in the nineteen years I served as a priest only twice did I indirectly, via media and clerical gossip, come across a case of child abuse among the priests that I knew.[24] Though I occasionally did come across priests who drank too much (two certifiable alcoholics), I never caught a priest stealing money, though I did hear a funny story or two about priests who did. The media now reports that there are many cases of these sorts but I don't find them funny at all. Even though I didn't like living with them, I admired and enjoyed the priests with whom I lived. In other words, priests in my experience are faithful to their vocation and stick to it. Sociological data confirms that most of them remain chaste, or try very hard to live chastely though they sometimes falter.[25] I would add my own testimony to the data, but I didn't merely falter, I flopped.

Second, to me priests live an odd life. Celibacy is odd no matter

23   Code of Canon Law #1394, 1395, and 194.

24   See *Bishopsaccountability.com* for a list of New York priests who were accused of child abuse and relieved of their priesthood. The list displays my naïveté.

25   Greeley, *Priests*, 36.

how you slice it, but more than the oddity of celibacy there is the clerical life-style that accompanies it. That men live their whole life in rectories with other men—unless they are gay—strikes me as unnatural rather than supernatural. Similarly, so are the sisterhoods and convent life. In either case you have to be made for it by nature or remade for it by grace (charism). I genuinely like and admire most of the priests I have known, but I came, through experience, to detest rectory life. At forty years old I still sat at someone else's table. The work of the priest is vitally important, yes, but the life of priests apart from their work is deeply repellant to me. I didn't like the seminary life. I didn't like rectory life, and didn't even like the life in the priests' residence at Catholic University where I taught (1973-1980). I wanted to go home after work, and I wanted to quit at 5 PM.

I never could, and still can't, take priests in large groups—in fact I don't like human beings in large groups, with the singular exception of forty thousand fans gathered in Busch Stadium to watch the St. Louis Cardinals play baseball. I don't mind that sort of gathering for it is when everyone watches something of import and no one watches me. I was initially drawn to the priesthood in part because of the attractions of the clerical state and then discovered that in the concrete, the state wasn't at all attractive. As I look back, the surprise was not the sufferings and joys of the priesthood but why it took me so long to leave what I didn't like. The priest is a public and communal figure and I wanted a private life. I wanted a job rather than a vocation. The priesthood calls for a modest but focused and easy extroversion while I am an introvert who pretends extroversion and finds it painful. As my wife reminds me I would have made a very unhappy pastor. I would have been utterly miserable as a politician or a policeman. The three things that, from beginning to the end, made powerful sense to me were preaching, celebrating the Eucharist and the sacrament of penance (reconciliation in the current terminology). They still do, though I am no longer allowed to do them.

Third, over the eight years of seminary training and nineteen years of life as a priest I was utterly unable to make any religious sense of celibacy. Study and prayer didn't do it. I could not raise myself (or, apparently, be raised) to the heights of understanding necessary to appreciate the "eschatological sign" celibacy is supposed to provide to the church and "the world." I admit that I wasn't able to make much sense of marriage during those years either—I fled from that when I was a teenager. For me celibacy was merely a sign of absence; it never became a sign of presence. Over the years, it dawned on me that a woman is the proper center for the life of a man, and how I fought this little insight! There is no substitute that I could find. I can only guess that priests who find celibacy an absence must love the work of a priest far more than I did and they must somehow find God in it to an extent that I did not. To me, living willingly without a woman is truly a form of holy madness.

Let me note two factors that are especially important to my story. The trouble I experienced in the priesthood was partly rooted in life-long low-grade depression that I have never fully escaped. This made life in the priesthood unhappy, as it undoubtedly would have made any way of life unhappy! A Jesuit theologian, Robert Doran, used the term "dispositional immediacy" for the set of feelings with which we greet and participate in life and which exist before and independently of how we think about life and what we decide to do with it.[26] "Dispositional immediacy" or "psyche" is omnipresent but often unnoticed and unknown. It is "unconscious." If those feelings cause enough confusion in life, they may well demand therapy. They become conscious when we notice and struggle to name them. I have been in a chronic state of mild depression for most of my life; I felt it and didn't realize it. I never regarded myself as depressed. I don't think the parish priesthood is the place for depressive and introverted men. I was both and very much remain the second.

I also had acute, as distinct from chronic, attacks of depression on several occasions that seem to me to have been crucial to my experience of the priesthood. These attacks occurred most of my senior year in the college seminary before beginning graduate work in theology, and again four years later in the several months before ordination, and again several times in the years 1969—1980 when, in hindsight, I was clearly on the way out.[27] Depression was a major sign of trouble. Just as I missed the "eschatological sign" character of celibacy, I also sidestepped the fact and implications of depression. It wasn't until the mid-nineties that I was clinically classified under the category "chronic depression," some fifteen years after my marriage. I was stunned when the psychiatrist told me. I brought to the priesthood a wounded psyche and carried it with me into marriage. Since the mid-nineties, I have taken low doses

---

26   Robert Doran S.J., *Subject and Psyche* (Milwaukee: Marquette University Press, 1994). 2nd ed.

27   The low scale depression or "sense of alienation" is, I believe, akin to the psychic roots of classical and modern Gnosticism as it is described by Hans Jonas in the most important and insightful book written on that Christian and Jewish heresy. Cf. *The Gnostic Religion; the message of the alien God and the beginnings of Christianity* (Boston: Beacon Press, 1963).

of mood elevators. I wish I had taken them long before, for I had a mood and it certainly needed to be elevated! But the depression and introversion were hidden even from myself in a cloud of extroversion, making it difficult to detect except by the woman who was close by in my downtime. In the episodes of depression, recognized as such or not, I constantly considered whether I belonged in the priesthood or, indeed, in the world. I think this qualifies as psychological alienation, certainly not in an advanced or crippling form, but real nonetheless. I always found significant relief in work.

Finally, Divine Providence is an undertow in all this. As notoriously difficult as it is to get specific about Providence, I must say that I have not been alone in this struggle over the priesthood and celibacy—except for some moments of acute spiritual homelessness, and even then the sense of God did not entirely fade. I also had friends who gave me help. Late in life (I am seventy-eight as I write this) my consciousness of God as the heart and horizon of my being and living remains as strong as it was when I was a child, perhaps even stronger. As used as I am to the study of atheism, the fact of atheism remains a matter of puzzlement to me—as much as my own sense of God must be a curiosity to atheists. Perhaps we sense the same thing and have different names for it. Perhaps we are divided by language rather than faith.

Getting Sacred

I found the eight-year education in becoming a priest intellectually and spiritually engaging and psychologically enervating. The tensions that were to preoccupy me over the following two decades surfaced there for the first time: a fragile psychic individuality coupled with stubborn, though surreptitious, resistance to domination in a religious culture in which domination is the name of the game. Dedication to a church community and a mind given to more questions than the community was likely to bear and I could not answer myself; a lot of genuine admiration for my seminary peers and my teachers joined to a suspicion that much of what I was taught was part of a clerically created myth. It was a nature that wanted to trust something or someone in a setting that insisted that trust in authority is requisite, and that a human being was expected to live supernaturally, a sinful nature expected to live virtuously. All in all these were tough years. Though I felt these tensions in seminary training, I did not know how deep and broad they were to become in the priesthood.

I had some good reasons for becoming a priest and some not so good reasons. The primary good reason was the love of God and the realization I retained from childhood that God is in fact here, present here and now as well as absent here and now. Even the absence of God is felt. If one were acutely aware of that presence and absence, if one were afflicted with the love of God in the 1950's, what else would a young male Catholic do but become a priest? What else would a Catholic woman do but become a nun? I was so afflicted. In other words, being a priest or a nun then made a great deal of religious, as well as social sense. There was still hope that God would be met more fully in that way of life, and that surely the sense of presence would grow and the sense of absence would recede. Both senses were quite strong. I was then and am now God-obsessed and church-obsessed. My wife and I share this joy, each in our own distinct way. For both of us God and the church is the cross from which we have not come down.

A second good reason was an ineradicable desire to serve the church. Ever since I was a child the church was the primary symbol of Christ in this world, the church here being people, priests and bishops. To be a priest was to embody that symbol (church) more fully and to participate in its reality in an intensified way, or so I thought. I didn't need the great Catholic theologians of mid-century, Karl Rahner or Edward Schillebeeckx, to tell me that, and as soon as I read their books on the church in the 1960's I recognized the truth of the sacramentality of the church itself.[28]

Pope Pius XII had written a lengthy letter on the church as the "Mystical Body of Christ" (1943), the church referred to by the later theologians as "the sacrament of the presence of Christ." The new atheists Dawkins and Dennett, Harris and Hitchens, prophets of the absence of God, and the older atheists like Ludwig Feuerbach, John Dewey and George Santayana who tried to pry religious experience free of institutions and propositions of fact, didn't lay a glove on this conviction of mine. Christ is really present in the church as He is in the Eucharistic elements. In fact, according to theologians old and young, it is the existing church that is the "Real Presence" preceding the Eucharist. This is the ground-level Christian truth upon which the hierarchy bases, unfortunately and illogically, its demand for total obedience and its sacralized authority. The church surrenders to The Church in which bishops and priests are the prime and indispensable actors. Inversion I would call it. But when I pick up such a book as Terry Eagleton's Terry Lectures, I can get another glimpse of Christ in the church behind the hierarchical

28   Karl Rahner, *The Church and the Sacraments*. (New York: Herder and Herder, 1963). Edward Schillebeeckx, *Christ, the Sacrament of the Encounter with God* (Lanham MD: Rowman & Littlefield, 1963).

falderal.[29]

As a Catholic, I believed that no job in the world could reach the level of importance that we attributed to offering Mass and ministering sacraments. This was a matter of childhood experience, not abstract belief, in the parish and school life in the east Bronx. The parish church was the beating heart of the neighborhood, the Mass was the center of worship, and priests stood at the apex of our lives as Catholics. Bishops were a long way off but the priests were *here*. Some of the solidity of this experience and belief I could attribute to the vibrant culture of 1950s Catholicism and the piety of my parents, but it runs deeper than the cultural practice of Catholics in that time and place. It—the belief in the importance of the sacraments, in the real presence of Christ in the Eucharistic elements, in Mary the Mother of God, in the symbolic nature of priesthood and the church –is the essence of Catholicism, the very things about it that Protestants don't seem to get. However, maybe they do get it in practice and object, not to it but to the Catholic doctrines of hierarchical mediation. Far more than statues, "The Catholic Church" presents a severe temptation to idolatry.

I wanted to "be there when the band starts playing," and I wanted to help others to be there as well. I wanted to share the spiritual and intellectual wealth of the Catholic Christianity. Both love of God and love of the church are as true of me today as when I was twenty, perhaps even truer as some of my internal turmoil has been quieted by time. I now find, sixty years later, that this love of God and the church still propels me. A professor of religion does daily very much of what the priesthood opened to me: deep personal communication with an engaged audience on matters of great importance in life. The move from the pulpit to the lectern seemed smooth while the love for God and the church flowed on undisturbed. At the lectern, however, you have to give all sides, be prepared to argue a case, think issues through, critically evaluate accepted positions, answer to the "congregation" of the classroom, and know a lot more than a seminary education would impart. But still the love of God propels me.

What were the not so good reasons for becoming and being a priest? The most distressing not-so-good reason was that I did it chiefly for myself. I pictured myself front and center stage doing holy things. The choice was less a selfless act than it was a self-protective act: I became a priest because I needed a shield. Next to my

29   Terry Eagleton, *Reason, Faith, and Revolution: Reflections on the God Debate* (New Haven: Yale University Press, 2009). Two American thinkers who deliver such a "glimpse" are Joseph Komonchak and David O'Brien. They break through the falderal.

hope and faith and intertwined with them was a profound felt-but-not-understood confusion over life and death. That confusion led to a rejection of ordinary life and a flight into an imagined sacred, safe, and unending life. Long before deciding on the priesthood, somewhere in the dark corners of my life as a child and an adolescent, I had linked marriage, family, and making a living with death. I had watched my mother and father. I had come to regard ordinary life as dreary and painful, the psychic equivalent of a slow death. My "dispositional immediacy" colored the world grey. The church and the priesthood became a refuge, a participation in the eternal life of Jesus, without the clutter, distractions and terrible sufferings of ordinary human life and death. I was fleeing the life my parents lived, as I picked it up from living with and listening to them, a life whose value was profoundly questionable to me. I had no problem loving them but was determined not to live like them. I observed precious little joy there but gobs of loyalty, devotion and honesty. It was clear that they lived for one another, and even more for my brother and me. But whence the sadness, what for the struggle? Where the joy that keeps us moving through the suffering and the loneliness? In God, of course, in God and the church, in its songs and celebrations, in worship and work for the kingdom where every tear is wiped away. (Revelation, 21:4)

Why are we here suffering? Hans Jonas long ago described ancient Gnosticism as an answer to that question: we suffer because we don't belong here.[30] I have an innate sympathy for Gnostic (and Buddhist) teaching about the genesis of suffering and the way to end it, namely, flight into a world of spirit. Of course, very little of my early conviction about suffering, death and the meaningless of ordinary experience, turned out to be true. It took a quarter of a century of clerical life, a decade of marriage and two sons for that confusion to work itself out. The priesthood is no refuge from suffering and it leads to eternal life no more surely than "ordinary life" does. Eternal life, whatever it may be, is a promise to all the disciples of Jesus, not to a clergy; and death is the fact that comes to all regardless of our religious and institutional circumstances. Even popes die, sometimes miserably and fearfully, for they are men, too.

The priesthood and the episcopacy, in my view, are at once a supernaturalist ideological imposition on the Christian movement and a natural development of specialized ministries in communities large enough to require them. The priesthood is one of the many specializations that come to a religion as it develops, along with mystics, prophets, miracle workers, and glossalaliacs, monks

---

30   Hans Jonas, *The Gnostic Religion*.

and nuns and a variety of administrators. The office of the priest and bishop is not a bad idea for service and organization, until the ordained ministry so completely dominates and controls the Christian movement that The Church, which runs and controls the movement must be called a corporation and its life a deformation. In the era of empires such domination must, in the natural course of things, find its root in divine decree. So a movement of interconnected communities becomes a religious system, leadership becomes ownership, and the holy becomes the sacred.[31]

I had supposed that by becoming a priest I was being raised up to some sort of sacred life but I later found that the Presence and Absence of God are tropes of human life itself. They cannot be attached with any special degree of intensity to a particular form of human life such as the priesthood or Catholicism. What a peculiar thing it is that religious ministries so easily turn into sacral castes, and even more peculiar that religious people like myself come to believe in them as a sacred sort of life!

I overlooked some large clues that might have earlier illuminated my flight from life and death into the priesthood: namely, the two acute spells of depression that remained unresolved in seminary: they were high-grade depressions. I turned my back on them, as if they were alien to my personality. They told me nothing about my ordinary life experience. If the seminary authorities and I had faced up to those clues I wouldn't have been ordained. A feeling of alienation and detachment from myself and the clerical world around me accompanied me for two decades of active priesthood and were in fact chronic. I wish now that someone in authority had said to me in those seminary days, "Get out of here and grow up!" and that I had listened. When Msgr. John Harrington, whom I disliked intensely, said to another seminary faculty member that he would campaign to keep me from ordination I thought he was wrong but he wasn't. When I sniped at him, challenging his authority, daring him in effect, it was perfectly clear that I didn't belong in the clerical caste. When my seminary rector, Msgr. Francis Reh (later bishop of Saginaw, MI) told me the faculty thought that I had a big mouth and must learn to shut it, I was amused. When my second pastor said he had begun to doubt the authenticity of my vocation because of my mild attempts at evasion and my evident distrust of him, he was, it turned out years later, correct to do so. I didn't understand or accept the institutional requirement for reverence and obedience and "priestly fellowship," ignoring then the

31   The "sacred" is the human attempt to control and direct the holy. See Darrell Fasching, *The Coming of the Millennium: Good News for the Whole Human Race* (iUniverse, 2001).

possibility that my religious superiors might have been right about some things.

It dawned on me in the years after ordination that life in a rectory was unbearably lonely and clerical life in general was every bit as distracted and maddening as "ordinary life." Although as always I admired priests, I didn't at all like the clerical life. Living in a rectory was even worse than living alone. Above all, I was attracted to the women with whom I worked. It took a painful series of love affairs over a decade to resolve this late adolescence. What should have in the course of nature been achieved by twenty-five years of life happened at thirty. Women suffered as I grew up; on their part, they thought they were dealing with an adult who knew what he was about when in fact he was mired in a maturity crisis.

In addition, years of teaching at the College of New Rochelle and at Catholic University in Washington D.C. and the possession of a Ph.D. provided me with a way to make a living that carried few of those connotations of the sacred that tossed me into internal conflict. I had developed a profession that I dearly loved, one in which the holy was not buried under the cover of the sacred and one that had at its core the issues that concerned me most deeply: life and death, meaning and truth, suffering and joy, the spirit and the flesh.

Between 1969 and 1980, the struggle over life and death became intense. I had no way out of the priesthood except by an act of disloyalty that I could not summon the courage to initiate, and so I fought to remain a priest. For well over a decade, I lived in a maelstrom of emotional, psychological, and vocational confusion and alternation. In the late December of 1979, after the Dean of the School of Theology at CUA threatened to turn me over to Cardinal Baum, the Chancellor of the university, I wrote to Cardinal Cooke in New York and told him that I meant to resign from the priesthood and marry. In the late winter (February 1980) I married Helene, whom I had known for a decade. I made some important mistakes in pursuing and practicing the Catholic priesthood, and discovering myself in my mistakes led me out of it. Never, however, did I manage to entirely cleanse myself of the sticky stuff of the clerical caste.

Going Profane

By "profane" here I mean "ordinary" or "non-sacral." In 1980, I started life a second time. Well, not quite, for I dragged a lot of the old Shea with me. I was 45 years old, I had no money (and I mean none) beyond the meager (and I mean meager) salary due me through Spring 1980, and I didn't have a job in the first few months though I had been searching for one for a year. I was in love with a woman who at the time was headed for a ministerial life; she was studying at Yale Divinity School, and would go on to earn graduate degrees in medical ethics at Georgetown and Saint Louis Universities. By marrying me, she unknowingly blocked her own path to Catholic ministry (the purity laws and contagion are taken very seriously by the hierarchy). Because I married civilly, I was suspended from the priesthood and excommunicated, and lost my tenured job teaching at Catholic University where the statutes forbade married priests from teaching and voided their tenure. I was thereby separated from the best community I had had as an adult. I hated to leave the faculty and students. I also lost twenty years of pension rights as a priest. I lost most of my friends and personal connections. Very few friendships have continued to this day.

In the summer of 1980, Helene and I rolled a U-Haul truck up to the side door of Caldwell Hall at CUA and added to Helene's meager possessions the several thousand books, a cheap couch and a coffee table, and drove off on US 95 on our way to Tampa. My stuff, added to Helene's, meant an attached trailer that baffled the inexperienced truckers when parking at motels, never mind the threat to other cars and trucks. Our trip south was paid for by Cardinal Cooke via CUA's administration.[32] I couldn't even have afforded to rent the truck without that "severance package." I didn't ask him for the support; he offered it. Two days later we arrived in Tampa with $2,000.00 left from Cooke's gift, looking forward to the first state pay check on the largest annual salary I had made up to that point, $18,000.

When I exited that vital Catholic theological and personal community at CUA, I headed for a teaching job in the Department of Religious Studies at the University of South Florida, a move that was to bring me new friends and many eye-popping classroom experiences. The context of my intellectual and social life had been Roman Catholic and now it was to become ecumenical and inter-religious as well. Where before I had not dared to think of myself as a theologian amidst the real theologians at CUA I now found myself,

---

32   To top things off, when the time came to ante up the "severance package" the vice-president of the university tried to clip $2,500 off the $5,000 promised by Cardinal Cooke. Golden parachute? Not even then! I had to appeal to the president Edmund Pelegrino to get the second half restored. The vice president dishonored himself and the university. Had president Pelegrino not reversed the cheap trick of his vice-president I would not have been able to pay the first month's rent and the security deposit on our modest row house in Temple Terrace.

at a state university, being called "The Theologian" by colleagues in religious studies, philosophy and humanities. In classrooms, I met witches, fundamentalists, Pentecostals, Jews, evangelicals, Gnostics, New Agers, Marxists, hyper-orthodox Catholics and what the popes call "radical feminists." I met a shaman who traveled in spirit to New York City on weekends while his flesh remained in Tampa, a woman utterly convinced that by believing in Jesus she would never die (John 6:47-50), some wonderful young Catholics and Southern Baptists, a Santerist *baba*, Raul Canizares, and the best student I had in fifty years of teaching, now an expert in American religions and a Master Teacher in that department, Dell De Chant. I found great professional satisfaction with those students along with some of my faculty colleagues. I learned far more from them than I was able to give. Among the latter was a serious Calvinist professor of Humanities whose criticisms of the Catholic Church honored the Master of Geneva; a Catholic professor of ethics who became a Lutheran right before my eyes; and one of the world's great Talmudic scholars. The three became friends of mine and influenced me profoundly. I remained a vigorous Catholic and was warmly received into the parish church of Corpus Christi in Temple Terrace, Florida.[33]

But more importantly, I discovered a center of affection, loyalty and life in one woman and, in a short time, two sons (1982, 1984). My psyche, never quiet, and my spiritual life continued as dense and bumpy as ever. My temperament remained high-strung, but there was considerable settling and steady purpose of mind and work. There has been the distraction and annoyance that infect everyday married life, (Do we get a dog or not? Do we buy a house? Do we need two cars? How can we shut that little bugger up so I can sleep?) but never any wavering. I suffered for nearly three decades over whether I should have been a celibate priest, but I have not wondered for even ten minutes whether I should have left the priesthood and married. I haven't had time or cause to wonder. I've been too busy making a living and trying to be a decent husband and father, in their own way as difficult as being a priest. I have never regretted marrying and I have never regretted being a priest even though I came to regard the latter to have been ill-founded. Leaving the priesthood was a relief. Constantly over the decades as a clergyman, I wondered whether I was fit for that life, and during those years I felt I was temperamentally unfit for marriage as well.

I am quite sure now that both the priesthood and the family were, and are, each in its time, well within the providence of God

---

33   The priests there were especially kind: Tom Glacken baptized both my sons.

for me, whether or not I was or am fit. Billy Watson, Helene's uncle, told her that he was concerned that some morning in the future I would wake and turn to see her head on the pillow, look at her and say to myself: "And I could have been a Monsignor!!" Never happened. When I wake, I say, "thank God!" I am a lot happier at being a professor than at being a priest, a lot happier with two in one bed, still deeply in love with Helene, and awed by the two young men who are my sons and whose maturity and integrity assure me that my marriage to Helene is blessed by God. True, had I not married my sons would not be, and had they not been I would still be wondering whether my life has been worthwhile. Funny thing how children justify the lives of parents.

As I left off preaching and celebrating Mass in December 1979, I experienced and still experience thirty years later a relief from the tension of the sacred. (See Appendix #6) Over the years several people have asked me whether I would return to the priesthood if I were invited. My answer has invariably been "Not a chance!" They couldn't pay me enough in this life or the next. These days I ask myself how I was able to manage it for close to thirty years. I simply couldn't live up to my idealized picture of priestly virtue.

Yet it remains peculiar, doesn't it, that I chose (repeat: *I chose*) not to pursue that Eucharistic joy I often experienced, or follow the joy through to some spiritual fulfillment. I cut it off as best I could with the supposition that the joy had more to do with its power over me than with the love of God. I still wonder about that. What I focused on was not the questionable invitation to consolation but on another spiritual motion: the powerful sense of the simultaneous presence and absence of God that had been a constant in my life from the time I was burned as a child through many bouts of depression and sin into what I now regard as "the profane" phase of my life. To put it perhaps too bluntly, constantly and almost without interruption I experience a presence of the Holy One and a failure of the Holy to act to remove pain in the world at the same time, and my own failure to achieve or even to desire any closeness to the poor of the earth.

Reflections

There are some things I have learned that seem worth pointing out—not unusual insights, perhaps more like common sense, but for me, at least, they were uncommon and took decades to come upon. Forgive me for getting didactic but I must pass them on.

- Martin Luther was wrong about a lot of things but he was

right about at least one thing: there is no work that is Sacred as distinct from work that is secular. If anyone thinks he/she has entered what The Church has named an "ontologically changed" way of life, he/she is deceived. All work, all ways of life are filled with the grace of God (the Holy One) and the possibility of sin. All life is destined to death AND promises eternal life at the same time. You escape from nothing by being a Christian or a priest or a nun, and you are not a fraction of an inch ontologically above a construction worker or surgeon or the homeless. If it is the Sacred that interests you, take a cold shower and move on. The Holy moves with you.

- Bernard Lonergan was correct when he wrote that "being-in-love" means a total reorientation of life.[34] He is simply reiterating what the Gospel of Christ meant to the Apostles and the first Christians that love, of the divine and of the human, is the "undertow" which brings us to harbor, such as we can know a harbor in this life. The undertow brings us through death to life with God.

- Know as much as you can about yourself when you make big choices and make them with confidence; be patient and forgiving of yourself, for you may be wrong, in fact you *will* be wrong about very big things in life, including your vocation. Go with the undertow.

- Stick with your family, your personal community, and the loves that God has given you. Don't move away from them without God's permission. In unusual circumstances you can get that permission. Be stubborn about sticking with your church or the synagogue or mosque or ashram: we are not saved alone. Be leery of sociological conversions, for you drag your old and true self with you.

- Don't become a priest or nun or monk unless you are definitively called to celibacy. If you are not called—as I was not—it will blow up in your face. Incalculable harm (and, to be fair, some incalculable good) has been done to the church community by the loony papal and episcopal obsession with celibacy within the diocesan priesthood. Be sure celibacy makes profound *religious* sense to you personally and not just institutional sense. If you are called to it, follow the call. If you are not, run for your life.

- Beware of ecclesiastical leaders. It's not that bishops are, by and large, bad people but they are ordinary people in very

---

34   *Method in Theology,* (New York: Herder and Herder, 1972), 105-113.

peculiar jobs who make as many mistakes as we do, and do far more injury than we can imagine, all in the name of God. Yes, bishops seem convinced and sure and even wise, but they have little insight into the torture their leadership can bring to Christian souls. If they are "ontologically changed" for the better by ordination they sure don't show it. It may seem a contradiction then to recommend that we all listen to Pope Francis but he meets all my criteria for a Christian saint with wisdom that comes from the Spirit. He seems not to be overwhelmed by his job or removed from our fate by his "ontological" status. He is a great bishop because he is a great Christian.

5. Change

Circa 1961-62, a pair of Belgian and Dutch Catholic moral theologians published articles on birth control that departed from the seminary theology I had been taught and from the teaching of Pope Pius XI in *Casti connubii* (1930) forbidding "artificial" birth control.[35] That coupled with my first year hearing confessions in Our Lady of Mt. Carmel church in Yonkers listening for the first time to penitents, men and woman, confessing birth control as a mortal sin led me to conclude that it wasn't sinful when it made good moral sense to the couple. Rather than reprimanding and attempting to dissuade the penitents as I had been instructed to do, I remained silent about birth control unless asked about it by the penitent and encouraged love and fidelity of the couple. An hour-long visit with Msgr. Daniel Flynn at the seminary along with a classmate, Fr. Mike Wrenn, informed me that any confessor who did not treat contraception as a mortal sin and attempt to dissuade the penitent from the practice would himself be guilty of "solicitation to a base sin." Under Canon Law, that priest would be suspended from the ministry, a suspension reserved to the bishop for absolution.

Beginning on the following Saturday afternoon (confession time 4 to 6, 7:30 to 9 PM), I was guilty of solicitation hundreds, perhaps thousands of times, and suspended every time. Over the next eighteen years, I remained silent. I never had any regret about my decision, but it was another step in a broadening separation between myself and the *Magisterum*. In 1968 in his letter *Humanae vitae*, Pope Paul VI, for whom I have great respect and affection, made the same mistake as his predecessor Pius XI. The thousands of priests and millions of people who did not follow "the authentic *magisterium*" were morally correct in my view.[36] Especially a sus-

35   Louis Janssens of Louvain wrote one in December in the *Ephemerides Theologicae Lovanienses* arguing in favor of the pill. Joseph Maria Reuss the Auxiliary Bishop of Mainz wrote an article in the *Tübinger Theologische Quartallschrift* arguing for the possibility of all types of contraception. William van der Marck OP argued for the morality of contraception in *Tijdschrift voor Theologie*.

36   "Authentic magisterium" is the term bishops and popes use to

pension of the thirty-nine dissenting priests in Washington DC by Cardinal Patrick O'Boyle (1968) left me convinced that the pope and the bishops had gone over the edge like lemmings on the trail of Pope Pius XI. Paul VI would not even allow bishops to discuss the issue in the Council, and then followed up by neutering the good advice given him on the question by his own commission. Hold on, I said to myself, there is something very big going on here! They are putting consistency in papal teaching above the conscience of married Catholics. Of course, there is a lot at stake, for if the *Magisterium* can be wrong in its noisy condemnation of artificial birth control it can be wrong about other pronouncements as well. *Casti connubii* and *Humanae vitae* may be low-lying logs in the hierarchical totem, but if they are pulled out, the totem all but collapses.

By the time I reached CUA in the fall of 1972, I had come far from my adulation of the church's bishops and their theologians for their good and unexpectedly successful work at Vatican II to the position that the episcopacy and the papacy were in more need of demythologizing than the New Testament. But I hadn't given up on them entirely, still thinking they were teachers who would learn that their positions in ethics are as good as the arguments for them. The arguments are often sound but if the arguments fail, the position fails, not withstanding the back-up appeal to the "Authentic *Magisterium*" and Holy Spirit which appears to be, like patriotism, the last refuge of a scoundrel. The church itself, in the lower clergy and in its laity, thoroughly rejected Pope Paul's reiteration of Pius XI's unqualified condemnation of "artificial birth control" in *Casti connubii*, and they were right to do so. Paul VI, John Paul II and Benedict XVI fell into the same papal black hole, and so the historic contradiction on this issue between the magisterium and the Catholic people continues, ironically supplying the best historical proof of the fallibility of the "Ordinary and Extraordinary Magisterium" of popes and bishops and a contradictory and equally infallible sense of what is true on the part of the laity and parish priests. The Catholic people got off the lemming line, perhaps definitively. It would not be the first time the Catholic laity had to correct erring

---

describe their binding teaching authority. Anything in doctrine or morals that bishops teach in communion with the bishop of Rome is true and *ipso facto* must be accepted by clergy and laity . cf. *TIME Magazine*. "Conscience and the Encyclical" (September 13, 1968). I signed the document along with several other New York priests a year later and we never heard about that from the New York chancery or archbishop. Had they been paying attention I would have been blocked from an appointment to CUA three years later.

bishops.

***

In 1968-69, while assisting the chaplain at the College of New Rochelle and studying at Columbia University I read a lengthy article in a Catholic journal arguing that the ordination of women had much in Scripture, history and theology to be said for it and little to be said against it. That, coupled with Joseph Komonchak's essay in a volume on women's orders and my attendance at a couple of conferences on the subject, left me convinced that the *magisterium* (the teaching authority) of the church was again mistaken in denying the priesthood to women. In spite of "definitive" statements by Paul VI, John Paul II and Benedict XVI, and now Pope Francis, on the unacceptability of women in priestly orders, I haven't wavered in this opinion. In spite of their suspect and even specious arguments that (1) Jesus didn't do it, (2) the church has never done it, and (3) women do not possess the requisite sexual organs to represent Christ in public office, the traditions in this matter amount to misogynism. It was difficult for me to understand how birth control can be a sin worthy of hell, yet clerical misogynism is a virtue. Had my bishop known my positions on birth control and the ordination of women he would have had to remove me from the confessional and the pulpit by 1970 and blocked my appointment to the faculty at CUA. They didn't ask and I didn't tell.

***

In this time period, my seminary professor of Scripture, Monsignor Myles M. Bourke, began to argue that there were no New Testament grounds for denying the validity of the Eucharist celebrated in Protestant communities.[37] I gladly adopted this position and several times after this received the consecrated bread and wine in Protestant and Episcopal churches. I followed this line of thought over the following years to the conclusion that Protestant "communities" (as the popes persist in calling them), are in fact "churches" and part of the "one, holy catholic and apostolic church." The sacraments, in whatever ways they are celebrated, are in the Catholic sense valid sacraments—even when the Protestants won't call them

---

37   M.M. Bourke with R. J. Neuhaus, "Dialogue on Intercommunion," *The Catholic Mind,* vol. 66 (1968): 12-18. See also Bourke, "The New Testament and the State of the Liturgy," *Worship,* vol. 44/3 (1969): 131-142.

sacraments. The exclusionist line drawn by the Roman Church at the Reformation had been a fearsome mistake. The Reformers, of course, made the same and even bigger mistakes. Schism is sinful, for it proceeds from a distorted love of the church and tears it. What a reprehensible thing the Reformation and the Roman reaction to it were! Dante would have put them all, Catholic and Protestant leaders alike, in one of the infernal circles.

***

Sometime in the mid-sixties (1967) I attended a private meeting of about forty New York priests at a church in the Bronx. The meeting was devoted mainly to the failure of Cardinal Spellman and Archbishop Maguire to establish a priests' senate in the wake of Vatican II — a priests' senate was taken by us priests as a mandate of the Council. I was then twenty-eight years old. In the course of that discussion, I said that I would give the hierarchy five years to allow priests to marry and, if they didn't, I would leave to marry. There was some shock among the priests present (see appendix #2). I am confident that the unobtrusive representative of Archbishop Maguire (Fr. Robert Stern) reported on this — and that my statement probably had something to do with Maguire's 1968 easy release of me to study at Columbia University. The official priests' Senate was established shortly after this meeting. I stuck around for fifteen years instead of five! The personal waters were murkier than I thought in 1967. At any rate, the waters were roiling early on. Preachers and theologians have often suggested that the basic sin of Adam and Eve was demand for autonomy of intellect and will. My attitude toward authority in these terms is an Adamic inheritance, with the teaching of the "authentic magisterium" representing the command not to eat the fruit of the tree of the knowledge of good and evil. I had taken a bite.

***

These are samples of my increasing unease with the "solidarity" and "communion" a Catholic priest should share with his bishop and equally samples of my solidarity and communion with the Catholic laity. They exemplify the vast changes occurring in the Roman Catholic Church at the time. As I approached a crisis with the priesthood in 1976, I was advised by William Connolly, S.J., an astute spiritual director of the New England Jesuit province, that the resolution to my problem would surely come and that the issue

would be settled when a moment of freedom occurred. I would realize, so he said, that the choice was mine to make. It arrived a year
later and I made the choice in the predicted moment of freedom
that was a pure gift, a *gratia gratis data*, a grace freely given. This
changed not only my mind about God, but my life as well. God
acted to set me free after a decade of the most frightful internal and
external hassle. I had feared from my childhood that God did not
speak, at least to the likes of me. Yet God did, without words and
by promoting freedom. It was still, as it had always been, Divine
Silence but now a freeing silence. All these years later, whenever
I think of those days, I feel again with gratitude the breathing of
God. Perhaps over all those years it wasn't God not answering, but
me not listening. I was essentially free all that time and only then in
a moment was I effectively free. I assume that God always has this
intention of effective freedom toward me and that I had to catch up.

For example, during that very same year, while at Harvard Divinity School (1976-77), I confronted in my mind's eye an image of
the Crucified. It occurred on the back porch of a Gloucester seafood
restaurant, down the road from the Jesuit retreat house, overlook-
ing the harbor after a fine dinner and a couple of Rob Roys (so I
can't claim it as a mystical moment). I "saw" the Son dying and
"heard" the Father's deafening silence. I have never been able to
understand how the Father can remain silent while His children
suffer and die. In fact, I have been outraged and offended by it ever
since my childhood. That night I wept and shouted on the porch:
how could you abandon Him (and me!) to this miserable world of
suffering and death? I no longer shout that, but the mystery lingers.
This is the religious root of my quest for autonomy and my lack of
confidence in ecclesiastical authority: the tooth and claw of nature,
and the Father's silence.

***

Years later, and by then married and a father, I made a couple
of weeklong retreats at the Jesuit provincial house in Baltimore under the direction of Frank O'Connor, S.J. On the second retreat,
the change was this: for most of my life, perhaps forty years, I had
feared death and life too. After a few years of marriage, I no longer
feared life. In a mid-week meditation, I realized that death is not an
enemy but a friend. In some ways, the priesthood had been a way
of avoiding death and the stream of ordinary life. The *fear* of death
and pain, I was guided to see, is far more the enemy than death and
pain themselves. I settled on mortality, accompanied by longing
for death which I now think secretly accompanied my fear of life. I

thought, and still think, that the fear of death, pain, and life itself, are the genuine enemies on the way up the hill of life and down the other side. They do pose a threat to the love we have for God, but the love and longing for God persist even while the fears call for despair.

In this mood, the crucifix has come to represent primarily the *creative* silence of God and God's *creative* abandonment of us all to history and nature, including pain and death, following in the wake of the Incarnation. If the Father could abandon the Son to life, pain, and death, death can't be the enemy. If God raised the Son from death, death can't be final. Fear of all this is the real enemy. God can be trusted and must be trusted. This was a sea-change in my mood and even, to a degree, in my dispositional immediacy which condemned me to a life of suspicion and doubt. I have remained a defensive grump but now a happier and less frightened grump.

***

I had begun an intellectual life in 1953-55 in the college seminary under the inspiration of a historian (Msgr. Joseph Nestor Moody) and a professor of English literature (Fr. David Rea), both of them extraordinary teachers. Why would anyone be intensely interested in 19th century French political history? Why fall in love with Alexander Pope's poetry? I can hear and see them still. I was nineteen at the time, a teenager looking for priestly intellectual models. By the time, I reached my graduate studies in theology (1957) I was bored by neo-scholastic philosophy and theology, the received forms of Catholic thought. Gradually, I became a surreptitious convert to an unlikely hybrid of Protestant theologies, Bultmannian existential hermeneutics of the New Testament and Barthian fideism on matters of Christian dogma (more Adamic autonomy, I'm afraid, and more distance from the Roman *Magisterium!*) Though I was enthralled by the study of the scriptures under the guidance of the best teacher I ever had, Msgr. Myles M. Bourke (how can one get excited by a *haplax legomenon?*), I was ordained in this negative state of theological mind in 1961. Now it seems that my mind bent toward forms of thought that lent themselves to preaching and teaching rather than those of an academic theologian. I have a very limited gift for philosophical theology or systematic theology, and none at all for biblical languages. I thought then that my interests were engaged by good teachers but I now realize that it was also subject-matter and method that held my attention and generated my enthusiasm. I could make sense of the inductive methods of scripture scholars and the narrative of the historians rather than the deductive and conceptual methods of the scholastic theologians.

A first overt step toward a formed and independent professional life other than the priesthood began with my choice in 1964 to
study at Columbia's school of philosophy rather than at Fordham
University's theology department. When I turned down the offer of
support to study at Fordham from the diocesan director of education, I was turning down a future in the work of the archdiocese. I
might even have become a monsignor!

At that point, I was skeptical of the intellectual viability of
Catholic theology—however, NOT of the Catholic way of religious
life of which I never despaired. I desperately wanted to know
how "the others" saw things. I got my fill at Columbia and Union
seminary. The professors there may not have been better teachers
than my seminary professors or as inspirational but they certainly were "other" in mind and spirit, and often attractively so. John
Herman Randall, Jr. (d. 1980), a professor at Columbia, intrigued
me the most, for he had no hesitation in directly and critically engaging Christian thought and practice, not always negatively. He
was a crusty naturalist historian of philosophy with a remarkable
synthetic mind, with respect for serious thinkers no matter their
metaphysical and religious convictions. He made it known that St.
Thomas was the "first medieval empiricist." It was on his work and
that of his teacher, Frederick Woodbridge (d. 1940), that I wrote my
doctoral dissertation. They were both labeled "Aristotelian Naturalists" because they sparked and lead a renewal of Aristotelian
studies in American philosophy, adding that study to the already
deep interest of American philosophers in Kant and Hegel.

Both were sons of ministers and both were atheists. They were
far too intellectually sophisticated to take any comfort in that label
but it did effectively distinguish them from the liberal Protestantism to which both were born. Without immersing myself in their
published works, I don't think I would have as sharp a sense of the
critical importance of atheism to the spiritual and intellectual life of
a believer (this believer at any rate). I would also lack awareness
of the Aristotelianism that bound them to Aquinas and the Catholic intellectual tradition as well. Atheism may be incorrect as the
solution to a significant intellectual issue, but it is far from wrong
about the silence of God or about the tensions between traditional
Christian doctrine and modern thought. Their chief problem is that
they are tempted, like me at various times, to take God's deafening
silence to mean that God isn't. Can't blame them for that, can we?
Who isn't so tempted? At any rate, studying their work intensely for several years both promoted sympathy for Naturalism and
confirmed my native Catholic Aristotelianism and Thomism dur-

ing those very years of their flowering in Catholic transcendentalist thinkers like Karl Rahner and Bernard Lonergan.

***

In 1965, four years after my ordination to the priesthood and in my first year of doctoral studies at Columbia and Union Theological Seminary, Frs. David Tracy and Joseph Komonchak returned from graduate studies in theology at the Gregorian University in Rome and argued me into reading Bernard Lonergan's *Insight: A Study of Human Understanding*, published in 1957. The argument took place in the small room I occupied in the rectory of Our Lady of Perpetual Help in Pelham Manor, a nifty little town caught between the Bronx and New Rochelle and a fascinating parish. As they told me of their teacher in Rome I said to myself, "Oh no! Not another scholastic epistemology text and not another Jesuit!" I happened to be reading Kant's *Critique of Pure Reason* at the time and was stunned when I read *Insight* to find that Lonergan demolished Hume, Kant, Locke and other Greats on the questions of what knowing and knowledge are. For the first time in my life I learned about "cognitional theory" and understood the reason for metaphysics and the anchors for its peculiar language. *Insight* belongs on every Great Books list; it tops mine.

Although in the following decades I continued to read him, I did not become an academic Lonergan interpreter, nor could I have been to be quite frank. I don't have either the brains or the temperament for that, any more than I could have been a professional interpreter of Thomas Aquinas, Hume or Kant). But Lonergan's "Generalized Empirical Method" became my map of mind and has remained so. I have read large swaths of *Insight* (1957) upwards of thirty times over the past forty-five years and became a devoted reader as well of his *Method in Theology* (1972). An important, but far from the only, change it fostered in me was the recognition that Catholics could think outside the scholastic box in serious dialogue with both the Catholic tradition and British empiricism, and, finally, with Continental philosophy. Such investigations as Lonergan's could turn up an often startling and lively Catholic intellectual tradition. His analysis of St. Thomas's epistemology is remarkable. I would say the same for Karl Rahner and a handful of other transcendental Thomists of the mid-century who achieved a synthesis of Thomist and Kantian thought, and placed both in a new intellectual and cultural context. Aside from them and from the numerous genuinely talented and expert Catholic scripturists of the period, the landscape of Catholic theology appeared to be a learned wasteland of intellectual abstractions and dogmas.

***

A few years later David Tracy's *Blessed Rage for Order* both fascinated and distressed me.[38] While reading it four times (I have to read an ordinary theology book twice to begin to understand it) my residual Barthian fideism and my ever active Irish Catholic devotion to practice and doctrine rose like the archangel Michael ready for the Final Battle. Tracy was a friend at that time whom I took to be, at bottom and like myself, a pious Irish Catholic, but his book smelled of Rationalism! A friend of mine is a Son of the Enlightenment? It took me five years and three published essays on Tracy's foundational theology to right myself (to which essays, by the way, I owed my tenure at CUA), but I still list to port. His best work was yet to come: *The Analogical Imagination.* (1989)

What was it about *Blessed Rage* that so deeply bothered me? Aside from his brief and regrettable foray into process philosophy under the influence of Schubert Ogden, Tracy's brilliant foundational theology cut at the roots of my fideism. My Barth-inspired naïveté fell under the wheels of *Blessed Rage.* The result of reading Tracy (and after him the Methodist Schubert Ogden) was an intellectual and spiritual whirl around the issues of knowledge, faith, belief and practice, a whirl that has taken forty years to slow and from which I have never fully recovered.[39] The experience fed my suspicion that I simply didn't have the intelligence to be a successful academic theologian on the level of the theologians at CUA. The fact is that I can't think clearly, abstractly and critically *a la Tracy.* I felt that my presence on the CUA faculty was a bit of a charade compared to my colleagues and friends. My doctoral dissertation on American naturalism (1973) and my book, *The Naturalists and the Supernatural* (1984) and my review essays of Tracy's *Blessed Rage for Order* display a good bit of this inner identity conflict. I seemed always to be wrestling with myself.

***

---

38   David Tracy. *Blessed Rage for Order: the New Pluralism in Theology* (Chicago University Press, 1992) and *The Analogical Imagination: Christian Theology and the Culture of Pluralism* (NY: Crossroads Press, 1998)

39   Schubert Ogden, *The Reality of God and Other Essays* (London: SCM Press, 1967). For the review essays cf. the bibliography of K. Parker et al., *Pluralism and Theology: Essays in Honor of William M. Shea* (Lanham MD.: University Press of America, 2009)

While teaching undergraduates between 1980 and 1991 at the University of South Florida I met my first biblical fundamentalists and conservative evangelicals. I had to ask myself, "How do they exist as genuine and full Christians without bishops, priests and sacraments?" and, "If *they* are genuine Christians without these Catholic institutions, what in heaven's name are Catholics?" It had taken me fifteen years to write a dissertation and a book about naturalist atheism; it took me the next twenty years to write one about evangelicals/ fundamentalists and Catholics. The two books emerged from a lot of face-time with atheists and bible Christians. Both books had existential and personal roots, the first during my years at Columbia as a student and the second in two decades of teaching in Tampa and in St. Louis in both of which cities biblical Christianity abounds. Catholic friends and colleagues told me that both the naturalists (John Dewey chief among them) and then evangelicals were not worth my intellectual effort (this was in the heyday of Continental philosophy and theology), but as usual I hoed my own row, and went where my intellectual and spiritual instincts took me. In both cases I was urged on by personal questions about the truth and meaning of my Christian faith, and in both cases I was wrestling with questions which the Psalmist and Job would tell me quite correctly were far too deep for me.

I found myself over those thirty years asking why I am not an atheist and why I am not an evangelical Christian. For me, the interests I took on and the work I did grew out of the existential and experiential, and rarely reached the level of theory. I am not a theoretician, nor by nature or grace a talented scholar. I got along in the academic world by virtue of hard work and a great deal of luck, and by making sure that I worked on academic material that no one else in my Catholic circle was interested in. Almost everyone I was around over the past fifty years was smarter and more learned than I. The constant reflection accompanying my academic work over all these years was that I was in well over my head. To accomplish what I so much liked to do, teaching and writing, required considerable muscling-up of "the little grey cells" as Hercule Poirot called them.

The simple answer to those questions about my religion is that I don't *want* to be an atheist or an evangelical; I *want* to be a Catholic. I looked hard at both alternatives and said, "No, thanks" to atheism and evangelicalism. Yes, in those thirty years my mind was changed in relation to atheism and evangelical Christianity, and, consequently, in relation to the Catholic thing. I concluded that Christianity as a religious stance and teaching makes sense to me, but that the Roman Church and its hierarchy are shamelessly obsessed with their own office and their spiritual eminence. They are driven to their obsession, I fear, by their robust sense of responsibility and the objective hopelessness of their authoritative position rather than by faith, hope and charity. In simpler terms, they take themselves far too seriously, so seriously that the only way they are able to talk about it is in terms of the supernatural. They *need* to stand in the penumbra of the divine in order to do their jobs as they see them. They seem as unable to accept finitude and its uncertainties as I was.

I know that pride is the deadliest sin but I was once proud to be a Catholic, through the forties and even into the nineties. I was proud to be an American Catholic—deeply impressed with bishops, priests, and the religious communities of men and women. I am no longer proud. In fact, I am sometimes ashamed. This is the most consequential change of mind in my adult life and the only sad one. The shame erupted when I closed on seventy years. It's not that I ever liked bishops (in fact I have never liked them!) even when I was proud of them and thought they were doing the apostolic job like the priests and nuns I knew well. I thought they were good priests who got promoted. Now I know that they abandoned children to clerical perverts, and because of their devotion to The Church rather than to the church, they hid the crimes and got promoted. The perverts are sick, yes, but the leaders of the Church are despicable, from the top of the hierarchical maypole to the base. If you cannot trust bishops and priests to care for children, what *can* you trust them to do? Can you trust their witness to the resurrection of Jesus? I think not. Can you trust them to tell the truth about important matters about the Church and the world? Not any longer can I do so. Timothy Shriver put it with a clarity that is rare: "If you can't trust the messengers, why trust the message? It is not too much to say that the crisis in the church is contributing to a crisis of faith in the Gospel itself. This is a crisis not of management nor of theology. This is a crisis of the spirit." [40]

For a quarter of a century, they have stumbled from one foul policy to another. They decreed an end to clergy sex abuse in 2002 only to violate again and again their own reform policies. Pope Francis sends each of them a letter ordering "one strike and you are out" policy on child abuse and large numbers of them ignore him.[41] Most recently (fall 2012), they have launched a ludicrous for-

40   *New York Times*, March 1, 2013.

41   See "U.S. priests accused of sex abuse get second chance in South America" *USA Today* (September 17, 2015), a report on priests who transferred from the USA dioceses to dioceses in South America after many more than one strike. The video of the investigation is worth attention.

mal "campaign" in favor of religious liberty in order to reassert the public posture of righteousness they lost a decade ago. Respect for them is gone. It will take decades with the sort of leadership that the current crop of bishops is unable and even unwilling to provide to restore it. The church needs new bishops. One can only hope that Pope Francis, a charming and righteous man, is a start in this regard.

As far as I am concerned several generations of American (and other!) bishops have been guilty of a betrayal of the Catholic people as ugly as the generation of British bishops who handed the Church over to King Henry and his insatiable penis, uglier even than the betrayal by Bishop Judas. Yes, the episcopal betrayal of children is morally more reprehensible than the betrayal of Jesus by his own. May God forgive them all, as I am sure God will, but I will not. This loss of respect and trust on my part bleeds through to my ecclesiology, even into doctrine itself and to piety. Their action and inaction, their deception, have left me without the "one, holy, catholic and apostolic church" I was raised in. I am scandalized by them even though I surely am not one of the innocent ones, and so I think of "millstones" tied around papal and episcopal necks (MT: 18, 6). They broke my Catholic heart, not that my heart counts in face of the ruined lives of children and the psychological and spiritual torture of their parents. But, it must be said, this generation of bishops merely continues the age-old infidelity of the Catholic hierarchy to the scriptures and to the confidence that the Catholic people and priests placed in them, generation upon generation.[42]

---

42   See the bibliography for books by Jason Berry and Gerald Renner, Michael D'Antonio, and the Investigative Staff of *The Boston Globe*.

6. Our Families and the Church

There was a time when Catholic clergy looked askance at Catholics who did not attend Mass on Sunday and bemoaned this fact by recalling the glory days of the Great Depression when, they alleged, Catholics filled the pews. "What we need is another Depression! *Then* they'd go to church!" establishing a causal link between misery and faith. I once worked for a pastor who reminded me of those glory days several times a month at the dinner table. He drove a Chrysler Imperial and drank Haig and Haig Pinch, his suits did not come off the rack; he could have hocked his cuff links if he needed cash, and he played golf regularly at the local country club. He said his own prayers and Mass without a Great Depression but he hoped for enough suffering for his non-attending parishioners to save their souls. Another pastor (not mine this time) explained his solid upper middle class clerical life-style by saying that he needed a Cadillac because he took Holy Communion to shut-ins and "Jesus should ride in the best," and he had two Cadillacs because the first might just break down. Our justifications have no trouble keeping up with our desires, it seems.

In the same line, some say, "There are no atheists in fox holes." Fear, after all, is the motor of religion, is it not? I once had a chairman of a religious studies department whose "introduction to religion" textbook was built around a narrative of a primitive man who got scared by a lightning storm. He fell to his knees in recognition of a dangerous god. Even Richard Dawkins can be expected to pray when the motor shells rain down, I guess. Alas, Christopher Hitchens gave the lie to all this nonsense by dying slowly of cancer with no sign of repentance. There is at least one atheist in the universal foxhole! The theory that comfortable people don't pray and when they are uncomfortable they will pray is demeaning both to the ones who do and the ones who don't. Historically speaking, is it the poor and oppressed who become converts? Ask the Jesuits whose glorious history displays the importance of getting the upper classes to convert, or at least to tolerate, before the lower classes can be effectively evangelized. In the early Mediterranean churches, the apostles needed the support of the well-to-do converts in order to preach the gospel to the poor. Yes, many times people need to be shaken out of their ordinary desires and fulfillments if they are to ask the sort of questions that lead them to faith. No, we don't need another Great Depression to fill the churches. If there is one thing that human beings don't need it's more suffering.

What's the point? It's this: there is something going on with religion that's far deeper in the human spirit than fear. That "something" isn't captured in the usual neat categories like fear and despair or whether we go to church on Sunday or even whether we are theists or atheists, something prior to what we choose to do or not to do. It even underlies the religious names we give it in our various traditions of prayer, worship and practice and it is, I believe, universal. Shades of Hegel, Schleiermacher and Houston Smith, you say. More modernism and liberalism and relativism! More Freudian psychological archeology! I don't think so! Read the documents of Vatican II, which tell us of a far more complex origin and foundation of the religious quest than fear of a lightning bolt or of the "first father":

> Men expect from the various religions answers to the unsolved riddles of the human condition, which today, even as in former times, deeply stir the hearts of men: What is man? What is moral good, what sin? Whence suffering and what purpose does it serve? What is the road to true happiness? What are death, judgment and retribution after death? What, finally, is that ultimate inexpressible mystery which encompasses our existence: whence do we come and where are we going?
>
> …From ancient times down to the present, there is found among various peoples a certain perception of that hidden power which hovers over the course of things and over the events of human history; at times some indeed have come to the   recognition of a Supreme Being, or even of a Father. This perception and recognition penetrates their lives with a profound religious sense. [43]

I am trying to fend off any misunderstanding of what I am about to say, namely that members of our families joined the exodus from the Catholic Church and into what might be called secularity (secularism is an ideology and no one in our families is inclined to ideology). But that exodus does not mean that the quest and its questions do not form the deepest and most intimate core of their being. Most, as far as we know, are dedicated to living de-

---

[43]   *Nostra aetate*, #1 & 2. October 28, 1965. The document, and the entire set of documents from Vatican II, can be accessed online at the Vatican and at the site of the National Conference of Catholic Bishops.

cently and lovingly, as the Lord commanded, and all of them are attuned to the mysteries of life and death.

Helene and I have the sense that from infancy to the present, and through all sorts of challenges to belief and practice, we have known what we are, where we belong, what to fight about, and even where we hope to end. I've already written out directions for my funeral Mass. I want the last rites. We know where to go on Sunday morning and why we go. We are both intensely critical of the leadership of the Roman Catholic Church and are baffled by their myopic defensiveness, their reactionary vision, and their shocking moral irresponsibility. They are threatened by the independence of lay people like ourselves (there are many others like ourselves!) and intend to restore "obedience," the old word, and "communion," the new word for the old. But all of this is part of the struggle for the soul of the church that has been going on since the modernist crisis of the turn of the twentieth century (and much earlier in other forms), and will continue until we have a pope who knows which end is up and appoints bishops who know it as well. Pope Francis gives us hope in this regard. The church needs pastors, not prelates distinguished by the hues of red and purple. But, sad to say, the bishops, including the bishops of Rome, have already had their way with our families. They left us with a moribund church and a suspect message.

My analysis of the situation of religion in the Shea and Lutz families is flawed from the beginning in the sense that I know very little about most of my relatives in respect to their withdrawal from the Church. A hint here and a clue there, but in our extended families we don't talk much about religion. In these latter days, Helene and I are the odd and old ones. Both of my parents, devoted Catholics, are gone. Helene's parents are still with us, practicing Catholics as they have been all their lives. I know only a bit about one son's reasons for quitting the church: "Believe it because it's been handed down" doesn't work for him. Perhaps our siblings left simply because they don't believe and they don't get the point of practicing. One son, four brothers and their children, a nephew and two or three nieces, and six grandnephews and nieces, amount to three generations lost to the church. Once we are gone there will be no more Sheas and Lutzes (I'm excepting son number two who is now, after years of absenteeism, vigorously practicing the Catholic religion and teaches scripture in his New Hampshire parish) in the direct line who are Catholic believers and worshippers. Several of the third generation are not even baptized, so it will be RCIA for them if they ever find their way back![44] With the exception of my

---

44   RCIA, the Rite of Initiation for Adults, involves six months cat-

first born son who attended a Benedictine Priory School and the College of the Holy Cross and left his Catholic practice at the latter, none of my younger relatives are educated Catholics. My brother, Helene, and I were entirely educated in Catholic schools, and my brother has ceased practice. Why, I don't know.

Let me say that I am not questioning the honesty, sincerity, character, salvation or, indeed, the religious dispositions of my relatives. I have a very high opinion of and affection for all of them. The appropriate issue here is not blame; it's the loss to the church and the loss to them. Why doesn't the church hold their hearts as it does ours? My nephew, in a rare and intense discussion of abortion, dismissed my view as a product of "Catholic brainwashing," a thing he apparently managed to skip or evade. I would want him to think of the value of what he left behind: along with Judaism the longest-lived and most vigorous ethical conversation in the history of Western culture where argument, not brainwashing, is the determinant feature. Those Christians who, in composing the *Didache* at the turn of the first century, condemned both pagan abortion and infanticide, were not brainwashed fools! They were thoughtful people who figured out the difference between a fetus and an acorn. They protected pregnant women and collected abandoned newborns from the hillsides before the wolves got to them, and that is what set Christians apart in the Roman Mediterranean: they had respect for life.

I am sure that the exodus of our relatives has little or nothing to do with the sex abuse crisis because all or most of the exodus took place years before the crisis broke in force in 2002. However, I'm just as sure that the abuse crisis confirmed decisions made long before for different and varying reasons, perhaps most of all boredom. But I'll try two questions: Are their individual decisions part of a larger picture of a steady decline of the church membership? Yes, for the background to their individual decisions is the massive abandonment of the American Catholic Church (and other Christian churches) over the past thirty years. According to the Pew Foundation, one third of American Catholics have left the practice of their faith. In other words, twenty million have swayed from the Catholic faith. Our family is a drop in the ocean of abandonment. The steady decline in European Catholicism over the past two hundred years is being matched by American Catholics at last. and Ireland and Poland, long the most Catholic of peoples, are now in the spiral. Historian and controversialist Hilaire Belloc once wrote

echesis before baptism and serves at the same time as a reintroduction to the church's message for those who have taken time off.

that, "Europe is the faith and the faith is Europe."[45] That wasn't the case even as he wrote it in 1920. He made a historical and cultural point but it is merely that. When it came to the Catholic Church Belloc was an incurable if delightful romantic.

My wife and I come from faith, just a generation or two removed from Irish and Bavarian Catholicism. Both were vigorous branches of the Roman church. My mother and her two sisters, one a Sister of Charity, were devout. My Power granduncle was not only a priest; he was a Monsignor! My father was staunch. He once quit a job when it would have forced him to miss Mass on Sunday, and this was in the thirties when jobs were desperately hard to come by. He checked with a priest in the confessional and was told to quit, and he did so with no means of support at hand. He certainly wasn't an anti-clerical but he had his reservations about just how well priests understood "life" (by which he meant marriage). He only had one vigorous argument against official Church teaching: he found that the common Catholic teaching about the reprobate character of Protestants and Jews was nonsense. He expressed this view forty years before the bishops at Vatican II got around to agreeing with him. Although I doubt he knew it, he was part of the on-going conversation, frequently enough underground, that is Catholicism.

All the other Sheas and Powers, McClearys and Drohans from the Bronx and Brooklyn showed up at my first Mass in St. Raymond's Church in 1961. It was the single largest gathering of the family in its American history (and the last). John Power, my mother's brother and his wife and three daughters, Aunt Catherine, Sister Peter and the rest of the Power clan filled the second and third pews behind my parents who sat in the first row, a place of honor for the parents of the newly ordained. One family of Sheas arrived a bit late and pushed their way into the front pew with my parents and brother. Aunt Catherine Power got more than a bit huffy when aunt Peg and uncle Barney Lyons and their family slid into that first pew. There was a pecking order in those days even in church, or perhaps I should say especially in church. Aunt Catherine was so bothered by this violation of protocol that she poked my mother sharply in the back to show her displeasure at this disturbance of the divine order of things. In other words, how dare Peg and Barney take a place in front when the Powers were relegated to the second row!

There were some later intimations. Uncle John Power's eldest daughter "ran off" with a married man who had children. In order to explain this familial anomaly, John commented, with a resigned

45   Hillarie Belloc, *Europe and the Faith* (London: Dodo Press, 2007; 1920).

sigh, "These days they live under the shadow of the atomic bomb." My father responded: "Bull shit, John. It's just hot pants." John Lyons, my cousin at whose wedding I had officiated, was divorced by his wife of a few years and invited us to a second marriage, this one to take place in the Congregational Church in Peabody MA. When John Lyons came to tell my father, and my father said he wouldn't attend an invalid marriage in a Protestant church, cousin John made the mistake of saying, "Uncle Bill, Protestant—Catholic. What's the difference?" My father responded: "You stupid bastard, I'll tell you what the difference is: five hundred years of Irish Catholic blood!" I attended the wedding in clerical collar but my father refused to do go. No one any longer thinks that those 500 years are worth remembering when it comes to religious loyalty. I do, but I really can't blame those who don't. To this day I retain the inclination, raised to a fever pitch by my father's stories, to suspect the British Protestants of constant crimes against humanity (i.e. Irish Catholics), a prejudice that has vanished among the younger Sheas.

All of that is lost now. All the historical and folk memory has perished as generation succeeds upon generation in the "new land" and with the passing of the Irish-American Catholic subculture. My family is no longer in a "new land" and the "old sod" is a sentimental memory. Had my father lived to see me leave the priesthood it would have been the most terrible blow possible to the family honor: a failed priest! I suspect that he would not have spoken to me again for the hurt and shame I gave to my mother and him. The generation before me didn't take kindly to such embarrassment. I remember clearly the night when, in a New Rochelle restaurant on Shore Road, I brought up leaving the priesthood; he replied, "If you go out that back door, you'll go out with my foot up your ass!"

My two Power aunts and one of Helene's uncles, faithful Catholics, refused to attend our religious marriage ceremony that was attended by most of our clerical friends. My father would not have attended; my widowed mother did because in the case of children the law must be bent, and even broken. She said that her sisters, one of them a nun, could turn down our invitation because they weren't mothers themselves, one of the few things she could hold over their sanctified heads. And their grandchildren and great grandchildren unchurched and attending public schools! Divorce! It entered in my generation and bloomed in the next: four already and others likely yet to come.[46]

---

46   In all this, the Sheas seem to have forgotten their own "foundational" scandal: my Shea grandfather had gotten Eileen Kennedy in the family way and ran, disappearing for five years before returning and marrying her and fathering eight more children. This return and marriage for

Why the exodus? Educational choices differ in different generations, and there is no Catholic education in the next generation
of Lutzes and Sheas. They won't even know that Jesus had, and so
the Christian churches have, a problem with divorce. A subculture
died, social status changed, parish attachment faded, the leaders
look and sound like moralistic grandparents, American individualism and autonomy all take their toll on the Catholic communal
conscience. It is a commonplace now that the Roman Church is
neither necessary to salvation (whatever that is!) nor attractive as a
religion, and you can stay in bed on Sunday morning. The church
is no longer a challenge, an invitation to goodness and virtue, a
bastion of truth about life and death, a harbor in a troubled world,
its very existence no longer a compelling message that Jesus is risen
and that the church is His body. The word "church" comes again
to mean the hierarchy (The Church) about whom there is little attractive and much objectionable. The leaders act out: they parade
in garments that no self-respecting male or female would take out
of the closet, or, indeed, even keep in the closet, as if Constantine
had not passed on to his just desserts and they were still governors
of provinces of the Empire. Who wants to be part of an institution
whose leaders are old misogynists who force their misogyny on the
young, raising pained questions about young women serving at the
altar as if their Christian consciences are offended by this desecra-
tion of the holy, and whose bishops who long for righteousness are
pulled into hypocrisy and deceit when scandal looms? It seems
that "The Church" is not only in the world, but of the world. It IS
the world in drag! To many The Church is simply another locus of
the adult phoniness that so put off Holden Caulfield.[47]

What about Helene and Bill? Do we object to secularization of
the family? We think they are mistaken, but we chickened out. We
decided not to oppose or reproach or even discuss the question
though we were both bothered. Their seats in the pews are empty.
We, Helene and I, miss them. We have been struggling all these
years with the responsibilities of belonging to the church. However,
our years have also been consumed with prayer, and there always
have been the Eucharist, the sacraments, the preaching and teaching, always the overwhelming Catholic intellectual and social trea-
sury, and always the Catholic friends, always the study of Catholic history. Other members of the family have not had so thick a

---

some reason so enraged his step-mother that she disinherited him and
"put them out on the road," reducing them to penury. It was a Protestant
neighbor who took them in.

47   J. D. Salinger, *Catcher in the Rye*. (NY: Little, Brown and Company:
1991; 1951).

Catholic context for their lives. Our life-long spiritual struggle has been over the mystery of God, the mystery of the church, and the mystery of evil. I doubt that such esoteric topics interest most of our relatives. They had and have real lives to lead and the church has precious little to teach them. They have their own communities of family, work and play. So why a religious community? Why another commitment?

From another angle, we might ask how is it that we, Helene and I, find God in the midst of this decade's long ecclesiastical maelstrom? How can we put up with church leaders who condemn the like of Charles Curran and Hans Kung, and the work of women like Sisters Elizabeth Johnson and Margaret Farley and dozens of other Catholic theologians, every one of whom has the good of the church at heart? Nothing could be more evident in the lives of the four mentioned. Catholic leadership is stuck in the vast misogyny, mindset and dogmatism of the ages, its own version of ecclesiastical original sin running alongside of historical Catholic hatred of Jews. How do we live with that, something we are reminded of every time we attend Mass where always one man presides and speaks, and even the young female altar servers are suspect and are forbidden to think of priestly ordination?

We rejoiced in the priority afforded individual conscience in *Dignitatis humanae* and in the historic reversal of the received teaching about Judaism in *Nostra aetate,* and other reform documents voted upon by the bishops of the Great Council. We admire the inspired group of bishops who led the rest as close to the truth as bishops had ever come. We rejoiced, too, when the American bishops condemned the arms race and nuclear weapons and wrote on the economic injustice in capitalism. These were the bishops of Paul VI. We have wept over the renewed papolatry and the two revisionist popes who undermined the Council again and again, and tried to drag the church back into the nineteenth century although both as young men were important participants at the Council. Both of us were brought up in deeply Catholic homes and received advanced Catholic education. We were called to Catholic religious life. Both of us still live in the remnants of the Catholic subculture made up of nuns and priests and theologically serious Catholic laity. Both of us love the church and still sit in the emptying pews.

As far as we can tell not one member of either family, aside from Helene's parents and ourselves and one of her uncles, are Catholic any longer or even religious. And we watch in sadness. We are not worried about their "immortal souls" (as one bishop recently put it as he worried about salvation of the benighted laity voting for Democrats) for they all have faith as we understand it, they are all obviously graced. We worry about the Church and its worship of God in spirit and truth, and we worry about the message of the freedom of the children of God. Yes, the church prays and lives on without them, and we fear the exodus will not be reversed. I surely will not live to see it.

Perhaps another sort of abandonment needs to be mentioned. My family left as Catholics generally have in the past without joining any other church. But some people who have been "family" to us for decades have abandoned the Catholic Church for life in other Christian churches. One colleague at the University of South Florida helped found a Lutheran community in his section of Tampa. He left because he could no longer put up with residual anti-Judaism in the preaching in his home parish. He is one of the few colleagues who have had decisive impact on my thinking. Another couple, friends for decades, are now Lutheran ministers. They left because of the disrespect shown to women and the laity by The Church. I wept when they did. And finally, a dear friend and his wife left Catholic worship and joined the Episcopal Church because he could no longer stand worshiping in a Church which demanded doctrinal conformity and was pronouncedly anti-intellectual. I feel like a bird left behind when the winter migration to the South has begun. I can't fly. When The Church loses people like this, my sky grows dark.

What about the church leaders' response to the Great Exodus? "The New Evangelization" announced by the popes doesn't seem adequate to the size and depth of the problem, and it certainly hasn't reached our families. It amounts to "get 'em back," but back to what? After all, the conciliar reform has been rejected by the current bishops and the last two popes. The impetus of Vatican II has faded. There are fewer and fewer young *fideles*, and more and more old *fideles*. It seems that Pope Benedict has gotten his wish, a much smaller Church of a saving remnant, made up of evangelical Catholics who whoop and holler when the pope waves, and a graying generation or two. If history's witness counts for much, the church will very likely survive and there will be a rebirth, perhaps too late for the Sheas and Lutzes. Where will they find their pointers to the Holy One?

Our faith, Helene's and mine, cautions us on any bleak pessimism. For one thing, the Holy Spirit and God's grace are invisible and very likely to escape our notice and judgment, and unable to be contained within any ecclesiastical boundary. I can sometimes discern where the Spirit leads me but I have no ability to tell where the Spirit leads others. I try to remember that the Spirit is in the world and not only in the church. The Spirit is for the world and not merely for the church. Who are we to judge where the Spirit is blowing others? All we can do is pray and watch for the action of the Spirit and finally the appearance of Son of Man coming in the clouds. (Mk 14:62) And second, even though the hierarchy may snooze, the human search goes on, in us, in our families, in every human spirit. Every time we reach out in love and compassion, we touch God. Isn't this the most important teaching of the second Vatican Council? And of Pope Francis?

7. The Upside

Being Catholic and Loving It

In spite of my own sins and miseries, the fact of the matter is that the priesthood is a life worth living and the church is a matrix of truth and spirit. Learning what life is about and how to live it is the basic practical value of a Christian community. The Catholic Church is chock full of the lessons and ways to deliver them as well as the corruptions which appall us. The church is still a learning laboratory. On the macro level of church life, one only needs to watch Pope Francis when he acts and hear when he speaks. His life and teachings are an impressive fleshing of the Beatitudes (MT 5:1-12). There are some bishops like him, not enough I'm sure.

But I didn't learn my Christian language from popes and bishops. I didn't need to do so, for I had Christian life and language teachers galore. As much as I admire Pope Francis, I don't need him to fix me close to the church. The family attended a large and vibrant Catholic parish in the east Bronx. As a Catholic, I had a not unusual mélange of parish priests, Sisters of Charity, Brothers of the Christian Schools and Marist Brothers who cared for me from first grade through high school. I met and prayed with Ursuline Sisters at the College of New Rochelle and Benedictines in St. Louis at my sons' Priory School, and Jesuits at St. Louis University and the College of the Holy Cross. I made prayer retreats with Jesuits and even once with Trappists. I sat in front of some remarkable men in the seminary while preparing for the priesthood. Just when I badly needed an intellectual path in life I was directed by two priest friends to read the work of the Jesuit philosophical theologian Bernard Lonergan, one of the very few people who "changed my life" while many have enriched it. I even was befriended by Rabbi and Professor Jacob Neusner, a renowned Talmudist, who encouraged me to be a better Catholic by his powerful faith-filled Jewish life. For a couple of decades he filled the role of an older brother, showing me how crucial Judaism should be to genuine Christian faith. Without the first, there is no second. After all, the New Testament is a series of footnotes, or better an appendix to the Old.

You never know, do you, how the grace of God will arrive? I

worked as a priest in four Catholic parishes where I was surrounded by admirable priests (with a few memorable exceptions!) and
taught in four Catholic institutions of higher learning where the atmosphere was palpably different from the state university. As good
as the state faculty was and as bracing an atmosphere as I found
there, there was not a very clear sense that there is more to life than
meets the eye and the academic mind. The Catholic schools had,
in my view, a strong sense of community that ran well beyond the
walls of the school, a definite moral/social tone, and a strong scent
of eternity. When I arrived at Saint Louis University in the summer
of 1991, I felt at home after eleven years of pleasant and valuable
exile in the University of South Florida. Serving on a national committee of Jesuit higher education for three years, I visited six other
Jesuit colleges and picked up that same scent of Catholicism I so
much loved at the Catholic University of America. When I walked
around the campus of the Marianist University of Dayton, I was
astonished to find that Catholic students *look* different than the students on the campus of the University of South Florida.

You could say, with some justification, that I am a cultural Catholic. But there is more to it than that. For all the crowded pool of
priests in which I swam and for which I remain most grateful, I
remember that the pool was fed, first and foremost, by my parents
whose Catholicism was deep and rich, not theoretically, not only
culturally, but spiritually (a much over used and undefined term!)
They believed and prayed their life long, and they invariably acted like Christians even when they suffered. They belonged to the
church, always a concrete community of faith, hope and charity. If
it is true (and I think it is) that faith is sometimes passed on through
a form of spiritual osmosis, and if it is true (and I think it is) that
faith is "learned" from the lives of others, then I am a Catholic
Christian because my parents taught me well the importance and
meaning of what it is to be a Christian. These teachings were always true despite bumps in life that my parents and I experienced.
Besides being always at the edge of economic collapse, they lost
three pregnancies, he had two year-long bouts of TB which kept
him from earning a salary, she suffered depression often, he had a
difficult job, she had to work unusual hours and odd jobs, he left
his parents behind in Ireland and never saw them again and that
broke his heart, her mother died when she was born and her father
died when she was a little girl and she blamed herself for the first
at least, he ended in the employment dust bin when the corporate
bosses changed, and she had stomach ulcers for years and nearly
died when she had surgery. They both worried about their first-
born and his priestly vocation, and she suffered bravely through

his vocation change, never wavering in her love and loyalty towards her son when everything she knew told her he was wrong.

They lived with two sons in a one-bedroom Bronx apartment building filled with working families, only a step or two above state housing. When they moved, after twenty years, into a four room flat in a two-story brick house in the same neighborhood, it was a significant step up. They were able to do it because one son went to a seminary college with no tuition and the other, an outstanding high school basketball player, went to the College of the Holy Cross on a full scholarship. They never made it, despite their efforts, into the middle class. Their sons followed the script: the second generation made it into the middle class, one a priest/professor and the other a commercial lawyer.

Like most lower class Catholic parents in those days of the Catholic subculture, the center of their lives were their children, their school, and the parish. However, at the center of their "spiritual life" was Sunday Mass. They prayed hard. I watched them at Mass even before I reached school and gradually learned that the Mass and prayer were crucial to a Catholic life. Not diamonds, not cash, not even health, not ease, not entertainment but holy bread, wine, and the rosary, Christ and His Mother, and being honest, never screwing people, and taking care of those poorer than you. This is what I saw for the first twenty years of my life. Even venal priests and bishops cannot put this flame of hope out, never mind the ordinary sins of ordinary Catholics, not even my own sins. Hope burned within me through my parents and I saw the value of the church and felt the presence of God. Should I have forgotten that? And moved on to what might have been greener pastures? Never! May my tongue cleave to my jaws if I forget what they showed me! (Ps. 137:6) And I won't because the same hope, love, and faith keep burning through me day by day.

Section 2.

Authority in the Church

8. Bishops, Archbishops and the Like

Irony, along with sarcasm and satire, is a form of humor that denotes the finitude of all human endeavors but especially the ones most prone to sacralization and pomposity. The divinely established and supported clerical caste needs sarcasm and satire, and the hierarchy itself desperately needs to cultivate its sense of the irony of standing in the place of the God-Man. It is difficult to make sense of terms like *In persona Christi* and *alter Christus* when they are used of priests and bishops. They must be meant to signal a religious ideal, for the terms contradict everything we know about the hierarchy and ourselves, and to promote reverence for a supposed supernatural ontological status when in fact the clergy are no more "ontologically changed" than a soda-jerk is by his work.[48] Beyond the irony, the titles become deadly when they provide a cover for the abuse of children and the seduction of young adult Catholics, male and female. The *other Christs* have done these things! Priest and bishop abusers have caused more "ontological change" in their victims than the sacrament of orders caused in them.

Sad to say, bishops don't seem to laugh at themselves in a way that promotes health, at least not in public. It is hard to imagine cardinals roasting one another annually or our seeing a pope sitting at a dinner table in the presence of hundreds of people as an American president must, hearing the savage mockery of this year's comedian. Humor is part of a democratic community's effort to keep the feet of its rulers on the ground. But such will not do for Catholics or their leaders: God is not mocked, and neither may be His stand-ins!

I sympathize with all bishops. They have a tough job and they are only human. I couldn't do the job; I couldn't even be a priest. The issue forced on us by the situation in the current church is not whether they are morally good or bad as individuals. Many of them are likely as good as most men are, and probably many of them are good bishops. They hate to be judged by others as I do. After all, Jesus said, "Judge not less you yourself be judged" (Mt. 7:1) and I all too soon will be judged. I must make my judgments where they cannot be avoided and make them with fear and trembling, fully conscious of my own sins. No, the issue is this: can they

---

48   I was a soda-jerk, a cemetery worker and an information clerk for the New York Central, and all of them transformed me "ontologically."

be trusted *as a sacred class* to lead the churches. This is an empirical question primarily, not a theological question. Many of them cannot be trusted. This is not a matter of theology or doctrine. They have proved themselves recently (and indeed, historically) to be threats to the wellbeing of their churches. Their recent history in this regard is frightful.

I have no right to judge them given my own history of moral irresponsibility and my character flaws. As Pope Francis has said: "Who am I to judge?" Jesus instructed his listeners: "Watch the beam in your own eye...." (Mt. 7: 3-5) Yet their major weakness has been their abject surrender to behavioral patterns of the Catholic caste system. It seems to be universally true that they won't discipline (or befriend!) their clergy or one another when it comes to serious moral matters—unless public scandal forces them to do so. Bishops like things quiet. Even when they make reformist moves as they did in Dallas in 2002 the most prominent among them don't follow their own rules through. They are stuck in clerical cement. They don't tell the truth either, a key ingredient in decent leadership. God knows they don't tell the truth to their churches. They won't take the steps necessary to protect children and families from clerical sexual predators, *even when they legislate the protective measures themselves.*[49] From the top to the bottom of the hierarchical scale, Catholic clergy have an irresistibly strong leaning in favor of protecting the brethren. This is the major flaw of the Catholic structure. The Church has failed the church. Unless offending bishops and priests are fired, unless the system called "clericalism" is eliminated, unless their ordinary way of doing clerical business is abandoned, unless the Light shines upon them, the church will again and again suffer harm at the hands of The Church. The Church needs to take a dive if the churches are to be healthy.

Think of the good bishops have done as a group. They kept the churches from Gnosticism in the early centuries, leading them to clear doctrinal standards and sacramental practice. Along with the monks and the new religious orders, they led the churches through the chaos of the so-called Dark Ages and some helped expand the churches' intellectual and spiritual life through the middle and

---

49   I need only mention Rigali in Philadelphia, Finn in Kansas City and Nienstedt in Minneapolis-St. Paul. Finn and Nienstedt resigned in June 2015. Their behavior made headlines a decade after the Dallas meeting had laid out the program of reform. For an example of the way an archbishop behaves under questioning in a deposition in a case of child abuse, see http://www.stltoday.com/archbishop-robert-j-carlson-deposition/pdf_8545e986-5a00-5e7b-81a9-a6eb04604585.html. This is as clear a case of a bishop protecting his "assets" as you could want!

modern ages. While they contributed mightily to the scandals that brought on the Reformation, they also secured the unity of the Catholic churches in the centuries following the Reformation with the help of the Jesuits. At the Council of Trent (1547-1563) they formulated the responses to theological criticisms of the Reformers and laid the foundations of practical church reform far more than did the nervous popes of the period who seemed more worried about the stability of their Petrine throne than about reform.[50] Above all, they preached and preserved an orthodox form of the Christian gospel (often!)

The fact there are bishops and priests is not the problem. The episcopal form runs the churches as well as any other form of government that other Christian churches have erected. The fact that there is a caste that pronounces itself sacred is the Catholic problem. A Catholic church is still in existence through the turmoil of close to two millennia is due in large part to their hard work. Unfortunately, they have used their position and their power to proclaim the sacrality of their own offices and their own immunity from the judgment of their churches and imposing the need for unconditioned obedience on the churches. They made themselves and their supporting governmental structure God's positive will for all Christians. They proclaim themselves "Successors of the Apostles." They assume that they run "the one true church" and are better or higher in the Christian order of things than the rest of us. This is what must stop. They need saving from their own self-protective and aggrandizing instincts, from using God to project their own will on the churches.

Church documents direct bishops to take special care of their priests. Bishops should carry themselves as fathers of the Fathers. I had a father, and a quite formidable one at that. He was strict for he loved me and he stayed close to me. I didn't notice much of that fatherhood in the New York archdiocese when I was a priest, with the exception of Terrence Cooke. Later church documents also suggest that bishops should cultivate relationships of trust and cooperation with their theologians who these days are laypersons rather than clergy. I didn't notice any theological coziness in the dioceses of Washington D.C., Tampa-St. Petersburg, St. Louis or Worcester MA. Quite the opposite in fact. What I detected on both sides was suspicion and distance. I am sure there are reasons for the distance between bishops and what are called their "theological cooperators" but I have no explanation for it. I wish they would explain it to me: why aren't bishops closer to their priests and to their theo-

50   John W. O'Malley, *Trent: What Happened at the Council* (Harvard University Press, 2013).

logians, and vice versa? Why doesn't mutual confidence reign? Could it be that it does and I just don't recognize it? I don't think so.

In my twenty-seven years in the Catholic clergy, I spoke with a bishop only four or five times, each time for less than ten minutes. I never spoke with a bishop during my eight years of training, not even with the bishops who ordained me to minor orders or to the archbishop who ordained me a priest.[51] Please note that in New York there were a dozen bishops to aid Cardinal Spellman and a thousand parish priests. That means eighty-three priests per bishop. None of them, with the exception of Terrence Cooke, Spellman's successor, knew me by name, and the reason Cooke did was that I was a seminarian when he was an administrator in the seminary. Once I asked for a transfer of parish assignment (Cooke). Again, I was told that my request to attend graduate school was equivalent to a betrayal of the cross of Christ (Maguire), and on the last time I asked for release from the priesthood (Cooke). The first conversation took place in 1964, the second in 1969, and the third in 1979, all at my request. Once I wrote a letter to Cardinal Spellman offering my services to the military chaplaincy during the Viet Nam war and received no response (thank heaven as I look back on it!) Thereafter, as a layperson I spoke with three bishops (once with May and three times with Rigali in St. Louis, and less than a handful of times with McManus in Worcester). No New York bishop, with the single exception of Terrence Cooke, ever spoke personally to me. They all failed to take any interest in me as a priest or a person.

Even Cooke took the minimum time possible, and only when I initiated it. I never had a chance to take an interest in them; in fact,

---

51   A slight correction: when I was a college level seminarian in New York I once walked with a classmate down Lexington Avenue toward Grand Central Station around midnight. We had been drinking 'twofers' at McSorleys Ale House for a couple of hours and were laughing our way home when, at 43rd Street we met Bishop Fulton J. Sheen head on. Sheen then at the height of his television career, out for his evening exercise in his clerical garb and black fedora with the episcopal cross on his chest. As he crossed the street coming at us unnoticed just as I was remarking that we had no cash and my New York Central pass wouldn't get us both home I said loudly enough to be heard, "Holy shit, we're stuck here in the city!" The bishop stopped, fixed us with his very intense deep stage glare, and then passed us by. We hoped he hadn't memorized our faces. As it turned out neither of us ever saw him again. What's more important is that he never saw us.

I made myself scarce whenever in sight of them. I was, I guess, supposed to grow up and take care of myself and join in the fraternity
of the lower order of clerics. And besides, bishops are very busy
men. In fact, in large archdioceses they are so busy with administration and sacramental ministry that they are nearly inaccessible
to priests and ordinary lay folk. In addition, they seem not to be
the kind of fathers one goes to for advice. Those years now seem
to me very strange, for they called for a way of living from which I
became increasingly estranged.

***

In 1985, the Leadership Conference of Women Religious sched-
uled Sister Margaret Farley, S.M., to be one of the speakers at their
annual meeting. Sr. Margaret had been teaching ethics for a decade at Yale University and had reached national prominence as a
leading academic ethicist, and was even invited by Bill Clinton to
a White House ethics conference. She was a mentor and friend to
my wife Helene at Yale Divinity School and the director of Helene's
doctoral dissertation on the ethics of assisted suicide. Sister Margaret had just run afoul of the Vatican by the unfortunate publication
of an ad in the *New York Times* with her name among the signato-
ries.

She had not been told of the publication in advance nor was she
asked if her name might be used. She certainly was not looking for
a confrontation with the Church. An outfit entitled "Catholics for
a Free Choice" (abortion was its issue) sponsored it. The ad stated
that there were other Catholic positions possible on the morality
of abortion than the "official" Catholic position, something that
would bother both the Congregation for the Doctrine of the Faith
in Rome and the American bishops.

This conflict was still being played out in the Vatican (it was
later resolved in Sister Margaret Farley's favor) when she was invited to speak to the Leadership Conference of Women Religious at
their annual meeting. Archbishop John R. O'Brien of San Francisco
and Archbishop (later Cardinal) Pio Laghi, the pope's representative to the United States of America government and to the American Catholic Church, had also been invited to speak and celebrate
Mass.

Since the sisters refused to rescind Farley's invitation at the demand of the Vatican and the American bishops' office, Laghi and
O'Brien refused to attend, speak, and celebrate the Eucharist for the

sisters.[52] At this point, I had one of my most intense ecclesiastical hissy-fits.

Since I knew Farley personally and was at the time president of the College Theology Society, I decided to write to Laghi and let him know what I thought of his decision. I knew at the time that the society's letterhead meant that he would probably read the entire letter (appendix #11). In a deliberately offensive tone I lambasted him for refusing to celebrate Mass with the nuns and with Farley especially, and I went further than prudence and civil deportment would advise: I said that Laghi would undoubtedly share tea and crumpets with military murderers in the Argentine government (he had been Nuntio to Argentina at the very time when Argentineans were "disappearing") yet refused holy communion with an American nun:

> Your refusal to speak with them and on the same platform with Sister Margaret is an insult to her and to them, gratuitous, calculated and cruel. In my fifty years as a Catholic and including twenty years in the clerical state I have never seen the like. You are a man with responsibilities of political sort, no doubt, and you answer to those who sent you. You would undoubtedly rush to break bread with politicians whose hands are bloody, with a Gorbachav, with a Reagan, with the leaders of the Argentine junta. Yet you would not speak to nuns on the same platform with a nun. My dear archbishop, I am ashamed for you. The act is close to being unforgivable. [53] (Appendix 11)

Who, in other words, did he think he is? Well, "who he is" was the Vatican representative to the American Church and to the Ameri-

---

52   Sandra Mize, *Joining the Revolution in Theology: The College Theology Society* 1954-2004 (NY: Sheed and Ward, 2007). Refusal to celebrate the Eucharist because a specific person is present is big stuff for Catholics. The cardinal-head of the Vatican's Congregation for the Doctrine of the Faith also attempted in 2013 to block an award to Sister Elizabeth Johnson, and the same group failed to fall in line. The hierarchical pique was evident. Difference is always defiance for them; error still has no rights in The Church!

53   The full text of the letters to Laghi and Quinn can be found in Appendix #11 and in the College Theology Society archive at the library at CUA. These are one of the very few "meaningful" exchange of letters I ever had with the hierarchy, aside from the letter from the Congregation of the Doctrine of the Faith dispensing me from celibacy.

can government, not someone who had to answer to me! [54] He was a Lodge and I was not even a Cabot! I received an answering note not from Laghi but from his companion, Archbishop John R. O'Brien, to whom I had sent a copy of my letter to Laghi. O'Brien reprimanded me for the disrespectful tone as well as the content of my letter. He was quite correct to do so of course, even though he mistakenly took me to be a priest when in fact I had been formally laicized three years previously. Being a priest would have doubled my guilt. I answered O'Brien as follows:

> I wrote to the *Nuntio* as I did because I thought he probably rarely gets spoken to directly and with some feeling and conviction about the way he and Rome behave. I did communicate my views to Cardinal Hamer in the same vein, and thought it responsible to give the Nuntio a dose of the upset and anger he aroused in some of us. Politically my judgment might better have been kept to myself and silence maintained. Or I might have sent a more diplomatic letter, masking my reaction. But I did what I thought best to achieve what I thought needed achieving, that is, informing him that I think he has well exceeded the minimal bounds of public charity expected of a bishop and that he would do well to think about that. (Appendix 11)

Predictably, there was no response. The "new evangelization" hadn't begun! I hasten to add that Archbishop Quinn is one of the good guys.

***

I met Archbishop John May of St. Louis in 1991 in the basement of my parish church, St. Margaret of Scotland. When I introduced myself he said, "Oh yes, I know you! You've kept me awake at night!"[55] I had just authored an article in *Commonweal Magazine* entitled "Dual Loyalties in Roman Catholic Theology." The title was inflammatory since bishops would regard it as a settled view that Catholic theologians have only one loyalty, namely to the teaching office of The Church (i.e. the exalted *Magisterium*). I was pleased

---

54   http://www.desaparecidos.org/arg/iglesia/vatican.html; http://laprensa-sandiego.org/archieve/2009/february20-09/Pio.Laghi.022009.htm; http://www.mosquitonet.com/~prewett/cardinalaccused.html

55   "Dual Loyalties in Catholic Theology" *Commonweal* 119 (January 31, 1992): 9-14.

and surprised to know that His Grace read it, and thought enough about it to lose sleep. I learned a short time later that Archbishop Stafford of Denver (now Cardinal Stafford of Rome) had also read the article and had been upset enough about it to shake a copy in front of his seminary faculty and warn them not to teach such "revisionary theologies" and "dual loyalties" to his seminarians. Since I had mentioned Bernard Lonergan and Karl Rahner in my essay, Stafford banned their writings in another example of decisive archiepiscopal insight and leadership! (Irony!)

***

May's successor, Archbishop Rigali, and I would agree that the priestly and episcopal ministries require both holiness and learning. Holiness is composed of a single-minded love of God and of neighbor. The learning required is knowledge of the Scriptures, history, and teachings of the church, as well as knowledge of the culture obtained by experience and an education in the liberal arts. In other words, priests and bishops need to know what they are talking about, and to whom they are talking, when they teach and preach. They need to have knowledge of the world we live in, civil as well as religious. Whether the individual bishop or priest does or doesn't have such knowledge is observable in the pulpit, the classroom, the discussion group, and his administration.

Gauging is the trickier project. Uninformed and culturally ignorant leadership easier to spot than a leadership professing ersatz or shallow holiness, but the latter too can be spotted and thus one becomes wary of that religious leader. TV evangelists do not impress me as being holy or learned. Some of the denizens of the Catholic television network (EWTN) impress me as being orthodox but not holy. Fr. Richard John Neuhaus, founding editor of *First Things* and a prominent spokesperson of the Catholic right wing, struck me as a learned man but not as a holy man. Instead, I saw him as a man who, like his friend Chuck Colson, would throw his grandmother under the bus to assure the ascendency of his righteous causes. On the other hand, Cardinals Terrence Cooke and Joseph Bernardin seemed to be both holy and learned men. One must confess to the fragility of all such judgments, but I do recall with a chuckle the sardonic remark of one of the seminary history professors, Msgr. Florence Cohalan: "Pius X was a saint and didn't know it. Pius XI was not a saint and knew it. Pius XII was not a saint and didn't know it."

The simple Christian rule for judgments of this sort, established by Jesus, is that you shall know the tree by its fruit. That applies to bishops and priests as well as the rest of the population of the planet. Paul extended the rule by listing the fruits of the Holy Spirit in quite specific terms. (Gal. 5: 22-23) You can tell whether it is the Holy Spirit or the evil spirit that is active in human beings and their movements by watching outcomes. If the fruit is good, the tree is good. Is the Catholic Church the true church, or even a true church? Watch it carefully and see. What has been going on in the Catholic Church since 1978 (the election of John Paul II) would make one hesitate. By this, I'm referring to the abuse of children and the deliberate masking of that situation by the bishops. Additionally, the intense effort of two popes with the collusion of their bishops to undo the laudable efforts of the previous generation of bishops at Vatican II to bring the leadership of the church out of Christendom into the twentieth century and to create genuine communities of Catholics. I don't think any of this abusing, masking and undoing is a good thing for the church, nor do I think the men who do it are holy. In fact, I think they are unholy and a threat to the holiness required of the church. Like Bill Clinton, John Paul II was a supremely gifted ecclesiastical politician rather than a saint, and such people have always been dangerous in the papacy.

But discernment of this sort is no easy matter. Ignatius of Loyola pondered the question "How does one know that God is calling one to a deeper faith and even a ministry?" One knows by paying close attention to one's spiritual "motions" in prayer—what, when one imagines it, moves one to joy in the good and to distress over evil? The health of what we call "conscience" is crucial to a decision. The heart, after all, has reasons that Reason knows nothing of.

While trying to assess the spiritual value of the revival called "the Great Awakening," Jonathan Edwards (pastor of the Christian congregation in Northampton, Massachusetts in the eighteenth century) traced out implications of the saying of Jesus and the writing of Paul: was that spiritual melee in the colonies building up the Kingdom of God or was it undermining it—as its detractors said? What were its fruits? He decided it was (there was the usual passel of religious lunatics on the loose!) an action of the Spirit of God as evidenced by the fruits of conversion in the life of his congregation. The evidence was there, before his discerning eyes, he said. He thought he could tell "by their fruits" who was genuinely touched by the Holy Spirit and who was not.[56] Similar to what American Catholic bishops claim, he could tell who was fit to be a communicating member of his church and who was not.

---

56   The irony here is that Edwards was fired by the congregation whose conversion he was documenting. See Patricia Tracy, *Jonathan Edwards, Pastor: Religion and Society in Eighteenth-Century Northampton* (Eugene OR: Wipf & Stock, 2006).

Ignatius and Edwards were both learned and holy, worth heeding. Even we ordinary Catholics must make judgments of this sort about ourselves but also about those who claim our obedience and loyalty. On no account are they to escape our judgment about their competence, their holiness and their learning. We need often to recall that Judas was a bishop. He, an Apostle, went "into the darkness." If Judas did, any apostle or bishop can. Jesus chose him and was betrayed. Jesus chose Peter and was denied. Whom shall we simple, half blind Christians trust? Which bishop? Which pope? A fertile field for irony I would think!

9. On the Way to Dallas

The Abuse Crisis

Shortly after the *Boston Globe* focused public attention on Catholic clerical pedophilia and ephebophilia, the suggestion was
made to the faculty of the department of theological studies
at Saint Louis University that it should consider public response,
and at very least a conference or a lecture series.[57] Typical of that
faculty at that time, the department members turned down the suggestion of public action of any sort. It was a timid department in
those days, still under the clerical thumb, and unlikely to call any
attention to itself or the problem. They were mainly clerics who
knew the rules of the caste, and academics who preferred neutral-
ity to anything that called for political commitment. While Boston
College, the College of the Holy Cross, and other Jesuit institutions
took significant steps to educate Catholics on the matter of corruption, the mid-western Jesuits maintained their well-deserved reputation for ecclesiastical caution.

My parish in St. Louis, St. Margaret of Scotland in the Shaw
neighborhood, under the leadership of Fr. Kenneth Brown, did not
ignore the crisis and held a six week Sunday morning, after-Mass
conference down-in-the-basement. Sessions were led by sympathetic Saint Louis University theology faculty members who had
some special interest in an aspect of the crisis, from family ethics
to canon law to ecclesiology. There were over four hundred regis-
tered family units in the parish and the Sunday morning sessions
drew over a hundred adult parishioners at each. The parish was
helped to cope with the shock and to answer some of its questions
about the scope and implications of the predation.

Cardinal Bernard Law of Boston, that most orthodox of American prelates, and his assistant Boston bishops, knowingly reas-
signed pedophile priests to parishes again and again, and passed
them on to other bishops and dioceses without telling the truth
about them. These priests (Geoghan, Shanley and dozens more in

---

57   The Investigative Staff of *The Boston Globe, Betrayal: The Crisis in
the Catholic Church* (Boston: Little, Brown and Company, 2002).

Boston) and others in Dallas (Kos), Louisiana (Goethe), and Fall River RI (Porter) and elsewhere committed hundreds upon hundreds of crimes against children and families. As the American Catholic public soon found out, four thousand priests abused tens of thousands of Catholic children. In my opinion, any bishop who knew of the predation and hid it should be removed. Any bishop who claimed not to have known that there were civil and canonical crimes involved in each incident is likely a liar or a fool and should be removed. Any bishop who turned his legal hounds loose on the parents who sought redress for the injury to their children ought to be removed from office. What those bishops, archbishops and cardinals must have thought was that the priests and the bishops should be immune from civil law, and that the bishop's job was to protect the priests and, if need be, to hell with the children and their families. Those bishops did not possess the moral insight and courage, not to say the holiness, needed in a bishop of a Christian church. No excuse is acceptable. This includes the one offered by auxiliary Bishop Timothy Dolan of the St. Louis archdiocese, saying that it wasn't until later that the bishops were told by the therapists that pedophilia is incurable as if this excused the bishops from their Christian duty to protect children and their families.

At the time, I was the father of two boys who attended a Benedictine Priory School. I would not have had to consult a psychiatrist or psychologist to know not to let such a priest within miles of my child. This is a common sense morality we are talking about, not some obscure case in Catholic moral theology or a delicate therapeutic judgment or a lacuna in Canon Law. Bishops enabled the predators to prey and they should not be allowed to continue on the "thrones of the Apostles." They have made a mockery of those "thrones" and of the civil law. Again, the Vatican shields Bernard Law in its sacred and exempt precincts to this day, keeping him from the justice he so deserves, as it earlier did Cardinal Pio Laghi protecting him from charges of collusion with the Argentine military dictatorship. The "Holy See" should not have been turned into a refuge for people who have enabled criminal predation. The Cardinal Law case is a scandal, this time committed on the highest level of church authority. What Law did to protect predator priests, Pope John Paul II did for Law, and Pope Benedict followed with his consignment of Fr. Marcial Maciel Degollado to a monastery for "a life or prayer and penance," and not to the civil authorities in Mexico where he committed most of his crimes. Benedict deemed Maciel "too old" to face even a Vatican court. Maciel should have died in a Mexican prison, and Cardinals Law and Mahoney belong in American courts of law and, possibly, in American jails. Is it a perverted sense of mercy that drives popes and bishops to treat their own men so gently—or is it the peculiar bond of clericalism and the conviction that civil law takes a secondary role to The Church and its Canon Law? Is the protection and welfare of children truly secondary to the protection of the clergy and of church resources?

Bishops and priests in the United States have been remarkably successful over the past two hundred years. They have done the job. I wonder if anywhere at any time, any group of bishops and priests have done the job better. The great nineteenth century archbishops were far above the present crop of American archbishops and cardinals in intelligence, virtue and energy. But clericalism is the chronic disease of a hierarchical system. It seems a virtue but it delivers corruption. It is arterial sclerosis and Rome is the epicenter of it. Married priests and women priests would possibly alleviate symptoms but not cure the disease. The hierarchy would find ways to weave those "outsiders" into the self-protecting, self-perpetuating sacred system. The solution must take a more radical form than that.

Tight adherence to orthodoxy is part of the hierarchy's function, but it is not a cure for this disease. The only cure within our very limited reach is sure knowledge that irresponsible behavior will result in public dismissal from office and public (secular) prosecution, from the lowliest of the pedophiles to the highest of the hierarchs. On this, the Catholic left and right agree—only the pope and the bishops don't. They shielded criminals. Granted, expulsion of offending bishops and priests will not entirely end the quest for preferment in the clerical state. Nor will it definitively end the ambition and caste privilege that seem always and everywhere attendant on the clerical state, but at least it will intensify clerical ambition's odor of contingency and the ambitious cleric's respect for the common good even if only for self-protection. As it stands now, an ambitious bishop can get ahead by pretending loyalty to the pope and by simulating piety.

Meeting of Parish Representatives with the Archbishop of St. Louis

Justin Rigali succeeded to the St. Louis episcopal throne of John May, a man beloved by the people and priests of St. Louis far more than any of his several successors. May had been a "pastoral bishop" appointed by Paul VI in the shadow of Vatican II. His immediate successors, Justin Rigali, Raymond Burke and Robert Carlson were church bureaucrats appointed by Pope John Paul II or Benedict XVI who busied themselves undoing much of the work of the Council in the name of hierarchical discipline and orthodox doctrine. Rigali and I were in St. Louis when the abuse crisis hit (2002), he as archbishop and I as professor in the department of theological studies at Saint Louis University. I had the chance to watch him as closely as an interested outsider could. We both read the same public reports but it is likely that he had intra-Church information about the extent and cost of the abuse crisis to which I had no access. I am sure he was as jolted by the scandal as I was but he kept a decidedly low profile about it. After all, he had been instrumental in the appointment of the bishops under fire; he had been a member of the Congregation for Bishops in the Vatican for a decade and then served for seven years as its secretary.[58] The Congregation puts before the pope the names of recommended candidates for the episcopacy. He was a close associate and friend of John Paul II., and, presumably, that pope's kind of man would recommend only that pope's kind of man. God forbid candidates with moxie should slip through the Congregation's net and land on that pope's desk!

Shortly after Rigali arrived in St. Louis (1994), he administered the sacrament of confirmation to the young people of St. Margaret's parish, and among them was my second son Christopher. I was impressed by the quiet and effective celebration of the sacrament by the archbishop, and especially so by his genial address and exchange with the confirmands. He is a little on the short side and a bit pudgy (I am much taller in height and wider in girth) but the vestments and accoutrements helped make him an imposing figure as they are meant to do. At the reception in the church basement, his geniality and gentleness were engaging to scores of parishioners. I thought that Archbishop May had a worthy successor. I continued to have a favorable impression of him throughout his oversight of the parish churches of St. Louis—though I knew that many priests did not. He had the studied charm of the Vatican diplomatic corps matched to an unconditional devotion to papal authority. The joke, often made in clerical and lay circles in St. Louis, was that Rigali would begin his sermons with a quote of Pope John Paul quoting the words of Jesus, as if the truth of Jesus' words counted on their use by the pope: "The Holy Father said that Jesus said that 'Blessed are the poor in spirit...'"

In accord with the policy of the United States Conference of

58   Rigali and Cardinal Burke were finally removed from the Congregation of Bishops in 2014 by Pope Francis. The quality of episcopal appointments in the United States has markedly improved.

Catholic Bishops requiring each diocesan bishop to meet with representatives of the laity to consult about the abuse crisis, the archdiocese of St. Louis held a meeting prior to the Dallas conference of bishops in 2002 ("public" is not the right term for the meeting—so far as I could see the press was not in attendance and there were no press reports afterward). Rigali later became the cardinal archbishop of Philadelphia and was disgraced there by his failure to deal with abusive priests, and auxiliary Bishop Timothy Dolan later became the archbishop of Milwaukee where he made cash grants to departing abusers and stashed diocesan funds in untouchable accounts to protect the funds from victims' law suits, and later was appointed the cardinal archbishop of New York. Both of these men met with about three hundred lay representatives of the two hundred St. Louis parishes on Sunday night, June 9th 2002 at the St. Raymond Church parish hall in downtown St. Louis. Rigali, I'm sure, would not have had a meeting about such a topic without the prodding of the Bishops' Conference, while Dolan is a man who would meet anywhere with any number and on any topic, and charm the ears off them.

That night the two bishops spoke for nearly an hour between them, turned the mike over to their panel of advisors on sexual abuse for brief comments, and then opened the floor to questions from the laity for almost two hours. The lay folk surprised and moved me with the respectful yet direct questions. I have never heard Catholics speaking so seriously and earnestly to bishops, nor have I ever seen a bishop take such tough questioning, or indeed any questioning at all.

The question session in St. Louis made plain some of the trouble that the assembly of bishops in Dallas could not or did not solve. The problem with the presentation and responses from the podium that evening is this: the "evil" to be extirpated didn't include, in the view of the two St. Louis bishops, the irresponsibility, deceptiveness and arrogance of their fellow High Priests who are in charge of priest-criminals. Rigali was especially visibly annoyed by criticism of bishops. He did not want to hear any of it. [59] Towards the end of the meeting, with Rigali and Dolan still at the microphones, I joined the line of questioners. When my turn came, I made three comments. First, I said that I hoped the Dallas solution to the abuse crisis didn't become a hunt for homosexuals in the priesthood. Second, I hoped that steps would be taken to be sure that innocent priests would be protected from slanderous accusations. Third, I

---

59   See my summary and transcript of the meeting, appendix #13.

hoped that the bishops in charge during the abuse and those who protected the offending priests, such as Cardinals Law and Egan, would be removed. Rigali and Dolan, for the first time, offered no response. Both men recognized me. Rigali simply turned from me and asked if there were more questions. He was not happy with that final suggestion. Had I anticipated his troubles in this regard as the future Cardinal Archbishop of Philadelphia, I would have suggested that he resign. I was vaguely aware at the time that Rigali had been John Paul's chief agent in selecting and recommending men for the bishopric, men who fell on the churches like fleas on the Lamb of God, many of them still gnawing away at the Rome synod on the family in 2014.

If the issue is abuse of power rather than sex, as several lay folk at the meeting pointed out, then what is the bishops' role in all this? After all is said and done, they are the ones with power. The bishops, some of them abusers themselves, were involved in hiding the truth and putting children at risk, and complicit in reinforcing the "power" of the priest abusers when they hid the crime and the criminals. What is the "transparency" to which bishops are newly called (Dolan) and how do they propose to induce it? Very little has happened in the following decade after the incident in Dallas that has helped to improve the area of transparency in the Church government. And what about transparency in the archdiocese of New York where Dolan now reigns? Or during Rigali's time in Philadelphia? It is a question of the leopard and its spots.

This problem can't be solved under the current Catholic system though it has to be solved by it. How will the "clerical circle" be expanded (Dolan), and how much transparency will be permitted? In the Catholic Church, there is no transparency, no way of investigation, no prosecutors, no public courts, no investigative journalists, no private detectives. There are only bishops immune from secular prosecution, whose duty is to the pope and not to their own people. Dolan especially sought to cover these faults with rhetorical tricks involving "transparency" talk, but to this day bishops resist "transparency" vigorously.[60] They file lawsuits to keep diocesan records from public prosecutors and courts, they turn over information only when ordered by the courts to do so, and they hide funds when they can. I'm sure what they do is transparent to God and some of it at least to the pope, but the rest of us remain shrouded in the inherited clerical opaqueness. Not very apostolic I'd say unless the Apostles were in fact oligarchs.

---

60   USCCB. The Charter can be found at http://old.usccb.org/ocyp/charter.pdf#page=11.

The argument, forcefully made by Dolan at that meeting, was that the bishops at the time were ignorant of the almost one hundred percent rate of recidivism among pedophiles and did not know that the pedophiles do not benefit from treatment. Although true, it is nonsense as a legal and moral cover for bishops. It seems to me that a loving biological father who had never given a thought to the psychological profile of a pedophile, would never let his son or daughter within ten feet of that pedophile again. You don't let a fox in the hen house. It doesn't take very much moral insight, not to mention education, to figure that one out. But bishops who were dealing with pedophile priests seemed not to have had that moral insight and sent them back for more pedophilia. If a bishop found a priest with his hand in the till he would assign that priest to a place where there are no cash boxes.

By this time in 2002, the ideological big guns from the Catholic's right and left were in place and firing. The right told us that the bishops haven't been faithful enough to core doctrinal and moral teaching (orthodoxy), and so sin and scandal followed. What Catholics need to do in the abuse crisis, they said, is to renew commitment to orthodoxy and get rid of homosexuals! The fault, they say, lies with the Catholic liberals in the aftermath of the Vatican Council of 1962-1965. The left tells us that the bishops haven't fully applied or extended the collegiality impetus of the second Vatican Council. If only we had had laypersons, especially women, involved in a more transparent church administration, and married men and women priests! Both sides agree, however, that the bishops failed, and the bishops admitted it. The visuals from the Dallas meeting in 2002 were stunning: a room full of aging Irish and German faces, with a few token Latin and African faces, staring glumly, fixedly, resignedly at the lay persons invited to tell the bishops what a bad job they had done and that they had better learn to police one another as well as their priests. Of course, they haven't done the latter, and they probably never will until their jobs depend on it.[61] They continue to "protect the Church from scandal" as they are sworn to do.

---

61   Margaret O'Brien Steinfels and Scott Appleby were the spokespersons for the laity. Their words seem spoken today, over a decade later. See http://old.usccb.org/bishops/steinfels.shtml. And http://old.usccb.org/bishops/appleby.shtml.

10. Constantine Does Dallas

Is the church a monarchy or a community? This is a false dichotomy, no doubt. Many argue that a monarchy is a particular political shape of community (papocentric, integralist and ultramontane Catholics would have to argue for this, would they not?) while others argue that monarchy is the antithesis of any genuine community, and ultimately, like dictatorship, the destruction of a community. I stand with the latter, as do the North Atlantic and European states and peoples. Monarchy was eliminated precisely because it didn't tend to the common good. We don't believe in absolute or divinely established monarchies, including the monarchy of The Church. God knows we have had enough of the latter—over a thousand years of it in fact—to show us the destructive potential of monarchy in the church.

However, this is not always the case, for not everywhere is the community of the church destroyed by the papal and episcopal monarchy (there wouldn't be any church at all if it were) but surely it is often damaged when that monarchy demands a "communion" that is doctrinally, politically and theologically conformed to a pope's ecclesiastical ideology. This is precisely what happened at the time of the eleventh century split between the Eastern and Western churches, and in the sixteenth century attempt at a Reformation in the west. A strong version of the same monarchical urge has been afoot in modern papacies, as in the famous story about his son's question to Benito Mussolini at the dinner table, "What is Fascism, papa?" Mussolini answered, "Shut up and eat your pasta." Later on, thinking he had not received an answer, the son repeated his question and *Duce* said: "I already answered you: shut up and eat your pasta."

Popes Damasus, Leo the Great, Gregory the Great, Gregory VII and their two medieval successors, Innocent III and Boniface VIII, set the ideals for the papal governance of western Christianity. This became known as papal primacy (not a primacy of honor but of raw power) over other bishops and universal jurisdiction over all the churches, in principle of the churches throughout the world and in medieval practice in the churches of western and central Europe. They even took themselves to be the superiors of secular rulers whenever they could. They consecrated emperors, and threatened to (and did!) depose them. Popes Gregory XVI, Pius IX, Leo XIII and Pius X, XI, and XII are modern examples of a vigorous clericalist view of the Church in modern culture, a culture which itself has its own profound distortions, naturally enough since we are still in "this world" where distortion is the name of the game.

The modern popes, like their predecessors, divinely established and guaranteed monarchs, engaged the secular rulers, and added to the ecclesiastical patrimony a critique of the political, social and economic culture that caused the gradual and decisive reduction of the Church's sphere of influence and the extension of secular primacy and jurisdiction. Both "hierarchy" and "Christendom" were premises from which flows a worldview where the higher clergy issue the cultural, moral and political standards and even the material property of the church belonged to them. Recent popes lost their war on modernity just as their medieval counterparts lost the war for control of civil monarchies, though it must be said that the medieval popes won more of their battles.[62]

The term "Christendom" doesn't appear in the index of the New Catholic Encyclopedia of 1967, and neither in the shorter Oxford Dictionary of the Christian Church. [63] In the Random House dictionary it denotes Christians collectively, the Christian 'world.' I am using it in a different sense.[64] Here and in *The Lion and the Lamb* I take "Christendom" to be an ideal, a dream deeply drawn in the Christian imagination over two millennia and which still holds the Christian imagination today in important ways like a tattoo which

---

62   The astounding thing is that anyone ever thought that the papal claim to secular and/or ecclesiastical dominion has anything at all to do with the Reign of God and the Son of God! While the Reign of God and the Son of God are mysteries, which cannot be penetrated, the reign of emperors, kings and popes present no mystery at all. It's the very human story of hard and often bloody work to control and direct the human environment within reach. Many Catholics, especially the hierarchy, take the growth of papal power to be providential. I have my doubts. Even God might have had a bit of difficulty stomaching that growth and its effects on the church. The Church today remains entangled with the Empire! In this sense Constantine still lives. Cf. Anthony Kemp, *The Estrangement of the Past: A Study in the Origins of Modern Historical Consciousness* (NY: Oxford University Press, 1990).

63   See "Christendom" in *The Catholic Encyclopedia* (1914). In the New Catholic Encyclopedia see discussion under "Holy Roman Empire," 7:92; and "Christendom" in Wikipedia.

64   For a quite different use of the term "Christendom," see Philip Jenkins. *The Next Christendom: The Coming of Global Christianity* (NY: Oxford University Press, 2011) 3rd ed.

remains when the skin sags.

In the late antiquity and the early Middle Ages Christendom took the form of an ideal of a single human society and culture under a single government practicing a single religion. The culture is normative and the religion is the true religion—where other cultures fall short and other religions are false.[65] In its western high medieval form (twelfth and thirteenth centuries, the centuries of Gregory VII, Innocent III and Boniface VIII), Christendom was an idealized symbiotic relationship between the civil and the ecclesiastical orders in which the religious officials counted on the civil order for the enforcement of the law of God and the Church. The civil officials relied on the ecclesiastical leaders for the consecration of the political order that needed to be sacred and to care for the spiritual (e.g. public worship) and charitable needs of the community. Christendom includes the state as well as the Church. In the ideal, this was a close as they could come to the establishment of the Reign of God.

In the Western form Christendom was led on its religious side by the Bishop of Rome and on its civil side by the Holy Roman Emperor. The pope established and blessed civil authority in the name of God and the emperor enforced the ecclesiastical monopoly of the pope. This was what may be called a "sacred society," namely a society originated, structured and blessed by God.[66] The ideal is rooted in the Jewish and Christian vision of a messianic kingdom that ends history, issuing in a supernatural society ruled by the divinely appointed messiah or by God directly (Rev 20-21). On the political side, this-worldly version began in the Constantinian era (313 CE Edict of Milan) when imperial decrees recognized the Christian church, formerly a despised and sometimes persecuted sect, as a legal religion, and shortly thereafter the official religion of the empire. Finally, the Catholic Church was the only religion permitted in the empire (emperor Theodosius I in 380 CE). The Church "triumphed" but what a sad day for the church![67]

The ideal was reflected upon by St. Augustine in the *City of God* (426 CE), in which Augustine, spurred on by the fall of Rome to Alaric the Visigoth in 410, worked out the relationship between the city of God (faith and church) and the city of man (civil society). Christendom was in its ecclesiastical version clarified for the Western church by Leo the Great (d. 461) with his drive to impose

65   Bernard Lonergan, *Method in Theology* (NY: Herder and Herder, 1972), 124, 301.

66   Darrell Fasching, *The Coming of the Millennium: Good News for the Entire Human Race* (iUniverse, 2001).

67   Rodney Stark, *The Triumph of Christianity* (NY: HarperOne, 2011).

Roman ecclesiastical rule on all the churches of the west (and, in principle, the east!) Leo's vision was of the whole church ruled by 'the successor of Peter.' The notion was applied with near fanatical literality in the papacy of Gregory the Great (d. 604) with the establishment of the Italian papal states as the secular base of the spiritual reign of the popes. It reached the apogee of its execution under Innocent III (d. 1216),[68] and the height of absurdity under Boniface VIII (d. 1303) for whom "all creatures" were subject to the pope. The Catholic apple had fallen far from the Christian tree.

The dream was not restricted to the west, for the Byzantine emperors and the Patriarch of Constantinople worked out their own version of it. So did the Czars and the patriarchs of Moscow. For example, in the last year of Gregory the Great's papacy (604), the Patriarch of Constantinople obtained the title 'ecumenical patriarch' from the Eastern Emperor. 'Ecumenical' meant worldwide, and this sounded a bit like Constantinople had jumped ahead of Rome in the ecclesiastical pecking order. Pope Gregory of Rome denounced the title as anti-Christian. But Gregory's successor in Rome, Boniface III, with nary a blink, accepted the title from the new eastern emperor within a year or two. Rome has never been shy about testimonies to its divinely bestowed role and has vigorously fought the competition to advance the popes' powers and rights.

The religious embodiment of Christendom in the west, then, was the bishop of Rome, and the political embodiment in the west was the Holy Roman Emperor. Charlemagne was crowned the first Holy Roman Emperor by Pope Leo III in 800 CE; the last emperor, Francis II, wisely resigned in 1806 after the empire lost to Napoleon at Austerlitz. Charlemagne ruled medieval politics as the "Vicar of Christ" and the "Anointed of the Lord," terms that were also used by the pope in his religious sphere. The emperor's function was to rule the *ecclesia Christiana*, not only as defender of the Roman bishop but also to establish the earthly version of the City of God. The emperor was the Lord of Christendom, theoretically universal and virtually omni-competent (like the Pope of Rome), and the terrestrial agent of the Divine emperor, to whom every *fidelis* owed obedience and fealty.[69]

---

68   Cf. the papal document *Venerabilem* in 1197 and the rape of Constantinople by the 4th Crusade in 1204, and Christendom's intellectual and spiritual nadir under Pope Boniface VIII (d. 1303). Cf. *Asculta fili* 1301 and *Unam sanctam,* 1302). See Fordham University's archive of medieval sources.

69   *New Catholic Encyclopedia,* (Farmington MI: Gale Publishing Co., 1967): 7:93d-94.

One decisive image in the complex set called Christendom is "two swords," one civil and one ecclesiastical, haunting the dreams and nightmares of popes and emperors, but also of the Reformers (Luther and Calvin) and the Catholic Counter reformation leaders (Jesuits and popes). They were fighting not only against other Christians whom each side regarded as heretics, but also to restore the old dream of a Christian commonwealth which would be either Catholic or Protestant, but not both.

Catholic Christianity in its fight against the sixteenth century Protestant Reformation kept a firm grip on the dream of a restored medieval Christendom, against Enlightenment secularism as well as the political and social changes forced on it by the end of civil monarchy, the rise of democratic and republican forms of social and political order and against the separation of church and state, all of which "evils" the Church blamed on Protestantism. In the middle of the nineteenth and into the twentieth centuries the popes continued to denounce the liberal capitalist West as well as the totalitarian communist East of the mid-twentieth century as departures from the ancient order of Christendom. Political democracy and republicanism fared no better in papal rhetoric. Still, at the end of the twentieth century the Catholic Church refused to use the word "church" of any other Christian body in the West. There can be only one true Church (i.e., it must include hierarchy and physically mediated succession to apostolic roles) even though Rome now admits and accepts pro-tem, the existence of other Christian "communities" of "separated brethren."[70]

Most disturbing to Roman Catholic leaders was the modern and objectionable notion that a civil order could have two or more religions, none of which were established by the state. The struggles during the second Vatican Council (1962-65) were between the bishops who favored abandoning the ideal of Christendom and, on the other hand, a powerful minority who favored maintaining it.[71] Christendom was ousted as a legitimate dream by the passage in 1965 of two documents by a huge majority vote of bishops: *Dignitatis Humanae* ("Of human dignity") and *Nostra aetate* ("In our

---

70   Pope Francis told visiting evangelical leaders that the church doesn't seek to convert evangelicals. Some say that the Catholic Church never changes! (Irony!)

71   The Lefevrist schism after the Council was based on two Conciliar departures from "the Tradition": (1) the repudiation by the Council and the pope of anti-Judaism; and (2) Council's acceptance of plurality of religions in a culture/nation (i.e., repudiation of a basic plank of Christendom).

age").[72] The Roman Catholic version of Christendom should have ended there.

***

The dream dominated to a significant extent the self-understanding of Protestant Christians as well in Europe and America. The European Reformers abandoned the papal version of Christendom but held on tightly to their own established national churches rather than a single universal and monarchical church. In the American British colonies, Protestants, in the official rhetoric, were joined to God in a covenant and were meant by God to be a "City on a Hill" to whom the eyes of the world would turn. They set up a church of saints who maintained hegemony over the political sphere—the hard hand of which showed itself in the exiles of Anne Hutchinson and Roger Williams from Massachusetts, the burning of witches and the hanging of Quakers, and the hounding of priests and Jesuits. In early New England, everybody was free except those who disagreed with the Puritan version of Christianity, in particular Quakers, mystics, Jews, Baptists, Catholics, witches and atheists. New England colonies established churches supported by public funds and passed laws excluding other religious groups until decades after the revolution and the national Constitution.

The dream was present in the American nineteenth century in the mix of Protestant denominations in the so-called Evangelical Empire and was expressed in the doctrine of Manifest Destiny, the religious and political sides of an American version of Christendom: others may be tolerated by "real" Americans but the government and civil society were to be Protestant. The emphases were sharply etched in the Nativist party in the nineteenth century and in a racist version in the Ku Klux Klan in the twentieth century. It still appears in the disappointed ruminations of Christian fundamentalists in the twentieth and twenty-first centuries who mourn the end of a "Christian, i.e. Protestant, America." They were also aghast at the "invasion" of America by the papists and Jews, and then at the rise of religious modernism in the seminaries and pulpits of Protestant churches at the beginning of the twentieth century. Restorationists still call for American law to conform to biblical laws and teachings.

Moreover, the dream did not just affect Christians. Even secularized Westerners who rejected both Protestant and Catholic Christianity and all "organized religion," hoped for a united city

---

72   John W. O'Malley, S.J., *What Happened at Vatican II?* (Cambridge MA: Harvard University Press, 2008).

of man ruled by the precepts of Reason and left no room in their ideal society for religious 'superstition.' The issue remains unsettled: how can you have one god and many religions, one faith and many peoples, one nation and many cultures? It is still a puzzle, and American culture(s) remains the laboratory, the great experiment to find out if and how it works.

I now recall that in my seven years at the Catholic University of America (1972-1980) I began to think seriously about the Catholic hierarchy's condemnation of artificial birth control. I thought about their methods of dealing with priests who viewed the issue differently. While I was still a priest, I proposed to myself that the entire schema of a hierarchy that would attempt to impose its moral will on parish priests and the laity without listening to them—and dismissing them on the rare occasions when they did—was based on the reigning Catholic conviction that popes and bishops are specially ordained by God to decide what is right and wrong and how to enforce the right. I thought then that the hierarchy (the bishops and the popes) are in more desperate need of demythologization than the New Testament itself! They need the pseudo-divinity squeezed out of them. How good it would be for them and their ministry if they could shake themselves loose of the Catholic myth of the inauguration of the hierarchical schema by Jesus at the Last Supper. This demythologization must be part of the solution of the present crisis. However, we need to remember that this is what Luther and Calvin tried and failed to do. Protestants and Roman Catholics alike seem afflicted by the desire to establish a proto-kingdom of God in this world in anticipation of a final reign of God.

***

Let me tell you what I "saw" in the Dallas meeting of all the American Catholic bishops in 2002: bishops, many shocked to their socks by the publicity explosion of the abuse crisis, battling to free themselves and their church from that 1,500 year old dream called Christendom. This myth became so embedded in the Christian psyche that, unnoticed, it still affects a lot of instinctive Christian leadership behavior, Protestant as well as Catholic. On the Protestant side it hides in evangelical hopes to make the United States a Christian America—meaning that biblical truths and principles at crucial points should govern our society. On the Catholic side, it is attached to the institutions of the Church, especially in those leaders whose sensibilities have been shaped by the Vatican ethos.

For them, secular society must be ruled by what they call "Natural Law."[73] The church that lay Catholics live and believe in is still, in the psyche and mind of its leaders, a perfect, independent society with its own goal, its own rules, its own divinely established governmental structures, its own Canon Law, its own courts, and its own special ways of dispensing the merits of Christ to the faithful (sacraments, sacramentals and indulgences). The Church should be *in* the world but it is not *of* the world said the Jesus of John's gospel (John 17: 13ff), and that came to mean the sinful "world" has no claims on the church. In Catholic Christendom the pope, and no one else on earth, rules the Church, the spotless Bride of Christ. He is the Vicar of Christ, he is Peter, in a mild Catholic version of reincarnation of the Dali Lama. "Feed my sheep" (John 21, 17) and "Thou art Peter and upon this Rock I will build my church," (Mt 16:16) spoken to every pope in the course of history became, in the hands of generations of popes, a church ruled by a monarch.

The reader might remember the old refrain, "In Boston, dear Boston, the land of the bean and the cod, where the Cabots speak only to the Lodges and the Lodges speak only to God." That is the WASP version of the Catholic hierarchical system. In the latter, the people may speak to the priest, the priest to the bishop, the bishop to the pope, and the pope, like a Lodges, speaks only to God—and to everyone else for God. In Dallas, for once, lay Catholics broke into divine conversation briefly and made it a public process by communicating their outrage to a captive audience of American bishops about the vice of some clerics and the irresponsibility of the solemn, purple-tinted men in front of them.

One of the rules in the Catholic perfect society is that nobody decides anything important without the approval of the bishop of Rome who speaks for God. In other words, the bishops themselves couldn't do a thing about getting the perverts out of ministry without getting the pope's permission.

A second one is that a bishop is responsible only to the bishop of Rome, not to his people, not to his fellow bishops, not to the civil community or even the civil law if it can be helped, but only to the bishop of Rome. A bishop therefore cannot be removed or censured by his brother bishops, no matter what his sin or crime, never mind

---

73   Msgr. John Harrington, my seminary librarian, advised us fifty years ago not to tell our future congregations that birth control is against the natural law. "These people are Americans," he said, "and they will want to know who passed that law and how do we get it repealed."

be reproved by his people.[74]

Clerical etiquette even forbids one bishop disagreeing or challenging, never mind criticizing another. Only the pope appoints and
only the pope removes, and in the furthest reaches of the dream the
pope is picked by the Holy Spirit (who, if so, has a lot to answer for
on the Last Day!) It seems that, under the present papal dispensation, removal of a bishop is rare indeed unless for a crime that has
become public, e.g., a Cardinal Archbishop of Vienna who had an
irresistible affection for young seminarians, or the poor Australian
bishop who had the temerity to suggest that Catholics may think
about ordaining women or dropping the celibacy requirement for
ordination. Who dares even hint at a disagreement with the Pope?
Who dares to shatter that sacred communion of belief? In that case
it is "my way or the highway" when the only crime involved is
breaking a papal taboo. John Paul and Benedict settled on repression as the method of coping with dissent: no conversation, no
disagreement. Bishops and Catholic theologians signed on to the
policy for the most part.

In 2002, the Catholic bishops in Dallas were going through an
ancient wrestle, one that has grown more intense and public since
the great majority of the bishops decided at the second Vatican
council (1965) to bury Christendom. The bishops thought they had
papal approval for the interment in 1965, but they have been struggling with the corpse for fifty years. At Dallas, two bones of the
old myth arm-wrestled the 250 American bishops. The first bone:
would they eject wretched, criminal priests from the perfect society
of The Church and turn them over to the civil authorities? Would
they drop the priests from ministry who sinned only once and subsequently repented? Or would they act as if Christendom was res-
urrected and continue to hide offending priests from the "secular
arm"?

In a decision applauded by those who care about the burden
Christendom imposes upon the church, the bishops in Dallas
pledged to cooperate with the civil authorities. Of course they still
had to get Roman permission, but this was a big historical moment.
To act as if the clergy were also citizens of the country and were
responsible to its laws was to surrender under considerable public

---

74   We are putting aside for the moment such ecclesiastical thugs as
Bernard Cardinal Law who, after decades of ignoring the vicious crimes
of his subordinates, slunk off to a Vatican apartment to avoid the civil
penalties of his crimes and the wrath of his people in the archdiocese of
Boston. John Paul II gave him sanctuary.

pressure.[75] Of course, they said just a little about their own conspiracy to cover up the crimes and protect the offending priests from prosecution. An ecclesiastical "perfect society" cannot be held responsible to the justice of the secular "perfect society"! No bishop was turned over to the "secular arm," though the priests finally were. Only one bishop, Robert Finn of Kansas City, one of several St. Louis priests to be forwarded to the hierarchy by Cardinal Rigali, was caught in clear violation of civil law, and was subsequently found guilty. He was removed from his diocese two years later after some fiddling in the Vatican. The archbishop of Minneapolis resigned his post in June 2015, as the state prosecutors readied similar charges against that archdiocese. Perhaps the civil authorities have turned a corner on the issue of prosecution of hierarchical figures and the institution.

A second bone remains. Bishops have no way in Catholic law and theology to dismiss or remove from office men who are, if it is conceivable, lower in the moral scale than the pedophiles, the doubly sanctified men who supported, protected, and passed on the vicious priest-predators to other victims. They, these archbishops and their ecclesiastical henchmen, shock the spirit of every Christian parent and the spirit of tens of thousands of decent priests that who can barely suppress their horror. The offending bishops didn't even have the decency to resign. Like President Clinton after the Monica Lewinsky exposure, they had a job to do! I mean not only Cardinal Law who finally did resign his office as archbishop of Boston, but also Cardinals Egan and Bevilacqua (RIP) and Mahoney, and dozens of lesser ecclesiastical lights who should have been shown the door. They, of course, are year by year slipping into a well-cushioned retirement that they do not deserve, and into a death that, if the book of Genesis with St. Paul in its train has it right, they thoroughly deserve. They will suffer some modicum of earthly punishment if the pope is still talking to the God of justice and God to him. Due punishment is not likely for bishops for, as the bishops did for centuries for their errant priests, popes now do for errant bishops. Constantine-spawned clericalism has many more than nine lives.

But the bishops would not, and perhaps could not, slay this dragon. Too bad; big historical moment missed! That second bone will have to wait for another day. But let us give thanks for what

75   There was a corresponding struggle on the side of the civil authorities over whether to prosecute priests. Police and prosecutors had not been inclined to do so. They certainly have hesitated to prosecute bishops.

the bishops did do. Christendom took another blow. Sooner or later Catholics will get that second bone. Perhaps the bishops will face up to themselves and chew on that bone when they no longer can avoid doing so. Until then the ghost of Constantine will prowl the halls of a fading Christendom.

11. The Archbishop and the *Mandatum*

W e turn a page now to an event that indicates just how out of touch the Vatican and the bishops are with the on-the-ground work in American universities and how little an American archbishop cared about that fact. *Mandatum* (mandate) is a word that appeared in the new Code of Canon Law of the Catholic Church in 1983. Canons 807 to 814 are the laws governing Catholic institutions of higher learning. Canon 812 reads as follows:

> Those who teach theological subjects in any institute of higher studies must have a mandate from the competent ecclesiastical authority.

The term and the canon kicked off a controversy unsettling American theologians and bishops for twenty years. First of all, no one seemed to know what a *Mandatum* is since the term had never been used in this context. Secondly, bishops giving "mandates" to a college and university professor is a notion abhorrent to American academic culture because it implies that bishops have some control over the professors' teaching. Academicians have even been suspicious of the influence that wealthy donors may seek to have over high appointments, such as an endowed chair that they underwrite financially. Granted, it's an unending vigilance they must practice but the cost must be paid in order to bolster professorial and administrative integrity. To introduce Church control over theologians in even muted ways is something to be avoided in the universities and colleges, Catholic or otherwise. Control may be acceptable in Catholic and Protestant seminaries but not elsewhere in higher education.

In the nineties American bishops, in concert with American Catholic college presidents and theologians, tried to find a way out of John Paul's and Ratzinger's mistake in their drive to control Catholic theological discourse. Representatives of American Catholic higher education went to the Vatican of John Paul II to plead for the excision of the canon from the proposed code; their advice was not taken. The American bishops proposed to Rome that, rather than a formal and legal relationship, bishops and theologians should keep the relationship "pastoral." Rome sent their proposal back and told them to rewrite. The American bishops decided (reluctantly, in my view) to go ahead with the legal solution as Rome preferred. *Roma locuta est, causa finita est.* The *Mandatum* is embedded in church law, a requirement to which bishops must adhere. The wise advice to the pope from both academics and bishops was ignored.

About fifteen years ago, in 2001, while I was teaching at Saint Louis University in the department of theological studies, the theology faculty accepted Archbishop Rigali's invitation to discuss the *Mandatum.* At a theology faculty meeting prior to the encounter with the archbishop, the faculty was urged by one priest member who had studied in Rome and was thought to know the ways of such ecclesiastics as Rigali, to "keep it cool" and simply ask questions at what was likely to be a formality rather than a significant exchange of views. Rigali was thought to be doing what the other American bishops had decided to do, and nothing more. No substantial discussion of the *Mandatum* would take place in this faculty member's view; as it turned out he was correct.

Rigali, a cannon lawyer by training and long a denizen of the Roman Curia, opened the meeting by speaking for about twenty minutes on what the pope thought of Catholic universities and colleges. John Paul II thought highly of them, to no one's surprise—we had all read the pope's allocution *Ex corde ecclesiae.* The archbishop then asked each member of the faculty to say what he or she thought about the *Mandatum,* or at least we *thought* that is what he asked. Most of the twenty faculty members told the archbishop in strong and clear terms that the whole idea is a mistake, that it would in one way or another do harm to the work of the theologians and so to the universities. They had good reasons to worry and stated them. Here are my notes on the substance of the exchange:

April 10, 2001. 4-6:15 PM at the Catholic Center, Lindell Blvd.

The archbishop began by quoting liberally from papal documents on universities and on theologians, as was his custom, reminding us of how highly the pope regarded us. The pope told the American bishops in 1983: theologians assist bishops and together they serve faith. Both study and explain scripture. A theologian's job is to offer reasons for The Church's doctrinal and moral teaching. The pope, Rigali recounted, spoke to theologians in New Orleans in 1987: bishops teach as pastors, and theologians serve the church in their teaching, yet they need

the charism of bishops and the bishop of Rome who vali-
dates the teaching of theologians. Again, the pope issued
an apostolic constitution on higher education in 1990, *Ex
corde ecclesiae*. In it the pope expressed profound respect
for Catholic universities and stated that he regards them
as the hope of Christian culture in our time. Bishops, the
pope wrote, should encourage theologians as they inves-
tigate Christian truth. In the face of the growth of the
media culture, episcopal dialogue with theologians becomes even more necessary. The archbishop concluded:
"We are gathered to reflect on the *guidelines* for the *Mandatum* application. The *Mandatum* itself has already been
approved." Now, he said, he would like to hear from
everyone, and he did.

I concluded later that I, along with other participants, did not
understand what the archbishop called upon us to do, for nearly all
of our remarks were on the *Mandatum* itself and not on the soon-
to-be-approved American episcopal guidelines about applying it in
practice. The archbishop was moving on to the guidelines when the
theologians hadn't yet swallowed the mandate itself.

At the request of the archbishop, each faculty member made a
short statement about his/her background and his or her work in
teaching and research, and then a brief comment on the mandate
and associated issues. At the end, the archbishop invited the 20 or
so theologians and school representatives to dinner at his residence
across Lindell Blvd. The meal wasn't half-bad and we had eight
fully uniformed nuns waiting on the tables. The archbishop proposed the toast to John Paul II and visited every table thanking the
theologians for their cooperation.

The archbishop's remarks during the meeting seem to have
cut the ground out from under the faculty's questions and issues,
for the faculty wanted to know what and why the Mandate is, and
what uses might be made of it. The archbishop, however, spoke of
the proposed Guidelines, about which the faculty apparently knew
even less. They were interested in "what," and he and the bishops
were interested in "how." Two ships passed in the night. I don't
think we grasped the reason for the meeting. Several months after
the meeting, letters from the Chancery Office were sent to the faculty members individually inviting them to apply for the archbishop's mandate. None were sent to ex- priests on the faculty (three,
including myself) because ex-priests can't be "mandated"—in fact

they are forbidden to teach theology at all. One was sent to a Protestant faculty member by mistake, causing some hilarity. Since the faculty did not discuss the mandate again, I know nothing of the responses of other faculty members, except the one by Professor Frank Nichols (appendix #15). There were no follow-up discussions; no "episcopal dialogue," as the pope called it, between theologians and the archbishop or his representatives ever occurred. The archbishop and his several assistant bishops did not regard such dialogue in any way desirable or fruitful. I was personally disappointed at this failure.

The discussion with the archbishop had no effect whatsoever in practical terms. If any of the theologians heard a word from him again he/she was silent about it. The entire Mandate discussion exposed this: neither the archbishop nor the theologians took it seriously, the theologians because they were concerned about the Mandate and its effects on the universities, and the archbishop because the Mandate was already a matter of law and he wanted to hear from us about the guidelines. The archbishop needed to check the Mandate box on his annual report and the theologians needed to protect themselves and their universities from the potential harm generated by John Paul II's bright idea. The affair is the perfect example of Roman Catholic formalism. I do believe that the pope took Canon 812 seriously, for he himself had rebuked theologians who got out of line and drove them from their teaching posts when he could. The American bishops took a step to the left (prudently without announcing it) and let the matter drop.[76]

Another instance: the bishop of Worcester MA, Daniel Reilly, showed no interest in the Mandate with regard to the College of the Holy Cross. He had a constructive relationship with the Jesuit presidents of the college and left matters internal to the college to the administration. The new bishop (2005), Robert McManus, asked to meet with the Holy Cross department of religious studies to discuss the Mandate. By that time the guidelines had been decided upon by the bishops. The bishop and the faculty met over lunch and discussed the issues, again everyone had his or her say, the differences remain and what has happened since I do not know.

We academics like to present "both sides" of an issue. Bishop McManus, when he met with the Holy Cross religionists, asked "Why?" A bishop would not be likely to discuss "opinions" in his own presentation, for his job is to preach and teach the faith held by the saints: Jesus is risen, no ifs, ands or buts. The tomb is empty,

76   Elizabeth A. Johnson, *Quest for the Living God: Mapping Frontiers in the Theology of God* (NY: Bloomsbury, 2011).

and this is not a matter of opinion. For a Christian, then, what's the problem? But for an academic theologian there is a problem: present "all sides" and "we're not bishops and we're not preaching or catechizing." The bishops and Rome didn't get or refused to recognize the difference.

In the course of our discussion with Bishop McManus it was clear to me at least that the theologians and the bishop were standing in different horizons of meaning and truth. It may have looked like they were contradicting one another, but they were not. The bishops' job is to preach and teach what the church believes; the theologians' job is to explain how the text is taken by different people at different times with different meanings and truths and for different reasons—without fudging the church's proclamation or her/his own belief. The professor in an American university, secular or religious, is not there to profess his or her religious faith and belief; he or she is there to profess how, when and why different interpretations of the texts or claims are offered. Professors are expected to be "fair," to present what is there in the historical record and what is there in current academic conversation, not to bury it in a profession of faith.

It seemed to me at the time that this was a perfect opportunity to get each party to explain to the other what he or she was up to, until some common understanding of the different tasks and stances was developed even if disagreement remained. I proposed to the chair of the religious studies department that we meet again with McManus for a quiet dialogue about those differences. The chair canvassed the senior faculty who turned my proposal down. This ended the only time in my long career when a genuine dialogue between an academic and a kerygmatic (proclamation) task might have taken place. It didn't. I think Bishop McManus was up to it, but the faculty was not. I do not think they wanted any more to do with him. I do know that I and another faculty member visited with him on separate occasions and tried to explain the encounter from our perspectives—as he did from his pastoral perspective. There is need for education on both sides. Neither side is a fox in the chicken coop, at least in this case. Rigali did not care enough about the complicated issues raised by the Mandate for American academics. McManus did care about them, but the academics were unwilling to sit down with him. So far as I can see the issue has been shelved after twenty years of concern on both sides. The Mandate is still the law but nobody wants to act on what it implies.

12. Authority in the Church

My problem isn't just with the Church. My personal problem is resentment of authority. *Pace* Freud, I never wanted to kill my father. I loved and admired him deeply but I feared him and his moral authority just as deeply. He was a model and a block to freedom all at once. I am still under his thrall, though he appears now only in my dreams, sitting at the kitchen table in his Clark Gable undershirt, challenging me to argue an argument I never win, and telling me, mostly by stories, how to live. The pope, for his part, doesn't challenge anyone to argue; he tells people how to live. That's his job. My father was the pope at 2502 Frisby Avenue and then at 2563 St. Raymond's Avenue, a loving and lovable pope like Francis, but a pope nonetheless. He was an admirable and determined man, and infallible or so he appeared to me.

I recall vividly that my mother, when I told her of my intention to marry, said, "You'd never do this if your father were alive." I was forty-five at the time. That was a confrontation that I had already had.[77] The resentment I felt as a child and adolescent toward adult exercise of authority spilled over into all phases of my adult life, causing conflict and confusion. It constituted a crucial layer of my "dispositional immediacy."[78] Oddly enough, I wanted to be told how to live, yet at the same time I resented it. I hated having decisions made for me and feared making decisions for myself.

Again and again over the span of my life, I found myself in conflict with myself over the authorities above me and sometimes in conflict with them: parents, teachers, seminary faculty, diocesan office holders, chairmen and deans and academic colleagues—and wife! I am pulled toward them to get things accomplished and to win their approval, and repelled by them because they judge my performance and block my plans. I envy what seems to be their self-assurance and fear their criticism. When authority is surrounded by an aura of divinity I am especially spooked. I am not a communitarian except in theory. I have convictions about the value

---

77   See appendix #3 for letters. I had had that argument, but my father saw no end to his responsibility to tell his first-born son how to live, or, better, how not to live.

78   Robert Doran, *Subject and Psyche, Ricoeur, Jung and the Search for Foundations* (Lanham MD: University Press of America, 1977). 1ˢᵗ ed.

of communities but I am far from a team player. You, dear reader, surely noticed this fact about my psyche in my account of leaving the priesthood. I can't stand being ignored or treated as an enemy or a threat. I long to be autonomous and immune from criticism, yet I want authority's approval.

Torn by emotional needs, I am almost incapable of rational argument when pressed and find it very difficult to back down from positions I mistakenly take or even to defend the ones that I correctly take. I want to do my thing and find myself resenting anyone who has the power to oppose me and undo what I value. I am quick to set up defenses and avoid contact, and I invariably suspect motives, suppose hostility and react accordingly. I love being retired now because there is no one to oversee and direct me—except my wife, God help her. Remember, all this has to do with the "problem of authority." In essence, I never grew up into a world of adults. I harbor and am moved by the feelings of a child under threat.

Let me give a few more examples out of dozens possible. One of the four New York parishes I served was populated by Catholics who had "made it" by the economic criteria common in American life. The *crème de la crème* of the creamy parishioners were easily identifiable by their association with the pastor, the senior clergyman. They served on the parish council, an advisory board to the pastor. Others were known by the mansions they lived in and the cars they drove. Don't mistake me here; these were all good and well-intentioned people whose dedication to the parish was obvious. But they had influence in the parish and on the pastor that a young assistant priest could not match (I had none!) I sloshed around in resentment, not only against the pastor who assumed toward me a directive and ultimately judgmental role, but toward his lay supporters as well. The pastor was my father without the love my father had for me. He was the boss.

I continued my childhood suspicion of wealthy and influential businessmen who had such enormous say over the lives of my low-income parents. I didn't like the rich and influential ("famous" didn't really enter the lists!) My developing proletarian antagonism was carried into the church itself. I came to dislike (I had always from a distance been awed by) bishops—they were the clerical version of the rich and powerful. Also, in my mid-twenties I switched political allegiance from my teen-age idol Senator Joseph McCarthy, from William Buckley my intellectual hero, and from the Republican Party to the Democratic party. This switch occurred in my first parish when I discovered that Republicans ignore the poor, and Democrats pay attention to the poor (and more than occasionally pander to them). There is a raw nerve ending here that grew from a concern for my parents to a full-fledged bias against anyone who had power over me (or them) and whose authority I was forced to bow.

Another example: when I was hired as chairman of the Department of Theological Studies at Saint Louis University in 1991, I was told by the interviewing academic vice president and the dean of the College of Arts and Sciences that it was the president's and their intention to make a mediocre department as academically sound as any Catholic theology department in the country. Notre Dame and Boston College set the standards to be met and even surpassed. In fact, I was told that they intended their department of theology to be "the best." I believed them (foolishly, as it turned out, for they had no more than a wish, if that), and I set out to accomplish their lofty goal.

In the course of my six years in the chair, I discovered that they had no intention of supporting the department in the task. No money, no new hires with immediate importance, and no further promises or excuses. I had been told by the chairman in Catholic University two decades before that I should "never trust an academic administrator until the check is cut," good advice which I failed to take. I assumed that the SLU administrators meant what they said to me.

By my last year in the chairmanship, I was pissed off and showed it. I had worked very hard over five years to improve the department[79] and had some success at significant cost to me personally. Suddenly, I found that for whatever mysterious reasons (something to do with money, of course) the administration actually decided to lower its level of support for graduate programs and concentrate on improving the undergraduate program. I and the undergraduate program director, Kenneth Parker, were unfairly and mistakenly accused by the Academic Vice President of ignoring undergraduate program development in favor of the doctoral program. I had given off a strong scent of frustration and the administrators picked it up. I've never been good at hiding my feelings. In the New York seminary the rector, Francis Reh, once remarked to the entire student body that when he wanted to know what the students were thinking, all he had to do was check my facial expression. My classmates joked about my ability to get two feet in my mouth and still talk. That is true to this day.

The Saint Louis University dean, as my six year term ran out and in response to my increasingly acerbic tone, accused me of being anti-Jesuit in my salary recommendations and of misinforming a job candidate about her prospective salary and lying to the

79   See Francis Nichols, appendix #15.

dean about it. None of those charges were true. The vice-president suspected me of setting him up for an embarrassing confrontation with the theology department over the level of support for the department and its graduate programs (at least a semblance of truth here, for I wanted him to explain to the faculty what I couldn't). He called me to his office and, with the dean present, suggested that I had emotional problems and needed an assistant chair to alleviate the stress. He was a psychologist. I told them both to jam it and walked out, daring them in effect to fire me with just a few months to go. I was then called to the Provost's office to permit him a look at the theology chairman who was becoming a problem. He listened respectfully as I explained to him my disappointment at the lowered sights of the administration with regard to graduate studies and, in particular, at the failure to support the theology department's efforts to improve itself.

I finished my term swaddled in resentment. I know nothing about what went on after this, except that on the fall semester's opening day the dean, with the new chairman at her side, appeared at the faculty and student luncheon to present me with a plaque for my service as chairman. As soon as I realized what was afoot I ducked out of the gathering and she had no one to accept the plaque. A month or so later she invited me to lunch to repair the breach and present me with the plaque. I refused, and suggested she not hang on by her teeth until I accept. She sent me the plaque in the mail and I dumped it. I don't like to be called a liar. I continued following another old rule of mine: three strikes and you are out. She had more than three at that point. The Messiah said that we should forgive seventy times seven, but the most I am able to manage is two. On the third strike, you're out. Not good, but then I'm not the Messiah!

What had grown like a fetid weed over the six years in the chairmanship was a near paranoid suspicion and resentment of the authorities who, I must admit now, had a much more delicate and consequential job to do than mine and who struggled, like I had, to do those jobs. I took their failure to support the improvement of the department personally when in fact they were simply doing the job they had been appointed to by a president who was widely regarded as brutal and domineering; they are the ones who deserved sympathy.[80] They managed, with one or two notable exceptions on my

80   Fr. Lawrence Biondi, S.J., has since been forced into retirement by a faculty and student revolt in 2014. I liked him and enjoyed him and stayed as far as possible out of his line of fire. I think that for a while and in some respects I was a good chairman. I certainly enjoyed the support of many faculty members and enjoyed the students in the classroom as I

part, to keep me in line until my time in the chair expired that May. But I felt the presence of my old spirit of suspicion and resentment toward those with authority over me, including now my successor in the chair. My hostility startled even me and must have worried them. I was so happy to be done with chairmanship that for two full years I breathed sighs of relief when I entered the humanities building every morning. I had entered a period of relaxation that has only been matched by being retired.[81]

I made a few notable and regrettable mistakes in the five years as the director of the Center for Religion, Ethics and Culture at the College of the Holy Cross, a job I enjoyed in a college I admire and am proud to have been a part of. Its administrative team was the best in five different institutions in which I had worked. I am sometimes verbally rough and insensitive in my dealings with colleagues, and certainly politically incorrect therein. When one colleague chided me for not fully appreciating "the Holy Cross way," I translated that as the "politically correct" way and dismissed her remark. But the fact is that I didn't, wouldn't, and couldn't support the mythical "Holy Cross way," that is, the student-centered and feminist ideology that I found oppressive. The students were the best I had taught and the faculty was the most talented and dedicated. But I had placed myself on the train tracks of academic retribution, and it had its own "way," the Holy Cross Way, with me.

One of the incidents involved my slightly overwrought verbal correction of a talented Muslim student for harassing and insulting an Israeli scholar I had invited to speak at the Center. The student filed a complaint against me. After a formal procedure involving discussions with me and interviews of colleagues and staff privy to the incidents, the dean admonished me in writing, threatening me with dismissal should I act so again. The student was not rebuked for insulting the Israeli professor, failure that stunned me. This is an example of the Holy Cross Way.

The other involved my ignoring a faculty member's criticisms of Center programs for not being sufficiently "inclusive." She had the dean call me in, and verbally provided him and me with a detailed list of my depredations in office. This was embarrassing and even more infuriating. The result was that I was forced to change the agenda for the program in accord with the wishes of the faculty

---

did in every one of the schools in which I taught. I am not a great teacher but I did find more happiness in the classroom than in an administrative position. Once again authority, even my own, threw me into emotional confusion.

81   The academic vice-president vacated his office a year later, and within a year or two became president of the Jesuit university in Chicago.

member. The charges amounted to what I expected: there was a "way" of doing things and I had not done them that way. I had long since begun to call that faculty member, among other things, "the Great Mother of Holy Cross." After the dean had told us to cooperate nicely for the good of the college I wrote an email to the faculty member (with a copy to the dean) informing her that, since she didn't understand me nor I her, I would require a tape recording on any conversation with her in the future. The dean did not like this at all. He sent me another note of disapproval. Both sets of charges appeared to me mistaken and biased, and I would not back down. After these two incidents the dean's and the president's attitudes toward me changed palpably, and I concluded that they were waiting for my term as director to end. It did in 2008 with an offer by the new dean's office to host a reception on my retirement. True to form I declined.

I think now that I should have been more discerning politically and even-handed interpersonally. It was typical of me to resent those who tell me, in authoritative tones, that I have misbehaved or misunderstood my place and role. Instead of attempting to clarify matters I reacted with hostility. It must be said in my favor that I did consult with five senior male faculty members, asking each of them for suggestions on how to deal with the female colleague with whom they had worked for decades, and in each case they said there was no way except staying out of her sightline. I tried, just a bit, to do that. I failed. To me, she remains a red cape, and I, an over matched bull.

What I mean to illustrate here is that your humble servant has a serious problem with authority which was exercised in the Roman Catholic Church and in the university, a problem much in accord with the fabled American adherence to individualism and its abhorrence of communalism. Just think what it would cost for a person with this emotional complexion to function easily and happily in the Roman Catholic clergy! I habitually tossed that wise and ancient advice, "If you want to get along, go along."

***

When I was a resident scholar at the Ecumenical Institute at St. John's University in Minnesota (winter and spring 1999), a fellow resident, a Quaker, responded quickly and simply to a question of mine. Is it likely, I asked, that the American public has gotten over its historical anti-Catholicism? No, he said, it remains below the surface and has not been eliminated. What adult American, he added, would approve of a church whose leaders insisted on treating its people like children? The Roman Catholic Church is an authoritative community that treats its members like children, perhaps the outstanding example of pure patriarchy left in the western world. This clash of spirits, mine and The Church's, precipitated intellectual as well as an existential concern with secular and religious authority. So, realizing my frequent inability to cope reasonably with authorities, I read a bit and thought a lot about my constant resentment towards them. Here are some of the conclusions I reached:

All communities have authorities. Dealing with them is a human problem, not specifically a religious one (the Mafia or the Federal Reserve for example). Some authority structures are tightly centralized and some are widely dispersed, but they are ubiquitous.

Authority requires reception as well as assertion. Authority is retained and exercised until people stop paying attention to it. When people do so, authority ceases and new authorities and structures will arise. (e.g. The American and French Revolutions; the Arab Spring of 2010.)

Authority has been a problem in the Christian communities since the first century. The New Testament scriptures witness to this perennial question of authority. Christians wrestle with the problem of authority as does every other social group, and rightly so.

Authorities have tended, throughout history and across cultures, to claim divine origin and support. The Pharaoh is the son of the sun, Alexander is a god, the pope is the successor to Peter and the Vicar of Christ, the priest is an *alter Christus*. Those claims to divine authority of some sort have been narrowed over the last few centuries. They survive in pockets of Christianity, in the priesthood (papacy) and the ministry. In the secular world kings, where the kingship has been retained at all, now are constitutional figures rather than absolute, divinely imposed and supported monarchs.

Christian authority has come in two forms since New Testament times: charism and office. I recognize both but don't trust either of them. The Catholic Church, firmly gripped by its structure of offices, has had tremendous difficulty with charismatic authority (e.g. with prophets, Gnostics, visionaries, healers, mystics, various antinomians, uppity priests and nuns, and anyone who says no). However, even the holders of office in The Church know that their form of authority cannot be cut off from the charismatics. They count on each other, much to their mutual dismay.[82]

Christians have undergone, in the last few centuries, large scale change in the exercise of authority, of perhaps the same degree of importance as (a) the formation of the Catholic ministerial structure in the first two centuries; (b) the invention of synods and councils (c) the rise of the papacy, (d) the Protestant reformation of the sixteenth century (a devolution of authority, often decentralization).

Over the centuries the Catholic Church's authority structures, procedures, and rules have changed remarkably but have done so under the principle: change carefully, slowly and wisely, and don't rock the divinely established ministerial hierarchy. We can expect this principle to continue in operation. The Catholic Church is the oldest and most conservative (of itself) institution in the West and perhaps in the world. For its structures and procedures it claims divine authority. It is an instance of the patriarchy that is far older than itself!

The consequential development in the Roman Catholic Church is the practical, as well as ideological, centralization of authority in the divine monarchy over the past two centuries in response to features of modern politics and culture. As much as the Church once copied the administrative divisions of the Roman Empire in its dioceses and archdioceses, the modern centralized Church parallels the development of modern centralized nation-states. It is ironic that the much despised Enlightenment is the occasion for increased Roman centralization.[83] Popes have gone from pony express to twitter but through it all have retained and reinforced their divine status.

Roman Catholic structures of authority are expressed in three doctrinal nuggets: the doctrine of Apostolic Succession of bishops, the doctrine of the universal jurisdiction of the

---

82   Archbishop Rigali liked to speak of the church offices as charisms, the papal charism, the episcopal charism, etc. If so, it is likely one of the lesser gifts of the Holy Spirit. See I Cor 12. One has to contend with the fact that St. Paul didn't know there were popes and bishops. The bishops and popes have lifted their offices into undisputed first place, in complete control of every other gift of the Spirit, another giant step in transforming the Christian movement into an organized religion, that is, the Roman Catholic Church in which all the gifts are ordered by one.

83   Joseph A. Komonchak, "Modernity and the Construction of Roman Catholicism," Woodrow Wilson Center for Scholars, Smithsonian Institution. Lecture, May 9, 1985.

bishop of Rome and the doctrine of infallibility of the *Magisterium*. The Eastern Orthodox churches agree with the first but deny the other two. Protestants deny all three, locating authority in the Scriptures (the Holy Spirit) rather than in episcopal teaching, but they retain a touch of divinity in leaders especially in sects.

There has been recent spectacular growth of the Catholic Church of many nations and tongues in the Global South, while the church shrinks and shrivels in the Global North where its claims that spiritual authority has been rejected by most and in South and Latin America where its corporation sole has run into serious competition with a powerful Evangelical movement. The Church's drive to unity (we *must* remain one church under the control of The Church, for that is what Jesus wanted) has created pressure for development of governance and the uses of authority as the church expands geographically, culturally and numerically (except in the West).

There have arisen (generally speaking) two distinct Christian stories of the origins of authority in the church, Protestant on one hand, and Catholic and Orthodox on the other.[84] Sometimes an ordinary story won't do and you need a story with God (or the gods) in it to get your point across. That's called a myth. All religions speak in myth talk. A "doctrine" is an affirmation that the myth is true as opposed to a myth that may have social and moral value but isn't true. Doctrines state the meaning of the myth in declarative sentences. The doctrine of *creatio ex nihilo* is the meaning of the Genesis myth(s), and the church states it and affirms that it is true, a fact, and not "just a myth."

In the Catholic Church, questions about the legitimacy of authority and its proper exercise gravitate toward the Bishop of Rome. This is the price of monarchy. He is the key figure in any consideration of power and its exercise. He holds "the keys to the Kingdom." (MT 16:19) In the Catholic Church's self-understanding authority is centripetal (power flows to the periphery from the center), not centrifugal (power flows from the periphery to the center). Parishes and Catholic religious orders exhibit a centripetal and centrifugal force. Another way of imagining it is in hierarchical terms: divine fullness exists at the pinnacle and emanates down through the ranks; or communal terms, divine fullness exists in the

84   W. M. Shea, *The Lion and the Lamb: Evangelicals and Catholics in America*, 18-21.

community that constructs its forms of authority. In my view, the latter is what in fact happened; in the doctrines of the hierarchy, the former is the fact.

The answers to questions of authority will emerge from the particular pope's (or bishop's or pastor's) exercise of authority and public recognition of that exercise—along with national bishops' conferences. For example, the American bishops' teaching on peace and economic justice won widespread support in the 1980's, while the papal encyclical on birth control (*Humanae vitae*) did not.[85]   Benedict XVI waged a surreptitious campaign to reinstate the old Latin Liturgy; it gets significant support from a minority of Catholics, and it was greeted by most American Catholics with supreme indifference. This is the inevitable fate of papal initiatives that proceed not from or for the good of the church, but from personal conclusions and commitments. The churches will occasionally ignore The Church when they have to. Recall what happened to Pope John XXIII's decree calling for Latin to be the language of instruction in all seminaries.[86]

The claim to Apostolic Succession on the part of Catholic leaders and to universal jurisdiction of the bishop of Rome are key claims to authority and are paramount in any serious dialogue with any other Christian church, Western or Eastern, and threaten to remain characteristic of Roman Catholic ecclesiology. However, I do not believe that these doctrines are true or that the myths they are based on are valuable anymore. The myths have lost touch with the actual history (e.g., there is little or no evidence that Peter was ever the bishop of Rome in any sense) and the doctrines have proved pernicious again and again. Over the centuries, they have become clerical clap-trap.

Authorities in the church must continue to earn the respect and adherence of the Catholic people by the way they live and rule. There was a point to the old protest movement in North Africa (Donatism) which I would put this way: if you want to bear authoritative witness to faith, then act in faith; insofar as you don't your authority dissolves.[87] The most ev-

85   Letters of the US Conference of bishops, *The Challenge of Peace: God's Promise and Our Response* (1983) and *Economic Justice for All,* (1986) (USCCB.org).

86   John XXIII, Apostolic Constitution, *Veterum Sapientia,* 1962.

87   The Donatists also thought that once apostasy occurred one lost one's standing in the church and had to be baptized again. I once heard Cardinal George of Chicago list his ecclesiastical lineage back to the pope

ident and applicable test stone of authenticity of church authorities is the New Testament and the traditions of church leadership. The bishops and popes are "shepherds," that is, pastors, not kings or secular lords. They should not act as High Priests whose authority is metaphysically bestowed and extends over the secular sphere as well as the churches.

A few words from William D'Antonio's *American Catholics Today* help to crystallize the problem in practical and current terms:

> An obvious case of the breakdown in accepted authority among Catholics is that the vast majority of Catholic couples use some form of birth control, which *Humanae Vitae* (1968) disallows, and the great majority do not see that their behavior is sinful... Further evidence that the teaching authority of the Vatican was seriously weakened during the middle period of the twentieth century is found in a series of polls asking American Catholics to agree or disagree with this statement: "Jesus directly handed over the leadership of His Church to Peter and the popes." In 1963 86% agreed the statement was certainly or probably true; in 1974, 71% agreed; and in 1985, 68% agreed... a decline of eighteen points in a span of twenty-two years... Catholics increasingly look to their own informed consciences in deciding what they will believe, even on such fundamental teachings as the Petrine principle of Church authority. [88]

Cardinal Timothy Dolan of New York said one of the major challenges for religions is this: "More and more people are saying, you know what, I don't have trouble with God, I don't have trouble with Jesus, I don't have trouble with faith, I do have some troubles with the church. That's a major pastoral challenge, not only for us as Catholics, but for the other revealed religions."[89]

To continue with my comments on these poll-established facts

who ordained a bishop who centuries later ordained George. It wasn't just the evangelicals in attendance (one thousand) who seemed stunned by this. Many Catholics were, too. Bishops actually think that the succession to apostolic eminence comes through a two thousand year string of imposition of hands.

88   D'Antonio, *American Catholics*, 91.

89   http://www.cbsnews.com/8301-3460_162-57577134/archbishop-dolan-pope-francis-a-shot-in-the-arm-for-the-catholic-church/

about American Catholics, The Church claims that episcopal authority rests on the stories of Jesus and the Twelve in the New Testament, on the Christian doctrine of apostolic succession (namely
that the bishops collectively succeed to authority of the Apostles
and that the bishop of Rome succeeds to St. Peter's authority), and
finally on long-standing church tradition (i.e., 1800 years of *de facto*
exercise of authority of bishops in and over their churches and the
1500 year gradual and ever-expanding ecclesiastical dominance of
the papacy). There were many challenges to the bishops' authority
over the centuries, from the third century Gnostics to the sixteenth
century Reformers, but all failed to stem the flow. Historically
speaking the only recourse to episcopal authority has been schism,
that is, groups breaking away from the authority of the pope and
bishop, and thereby ceasing to be Catholic such as in the case of
the Reformers during the sixteenth century.[90] The key to that disaster was the conviction common to popes, bishops and reformers
that they didn't have to listen to one another. Their pretended dialogues were in fact monologues. Schism is the curse of Christianity.

However, the bishops' and popes' moral authority has been di-
minishing significantly since Vatican II [1962-65], at least among
American Catholics who for the previous two centuries had been
the most loyal Catholics to the traditional authorities.[91] Why the
diminishment? Some say the overarching reason for it is the assimilation of Catholics to the "American Way," or their entry into
American economic and cultural mainstream, or, as some put it, the
breakdown of the American Catholic sub-culture. But the "reason"
for schism and diminishment of adherence to traditional authority
has been in force in Europe for five hundred years. Assimilation to
American culture is not much different.

Humanae vitae is Pope Paul VI's encyclical letter continuing a
century long ban on artificial birth control for Catholics because it
is deemed a sinful violation of marriage and against "the natural
law." While the Council (1962-1965) was received with enthusiasm
by most American Catholics, the encyclical was rejected by a majority. Since most American Catholics have decided to make up their
own minds about Catholic teaching on sexuality, they have also
taken a dimmer view of the judgment of the male hierarchy of the
Church on the so-called "pelvic issues." American Catholics do not
seem to think that the *Magisterium's* answers to these moral questions are central to their Christian faith.

90   Of course, there is the third way that has been frequently taken by
Catholics: pay attention to them when you think they are right and don't
when you think they are wrong.

91   See D'Antonio, *American Catholics Today*, 98, figure 6.2.

Democratic authority practices and structures that Catholics have become accustomed to (D'Antonio calls these "rational-legal") are in sharp contrast to the "traditional" authority exercised in the Church. In the nineteenth and twentieth centuries, monarchical "Christendom" gradually chocked to death. Current Church authority is a remnant of this demise and stands out starkly in a "modern" or "post-modern" culture, not that "standing out" is entirely and always a bad idea. Bishops apparently like to think of themselves and their moral teaching as "counter-cultural," and they take some pride in that label. In some respects, there is a genuine clash, even a contradiction, of Christian church and American culture. Think of the common Catholic teaching on capitalism and labor and the role of government in caring for the poor, teaching which many American Catholics simply ignore.[92]

Catholics along with other Americans have seen large changes in the civil, social and political orders and are used to seeing varieties of people influence the shaping of public policy. The Church seems to work in the opposite direction, from top (God) down. Popes and bishops don't seem at all interested in what their people think or believe, except to correct it. The "teaching Church," the *Magisterium*, is thus *very* slow to learn.

Again, membership in the Catholic Church is now voluntary. No one is required for social or political reasons to accept church authorities. In fact, they may disregard them if they choose and remain Catholic at least in name and even in religious practice. In religious matters, it would seem that individual and well-informed conscience is supreme. As an example of this, recently a priest who is a member of a missionary order of priests, brothers and nuns (Maryknoll) was expelled from his order and excommunicated from the church because he continued his public support and involvement in the ordination of women into the priesthood. He refused the commands to halt his support because, he claimed, he would not violate his own conscience. Similarly, an Irish Redemptorist priest has been threatened and rejects the threats on the same grounds. Theoretically, of course, this appeal to conscience is reconcilable with Church doctrine, but in practice the Catholic authorities tell us that "your own conscience" must be shaped by what the bishops teach, that is, when there is a difference in belief or practice the bishop is correct and you are not This is nonsense unless one believes that the bishops are possessed of divine guidance and the priests and laity are not. After all, it is the church that will prevail against the gates of hell, not the episcopacy and papacy. (MT 16:18)

92   See Pope Francis' Apostolic Exhortation, *Evangelii gaudium* (2013) and the controversy surrounding it.

Education and information levels have increased among the laity and now often surpass that of the clergy.

Since the Council American Catholics have fallen into sub-groups distinguished by their quite different attitudes toward church authority and by connotations of the term "Catholic," among them: Traditionalists groups who repudiate the Council and question the legitimacy of the popes elected since 1958; "Traditional" Catholics who remain devoted to the pre-conciliar Latin liturgy; Conservative Catholics who accept the authority of the Council, Rome and the bishops and who cling to their decisions and rules and many of the older religious practices; Progressive Catholics who want to see the reforms of the Council continued and extended even further than the council Fathers anticipated; Liberal Catholics who want to see democratic structures introduced into church governance; and small single issue "radical" groups like Womenpriest and Catholics for Free Choice who contradict Church authority on issues of morality and traditional practice. Even the bishops in the USCCB seem to fall into groups more or less conservative depending on the issue. As for myself, I fall into several camps at once: conservative, progressive, liberal and even "radical" (in ecclesiological issues).

All this is to say that the "problem of authority" is far more complex than it seemed when I thought it was a simple matter of obedience and disobedience. I gradually evolved politically from a right-wing Republican to a far-left Democrat and finally to a democratic socialist (is this evolution or devolution?), so I skipped from the 1950s common sense definition of a Roman Catholic to a deeply critical ecclesiastical left-winger. The journey in both cases seem to be best described as a gradual recognition that political and religious authorities are like me, and as Pope Francis said, "Who am I to judge?" Well, who are they to judge?

13. Why I Am Not a Catholic Theologian

Even Though I Talk Pretty Good Catholic

"When you put ten Protestants in a room they will talk about anything, and when you put ten Catholics in a room they will talk about the church." I don't know whether this is a Protestant *bon mot* about Catholics or a Catholic *bon mot* about Protestants, but it strikes me as typologically just. I do not intend to violate its spirit here.

I have never laid eyes on Pope Benedict or on his previous incarnation as the Cardinal Prefect of the Congregation for the Doctrine of the Faith. Photographs and videos of him warm my heart, but then so do the photos of every other one of my eight popes. Being a Catholic and an academic who has inhabited departments of religion and theology for the past forty-five years I have dwelt in this short man's long shadow. I think he is a very fine theologian who has explained again and again to us academics what it means to be a Catholic theologian. He is a highly qualified academic and practiced scholar in addition to being a devoted bureaucrat. He has been on the job throughout his whole adult life and has gotten the job done. His papacy ended sadly and bravely.

Having said this, I find myself in a peculiar, even tortured relationship to him—in my head and heart! During most of an extraordinary life in the service of the church he has been in a position to "lay down the law" on what a Catholic theologian is. He has done this so clearly and so effectively, in word and work, I have concluded that, by his standards, I am not a Catholic theologian. In my view, the theologian serves the good of the church (and The Church!) by studying God's presence in nature and history as well as revelation, and by constant dialogue, conversation and even argument with all Christians (i.e., the church and The Church). Tradition is part of the subject matter of the theologian. Establishing Tradition makes up the work of a Catholic theologian. Argument is part of that effort. The *Magisterium* of the Catholic Church is an important dialogue and argument partner of the theologians.

Thirty years ago, Cardinal Ratzinger made this comment about theologians:

> Broad circles in [Catholic] theology seem to have forgotten that the subject who pursues theology is not the individual scholar but the Catholic community as a whole, the entire Church. From this forgetfulness derives a theological pluralism that in reality is often a subjectivism and individualism that has little to do with the bases of common tradition. Every theologian now seems to want to be 'creative.' But his proper task is to deepen the common deposit of the faith as well as to help in understanding and proclaiming it, not to create it.[93]

Twenty-five years ago in his capacity of Prefect of the Congregation for the Doctrine of the Faith, Cardinal Ratzinger, with the full approval of Pope John Paul II, made similar comments in *Donum veritatis* on the relation between the theologian and the Church's teaching authority:

> In theology this freedom of inquiry is the hallmark of a rational discipline whose object is given by Revelation, handed on and interpreted in the Church under the authority of the Magisterium, and received by faith. These givens have the force of principles. *To eliminate them would mean to cease doing theology* [DV #12]... the Magisterium is, in its service to the Word of God, an institution positively willed by Christ as a constitutive element of His Church [DV #14]... Consequently, the documents issued by this Congregation expressly approved by the Pope participate in the ordinary magisterium of the successor of Peter. [DV #18]

Donum veritatis, if not a masterpiece of teaching, is a masterful presentation of The Church's view of itself in relationship to theologians and the believing faithful. It is Ratzinger at his systematic best, quite straightforward and logical, easy to read and hard to comprehend, with a depth to it that escapes an ordinary mind like my own. Additionally, while he underlines the responsibility of the pastors, the theologians and the faithful clearly, he also forces to the forefront of my mind that old bugaboo of Catholic scholastics,

---

93   Vittorio Massori, ed., *The Ratzinger Report* (Ignatius Press, 1985), 77. See also *Donum veritatis* [1990], "On the Ecclesial Vocation of the Theologian," Joseph Cardinal Ratzinger and Archbishop Alberto Bovone.

Immanuel Kant, who said that the believer must take responsibility for his or her believing, and cannot palm it off on the Guardians.[94] The primary "Guardian" of Catholic faith has been Cardinal Ratzinger in his capacity as prefect of the Congregation for the Doctrine of the Faith and then pope.

If I understand Benedict's words correctly, he presents an American university theologian with a dilemma. But it is not the situation of theology in a university that interests me here so much as whether the subject who does theology is "the Church," as he puts it, or the individual Catholic theologian, or even theologians as a guild. If he means that theological reflection is done not only *in* the church but also *by* the church, thereby excluding "subjectivism" and "individualism," I don't see how theology is done *by* the church any more than it is done *by* the university in which the theologian works. The individual theologian, in Ratzinger's view, is subsumed by a higher ontological reality and takes on the goals and limitations set by that ontological reality, 'The Church.' The theologian's reflection has no standing *as theology* until the Church owns it, meaning, I think, the Magisterium—with the immediate implication that what you read on these pages is not theology but something else.[95]

A Catholic theologian is trapped in the web spun by Ratzinger in the name of Pope John Paul II. As brilliant a gem as *Donum veritatis* is, and as beneficial as its traditional thinking has often

---

94   Immanuel Kant "What is the Enlightenment? " Columbia University, trans. Mary Smith. "Enlightenment is man's emergence from his self-imposed nonage. Nonage is the inability to use one's own understanding without another's guidance. This nonage is self-imposed if its cause lies not in lack of understanding but in indecision and lack of courage to use one's own mind without another's guidance. *Dare to know!* (*Sapere aude.*) 'Have the courage to use your own understanding,' is therefore the motto of the enlightenment."

95   CTS Presidential Address published as "Theologians and their Catholic Authorities" in B. Prusak, ed., *Raising the Torch of Good News* (Lanham MD: University Press of America, 1988): 261-275; "Dual Loyalties In Catholic Theology" *Commonweal* 119 (January 31, 1992): 9-14; and "The Subjectivity of the Theologian" in *The Thomist* (Spring 1981): 194-218. All three evidence a deviation from the norm of Catholic theology as conceived by His Eminence. It would not be difficult to list another dozen essays and chapters supporting the claim that I live in the shadows. The latest are the last two chapters of *The Lion and the Lamb: Evangelicals and Catholics in America* (NY: Oxford University Press, 2004). It seems to me that orthodox Catholic ecclesiology is evaporating there.

proved to be, for me it became not liberation, but a straightjacket.[96] That handful of my colleagues who warned me that there is too much of the Enlightenment in my thinking turned out to be quite right. Kant on conscience tops Ratzinger: Ratzinger thinks that The Church does the thinking for the church and Kant would think that The Church, the Guardian, would stifle thinking in the church by controlling the outcome of thinking. I believe Kant with this un-Kantian proviso: pay attention to the Guardians because they often know better than you do, but don't when they don't.

I am one of those whom Cardinal Ratzinger accused of wanting to be "creative," that is, of wanting to step outside the bases of the common tradition, of being in that "broad circle" who are "forget-ful" of the nature of Catholic theology, and who shape a plural-ist, a subjectivist, an individualist theology if, indeed, it is theology at all (clearly it isn't *Catholic* theology!) Consequently, as Lucifer fell from grace by refusing to accept the incarnation of the Word, I fall from theological grace by not accepting the limits placed by His Holiness on my lifetime of thinking, writing and teaching. It is precisely because of the role assigned the *Magisterium* by Ratzinger that I resolved early on not to write or, so far as I could avoid it, think about doctrines. As a matter of fact, I don't recall ever accept-ing those limits even when I was circumstantially bound by them. I am not a Catholic theologian under Pope Benedict's list of basic qualifications.

However, I have not forgotten what Joseph Ratzinger means by "the proper task of theology." In accordance with orthodox tradi-tion I would have to agree with him about that task and even cede to him the right to define that task, although some, perhaps many, theologians would disagree with me here. They would not cede to His Holiness the right to define theology for us all; indeed, they might today define it in ways unacceptable to him. In fact, if you might think about theology differently or wonder about the truth of certain teachings of the *Magisterium* your problem, in their view, isn't intellectual at all; it is spiritual. "Dissenters" would be repre-hensible individualists in his view.

I agree with him nonetheless: the sources of Catholic theology as he defines it are found in the Catholic tradition and nowhere else; the goal of Catholic theology is to deepen the church's under-standing of that tradition and nothing else; the guide and judge of the theologian's product is the Catholic hierarchy, and no one else. I do not think one can argue Ratzinger down *from Catholic sources.*

---

96   One example of the excellence achieved under Ratzinger's own rules are his volumes on *Jesus of Nazareth,* published after his accession to the chair of Peter.

Recognizing all this, I have been unable to call myself a theologian for the past four decades. I confess that long before I read his books I suspected that fact about myself and I take his words as confirmation of my own insight.[97] There is no place for me in the ecclesial theology outlined by the cardinal who is now pope *emeritus*.

Ratzinger was also right to insist that the social context of theological or any other reflection, if it can be deservedly called a "Christian reflection," is an active life in a Christian community.[98] It may seem at times that we academics work alone and think alone with our books in our laboratories, but in fact, we work and think in communities. After all, an entomologist has a community. We might "forget" that, too. Ratzinger reminds us, and he especially reminds me, that the tug between the individual and the communal marks a difficult struggle in the theologian's professional and religious life. Rather than face up to the rigorous conditions placed on theology by 'the Church' (i.e. Ratzinger), I abandoned the notion that what I have done can be considered theology or that it might contribute to the church's understanding according to Ratzinger and his theological colleagues. I have a broader and less exclusive notion of the church than he does and, in that context and without the limits he prescribes, I may be a theologian of some sort. If so, I might well be a *Christian* theologian thereby slipping the Guardian's leash. But still, he would insist quite rightly, my matrix is the Christian church. There's no escape from the church's essential communalism.

Nonetheless, in spite of my seeming American individualism, I am a communalist. For me the Catholic Church's life and traditions, its texts and liturgies are the prime source of my life, my preaching, my teaching and my thought—but I find other sources as well and I have other communities as well. For him the Roman *Magisterium* sets the limits of religious thought and judgment; for me it does not. For twenty-five years before his election to the papacy, he was the person in charge of drawing the lines for theologians, lines of consideration, expression and judgment that they dare not cross.[99]

---

97   I am a conservative Christian when it comes to doctrinal matters with the glaring exception of the ecclesiological. Although it has taken me years and even decades to work out what a theologian is and whether I am a theologian, I can date the decision to abandon the theology that Cardinal Ratzinger promotes to the year I entered the Columbia University department of religion rather than the Fordham University department of theology (1964). I had itching ears even then (2 Tim. 4:3-4).

98   *Donum veritatis*, #1.

99   Think of the dozens of theologians he has silenced and forbidden to publish over the years and, as many as he could manage, put out of

The lines make a certain bit of sense given his ecclesial context but they fall far short of the universality he accords them.

It seems to me that I have indicated at least some of the points at which Ratzinger and I differ, and so I move on. I have a few convictions that I should mention which play on the work I have done whatever it might be called. I'd like to put them on the table here.

First, if anything is, God is. This is one of the very few things I know—as distinct from think or believe. The presence of God is a given to me rather than a conclusion of mine. I don't *argue to* the existence of God so much as *start with* the presence of God.[100] At one point or another, arguments help me to articulate what I already know without them. I know that God exists before I make the judgment as a result of philosophical reflection that God exists. All sorts of people, the vast majority of people over the earth, know that God exists without anything close to philosophical reflection. Indeed, explicit philosophical reflection on the existence of God often unsettles and unnerves them as it did and does me.

The knowledge of God, coming with the operations of human consciousness, is the sort of knowledge you can have without noticing it, without understanding it. The odd thing is unbelief, not the knowledge of God. I am awed by Richard Dawkins and Christopher Hitchens, not by their beliefs (i.e., there is no God) but by the fact that they believe them. How, I ask myself, could a human consciousness essentially like mine, not get it? It seems so obvious to me! For me God is *there* and *here* and we know God, so the important and difficult *philosophical* questions are: in what manner God is *here* and *there*, and how do we know it? How do we speak best about what is given to human consciousness?

Culture shapes nature and the two are intricately intertwined. As hard as I try, I am unable to untwine them, and so I am acutely aware that I would have no language to speak of God and to God were it not for my religious community which speaks of God and to God incessantly and with confidence. Nonetheless, as much as the language for God is cultural, I think that the knowledge of God is "natural" in the first instance.[101] No matter what post-moderns sug-

---

their academic positions, some exiled, some forced to change their ecclesial matrices. We should not forget these little ones. The 'lost sheep' did not tempt the Prefect from protecting the flock! [MT 18:10-14] He flicked them off as one would a flea on the Lamb of God.

100   There is a big problem here, one that has plagued Western philosophy since Hume. I am aware of it.

101   "The Natural Knowledge of God," "Belief: Today's Issue," and "The Absence of God in Modern Culture" in Bernard Lonergan, *Second Collection* [Philadelphia: Westminster Press, 1975], 117-33; 87-99; 101-16.

gest, Being is not language and God is not a word or a proposition. God is distinct from and prior to language and everything else. Nor is God a being, supreme or otherwise.

Stephen Hawking appears in a documentary entitled "Why God Didn't Create the Universe." Benedict Cumberbatch gives him voice, and concludes that God couldn't have done so because time didn't exist before the Big Bang. How, then, could God create if not in time? For Hawking God is another being! God must be a being and so God cannot exist because beings require time. Nothing existed before something existed, including God who is something, and therefore God cannot exist. An astounding statement!

I've never been able to think anything, or say it, or see it, or love it without loving and "seeing" God. I have tried over the decades to think myself into atheism or agnosticism but I have failed miserably. Like Michael Corleone and his Mafia, I kept trying to escape into the wonderland of atheism wherein what we see is what we get and no more. However, I kept being pulled back into the church where there is Christian faith and hope and far more than we can see, a community that holds to the notion that God is not a thing in time, not another being at the start of the Great Chain of Being, but prior to time and beings.

This sense of God, a kind of implicit faith if you will, is a gift that accompanies being human.[102] Some think it is a form of self-deception even if it is biologically required for human flourishing![103] I am happy to call this immediate "sensing" of God an act of metaphysical insight common to all human beings—if mentioning metaphysics doesn't scandalize you and as long as no one thinks that by insight I mean a conclusion to a 'rational' argument. Be that as it may, I am most grateful to have it, and for that reason I call it a grace. For me it serves the same foundational function as the evangelical second-birth. In fact, the second-birth is a matter of being flooded with an awareness of what was already present to us, what we already knew and had not up to that point been willing or able to acknowledge. The second-birth is the acknowledgement that God has been with us before we knew it. However, I don't think we

---

102   In their 'revisionist' theologies Schubert Ogden and David Tracy made similar arguments that faith is implicit in all human action, Tracy in *Blessed Rage for Order: the New Pluralism in Theology* (NY: Seabury/Crossroad, 1975) and Schubert Ogden in *The Reality of God and Other Essays* (NY: Harper and Row, 1963). See also W. M. Shea, "Revisionist Foundational Theology" in *The Anglican Theological Review* 58 (1976): 263-279.

103   As in Nicholas Wade recently from the point of view of evolutionary biology: see *The Faith Instinct: How Religion Evolved and Why It Endures.* (NY: Penguin Books, 2009).

are born again as the outcome of a philosophical reflection.[104]

A corollary of this is the following: I have little or no positive *knowledge* of this God whose existence is surer than my own.[105] True, on a good day I can think about what God *isn't* with some confidence (God is not material or temporal or otherwise limited). On my own I cannot say much about what God *is*, what God is up to, what God is like, whether God speaks and I may speak back expecting to be heard.[106] So confused am I in fact that I may easily deny or doubt God's very existence even when sensing God's presence, for God is well outside my native way of knowing. For 'knowledge' of this sort, of the sort that many classify as religious or even theological 'knowledge,'[107] I turn to the Catholic people (and others!) who have some collective and traditional wisdom to lend me on the subject, and I believe them and do what they do. I think that the teachings of Christianity in its order of doctrine are true, but I don't *know* that they are and so I can say truthfully and exactly that, "I believe." The "I believe" is entirely derived from the "we believe" of the ancient creeds still recited in the churches. This becomes especially clear to me on occasions of worship in the community, and otherwise where and when, on rare occasions, I can summon the energy and concentration required to think straight about it.

These beliefs that I have pronounced in the Christian creed

---

104   This is an Augustinian and Bonaventurian way of coming at the matter, and one which would be recognized as such by Pope Ratzinger who himself has been called a Bonaventurian as distinct from a Thomist. The best Thomist theologian I ever knew, William Hill, O.P., once said to me, at the end of a talk I gave on religious experience, "I have a hard time believing this, but I suspect you're a Franciscan!" that is, a Bonaventurian as distinct from a Thomist. Hill was surprised because he knew me to be a devoted reader of Lonergan's *Insight.* He supposed some disagreement on the knowledge of God between the Bonaventurian and Thomist traditions.

105   See Bernard Lonergan, *Insight,* 658-669. Lonergan knew a great deal about God by unpacking the "idea of God." One must have read the six hundred preceding pages in order to follow these ten. He has a more metaphysically chaste discussion in *Method in Theology* (NY: Herder and Herder, 1972), fourth chapter, on "Religion."

106   Lonergan, *Method in Theology,* on the inner and outer Word; also Karl Rahner, *Hearers of the Word* (NY: Continuum, 1994).

107   I call it belief rather than knowledge, preferring to use the terms knowledge and knowing in the more technical sense as Lonergan develops it in *Insight;* see the index under knowledge and belief. See as well *Method in Theology,* 41-47 and 115-119 for clarifying discussions.

weekly for the past seventy years, even now at my advanced age and with a decent education, sometimes shake my poor mind into a state of wonder. The Incarnation? The Second Coming? A Virgin Birth? A Holy Spirit? "Why would anyone believe, or want to believe, these curious claims," I say to myself, a man who hopes for a church funeral and burial. Who would be able to believe any of this after reading and hearing this new century's antagonists of religious faith, the supremely rational Dawkins, Hitchens and Sam Harris—men who loath my religion and my church and think the world better off without them?[108] Yet I want to believe the doctrines and do. With regard to specifically Christian beliefs I am, by myself, every bit as much in the dark, clueless, and trusting as I was when I first believed. Alas, I haven't learned much about them over the decades. I follow the light I was exposed to by my father and mother, by the Sisters of Charity, by the Brothers of the Christian Schools, and by the priests of St. Raymond's Parish in the Bronx, and, over the years, by people like Archbishop Fulton Sheen, Dorothy Day and a convent of Ursuline nuns at the College of New Rochelle.

The church as a community utters strange and deep things about God that I would not have a clue to by myself. For example, the church and the Scriptures say God favors the poor, and that so should I—that's a lot deeper than anything I could guess or imagine on my own. I would not ever think *that* to be true in the face of what happens every day in the world I inhabit. On my own, I would think that God has it in for the poor (good luck to them!) On my own I would say that God has a preferential option for the rich, favoring Goldman-Sachs and Citicorps and, up to recently, Bear-Sterns and Lehman Bros, and for decades Bernie Madoff (like Job, Bernie has slipped into bad times—I can only hope he now hears the Voice from the Whirlwind) (Job 38). On my own I might even think that evangelical prosperity teachers have a point!

When I sit and pray, my spirit is bourn up by the assertions made around me by believers, especially those successors to the apostolic witness who talk as if they know what they are talking about. The successors *believe* what they are talking about but they don't *know* what they are talking about—at least in reference to Jesus. Not one of them *knows* that Jesus was raised from the dead any more than I do. I admit that even I talk with conviction about the

108   Richard Dawkins, *The God Delusion* (NY: Haughton Mifflin, 2006); Christopher Hitchens, *God is Not Great: How Religion Poisons Everything* (NY: Grand Central Publishing, 2007); and Sam Harris, *Letter to a Christian Nation* (NY: Vintage, 2008). These are valuable books for someone who has been reading anti-Christian and anti-Catholic literature for the past fifty years but they are also boring and exasperating.

Resurrection of Jesus when the Spirit moves me, but it is not with knowledge that I speak, it is with passionate faith and hope. In fact it may well be that even the original apostolic witnesses did not *know* that Jesus was risen but had the same sort of faith and belief that Christians have today.

I can only suppose and hope that there is a connection between the mysterious God present to me and the beliefs the community has taught me to profess. I pray "our Father" as our Lord taught his disciples. I have chosen to live my life in the communion of that apostolic generation. I will die in that communion, God willing. But this is not to say that I *know to be true* now what the popes and bishops tell me. [109] What I do *know* is this: it is important and good that I believe them and stand with them in hope and faith even when I disagree.[110]

Now the twist comes. I rely totally on the word of the church for my beliefs about God and Christ. Yet the structural order of the Roman Catholic Church is an increasingly odd matter indeed for me, and it lies far down the road in importance from knowledge about and belief in God and the gospel of Jesus, even though it is only through the church, primarily through my parents, that I have come to believe what the church believes about God and Christ. The Church on its structural side, is not the object of a metaphysical insight nor is it itself any longer for me a matter of religious belief. In fact, of all the things that the Catholic Church teaches, the most unbelievable is its teaching about its own structure and ontological status, and the most objectionable is its immense pretensions for both.

The Protestant Reformers and their evangelical offspring have helped me to wonder about the claims that popes, bishops and theologians have made for the hierarchical Church with regard to its divine authority. This is where the pope, bishops, and I part company. In other words, I don't think, much less believe, that the

---

109   Ratzinger also writes that doubt accompanies Christian belief— as it does the mind and heart of the agnostic and the unbeliever. I agree: human beings are "programmed" to doubt as well as believe. See his *Introduction to Christianity* (NY: Herder and Herder, 1970).

110   Does belief ever become knowledge? In the empirical realm, yes, it often does but not easily. When Stephen Hawking proves a unified field theory, he will *know* that there is a unified field. Until then, he hopes and believes. Until the Last Judgment, we believe what God is up to, but don't know. I do not know there is resurrection from the dead until I am raised. Until then, I believe. However strong our beliefs may be, however "certain," they remain beliefs. Christians often sound as if religious belief is personally generated knowledge but it isn't.

"One, Holy, Catholic and Apostolic Church" *subsistit* in the Roman Catholic Church any more (or less) than it does in other "ecclesial communities."[111] When the popes and bishops talk about themselves in eulogistic terms, I detrain, as perhaps many, if not most, American Catholics do. Even as modern popes, bishops, theologians and councils are caught up in endless chatter about the hierarchical nature of the Church and its divine origin and authority, more and more laypersons wonder why. To what end is the chatter? Perhaps it is a cover for their spiritual nudity or for their own fear that what they witness to may be untrue.

But, but, but... still there is another side to the church (this Catholic Church is the only one with which I am genuinely familiar), and that is the gravity of its gathering of men and women and children. Here, we pray, hear the scriptures read, and hear a homily spoken to our hearts, to remember a common past and look for a common future, to tell a story that includes everyone as characters, even me, to share the holy meal and to "go in peace to love and serve the Lord." There is something about the gathering and what is done in it that makes the church indispensable to me and to hundreds of millions of attendees, and makes the church inviting for some and irksome for others. Your gathering, whatever brand it is, possibly does the same thing for you. I would never go to the same old play or movie once a week, but every week I go to church for more of the same old thing. I could watch Mass on TV but I never do. I don't understand this fact about myself. I don't fight it, I don't get it, but I "let it be." When I go I am aware that I am doing the right thing. I *know* that it is good that the Old Words be spoken again and that the Old Things be done, in addition to believing the Old Words and participating in the Old Things. I hope dearly that my sons, their wives and their children will follow me and their mother in this as we followed ours. In matters of faith, hope and suffering, their mother, like Mary, is a font of wisdom.

I strongly *suspect* and I don't *know*, that the millennium-old self-eulogy that the Catholic hierarchy and clergy deliver about The Church is an expression, distorted as it may be, of the mysterious fact that people still come to hear the story and pray with them. The fact of common worship is a wonder (a *res mira*) but the self-referential doctrine and ecclesiology is a scandal (*causa offensionis*) so far

---

111   See the Vatican Council's "Decree on Ecumenism" (*Unitatis Redintegratio)* and *Lumen Gentium* #8 for an explanation of *subsistit in ecclesia Romana*. See also the comments of Cardinal Ratzinger in the CDF documents *Dominus Jesus* (2000), part IV; *Donum veritatis* (1990); and "Responses to Some Questions regarding Certain Aspects of the Doctrine of the Church." See Vatican.org under documents of Vatican II.

as I can make it out. It is an etiological myth gone mad and an insult to the Christian people. What bothers me particularly is the claim that it (*Ecclesia Romana*) is the One True Church of Christ in the Full Sense and that no other church is quite as true and real; that its social organization is a matter of Christ's own will and commission; and that it is monarchical in nature.[112] These specific beliefs about the Church amount to a large part of what Cardinal Ratzinger, now retired Pope Benedict, means by the Deposit of Faith. According to him only by accepting these claims among others as essential can a reflection be called theological and Catholic. He was in the driver's seat, of course, but still I think him mistaken. He and his high clerical cohorts can accomplish what the church needs without slathering themselves with divinity.

I suspected decades ago, while walking the pavements of the Catholic University of America in the 1970s that the hierarchy needed to be taken down a peg or two. Specifically when the pope and the bishops put us through their birth control wringer, but for some time now, I increasingly am astonished when I see and hear them, and I am sad that the course of history and their own choices have taken them to this point of self-understanding. Once again, I do not object to their governance (someone has to do the job) but I do object to what they have made of it in church doctrine about itself and in their own souls. Most New Testament exegetes would allow for the possibility that Jesus did not attribute messiahship and divine sonship to Himself during His lifetime, or was very circumspect and indirect in claiming a divine status, a modesty that The Church might well imitate.

So, to sum it up, let me say (a) that the existence and presence of God are overpowering to me—they are the other side of my finitude; (b) the story and the gathering are for me fatefully gripping; (c) the doctrines of great creeds are at once illuminating and impenetrable, and worth believing; and (d) the Catholic Church's teaching about its own nature and divine status is arguable for one who does not pretend to be a theologian. But, and I must add this in all honesty, for Catholics like myself the Church catholic is more than the churches! There IS something divine about it no matter how it is organized, though we seem bent on distorting that as soon as we open our mouths. In no way would I locate the divinity of the church in its leadership or its ecclesiastical structure any more (or less!) than I would in the Archbishop of Canterbury or the Stated Clerk of the Presbyterian Church, though all of them are human

---

112   The Latin usage at the Council is that the church, willed by Christ and handed over to Peter as its shepherd, *subsistit in ecclesia Cattolica.* Cf. *Lumen Gentium*, #8.

beings who walk in darkness yet have seen a great light. After a lifetime of experience with them I would have to say to the pope, the cardinals, and the bishops, "Get off it!" and "Get over it!" And, I suppose, this is why I am not a Catholic theologian.

Section 3.

Which Way to Reform?

14. "The Church that Forgot Christ"

Jimmy Breslin wins the argument if all before us are Cardinals Law, Mahoney and Egan and, more recently, the legal performances of Archbishop Carlson and the resignation of Archbishop Nienstedt, men who don't seem to remember anything that ever happened to them. [113] With the many sins and crimes of the bishops and of the popes in this last century, we Catholics seem to have reached the bottom of the ecclesiastical barrel. The bottom in this past century, in my view, was reached between 1933 and 1945 when the bishops of Germany, France and Italy did next to nothing to support justice for the Jews of Europe and next to nothing to oppose the madman's war in which over fifty million died. With the clerical abuse crisis we Catholics *are* the bottom of the ecclesiastical barrel, a new bottom to our old barrel. Even Luther and Calvin, who thought they knew the score on the "Romish" church, would gape at what the Catholic clergy (high and low) of the second half of the twentieth century have wrought across the globe: a flash-flood of child rape and the seduction of young men. Who would have thought? Not me! Up to my middle years, I was convinced that crimes of the episcopacy and papacy were a thing of the darkest of ages. I thought we had a string of great popes, and honest, talented and standup bishops, and I basked in the glow of a morally superior Church. Now I have to explain to myself and others why I want to remain a Catholic.

The moral facts about the Church seem clear enough now. The question is what to do about them. There are not many options present to ordinary Catholics. Thirty million American Catholics remain churchgoers, following the practice of most of our Irish, Italian, German and Polish and central and southern European ancestors. Another twenty million retain their Catholic 'union cards' but attend church far less often. In the United States, twenty million more people in the past few decades have made their decision, ripped up the 'union card' and left the Catholic Church. I expect that over the next decade millions more will follow, for the corruption shows little signs of abating and many people grow tired of it all. I am tired, too, but leaving is not my choice. I have not left and

---

113   Jimmy Breslin, *The Church that Forgot Christ"* (New York: Free Press, 2004).

have no intention of doing so, as long as I can find a parish where the sacraments are worthily celebrated, the preaching is orthodox and insightful, the Scriptures are seen as the measure of a Christian life, the perverts have been sent packing and the pastor can put up with my odd opinions on The Church.[114] I haven't had difficulty doing so for the past thirty-five years.

I do not wish to be unkind, unjust or hyperbolic, but this is what it looks like to an interested Catholic father who reads secular and Catholic papers and magazines and even an occasional book on the sexual corruption of the clergy.[115] Negligent and evasive popes have, over the past thirty years, installed negligent and evasive bishops who have in turn ordained priests with disturbing sexual interests, and then hid them when they raped children and young men. Not being willing to cause stress to the Holy Father who appointed them by acting privately or publicly to correct the situation (and so calling negative attention to themselves), they follow in the *Omerta* of episcopal ordination. Many, perhaps most, remain willing to double-cross children and their parents in order to 'save' their errant priests (and themselves, it must be said).

"*Omerta*" is the term the Mafia calls the pledge of silence taken by "made men" that protects its hierarchy. The clerical world generated such a pledge long ago, its basis being an agreement passed on from one generation of clergy to the next that you don't turn the perverted priests and bishops in to the civil officials, and that you remain blind and dumb in the case of your fellow bishops and priests who aren't up to the job in ability and/or morality. The Church runs the church with a remarkable tolerance for the sins of the clergy while it (The Church) insists on dunning the churches with warnings and denunciations of the sins of the laity. When confronted with the clericalism problem the pope calls for a synod of bishops on the problem of the family and invites but a handful of married couples with neither voice nor vote.[116]

With millions leaving the practice of Catholicism perhaps a tiny spark of memory flitted across the mind of Benedict XVI who some years ago, before his elevation, suggested that we need a smaller

114   Orthodox not by my definition but by the creeds of the ancient churches. The ancient Church got it right on the big doctrinal questions of the era. The modern Church has gotten it right on most issues with the exceptions of ecclesiology and sex. It's when they start talking about themselves that they go all screwy.

115   See the bibliography for books by Jason Berry and the Boston Globe investigative staff, etc.

116   To his eternal credit, Pope Francis ordered that a survey be taken of opinions in the churches before the Synod of Bishops.

and leaner church. He's getting one, at least in the West, and good luck to him. But the exodus worries me and radically undercuts my understanding of the peculiar character of the Catholic Church where the cold and lukewarm are as welcome as the warm and hyper-warm. The church is not a sect crowded with the saints; it's an oasis for sinners, even for episcopal and sacerdotal sinners.

So, in order to open up the options before me, I entered into a dialogue with a book by an old-timey Catholic like myself (Jimmy Breslin) who *has* left the church and makes his case in print for refusing communion with the bishops of the current Roman Catholic Church. More briefly, I encounter another man (Garry Wills), an intellectual who hasn't left and who has given his reasons for sticking it out.[117] I chose them because they are my kind of Catholics, men whom I have admired for decades and whose integrity of mind seems obvious to me. In addition, they are laymen and not professional theologians.

Frankly, both of them know more about the church than I do. Breslin knows Catholics and their way of religious practice as he knows the people of the New York street, and the priests and nuns of New York who make the church catholic; Wills knows the church by way of historical and cultural study and life-long Catholic practice evidenced in several of his books about the church.[118] Maybe, I said to myself, I might find illumination and even inspiration in what these two men have to say. Maybe I'll be able to articulate reasons of my own for what I already know I want to do. In this chapter, I'll recount the devastating charges made by Breslin and disagree with him, and at the end of it, I'll listen briefly to Wills as he tells us why he hasn't jumped the ecclesial ship.

Now, to be honest I do have to own up to two things, for I live in a glass house. First, it is highly unlikely that I would have followed the historical Jesus—too rough, too prickly, too sure, uneven and unpredictable, too landless, too unconcerned with ordinary life, far too assertive and authoritative and too much over my head in his preaching. To this day I keep a jaundiced eye on peripatetic preachers of kingdoms to come, Catholic and otherwise. I don't like the ones whom I have heard. Likewise, had I not been born and educated a Roman Catholic Christian I almost certainly would not have become one (in both cases I put aside the grace of God). As I find Jesus odd and objectionable, I find the leadership of the Catholic Church alternately vapid and morally offensive. The lat-

117   Jimmy Breslin, *The Church that Forgot Christ*; and Garry Wills, *Why I am a Catholic* (New York: Houghton Mifflin, 2003). I am confident that Breslin would not classify himself as an intellectual or a scholar.

118   See bibliography.

ter I decided decades ago when I realized that they failed to help European Jews between 1933 and 1945. Being a chicken myself, why would I want to join a church led by chickens? Besides, the Apostles, according to the stories, weren't chickens, except once and then only for a day or two, dunces maybe, but chickens not, at least according to the *Mythos*. I could be mistaken here, but the Apostles would object to sharing their eschatological thrones with the likes of Law, Burke, Mahoney, Egan, Chaput, Nienstedt, and George, our latter day archbishops. Yet here I am, a chicken in a church led by company men.

Second, and this is even more painful to admit, had I been a bishop or a chancery servant of a bishop in the church of the last fifty years I would have done exactly what the bishops and their servants did: covered up for deviant priests and bishops, and switched them from parish to parish and diocese to diocese. I say this because, having been in "the system" for twenty-nine years, I have a feel for it especially at its lower levels and it had its hands around my neck. I know the odor of its breath. It is a system built on conformity and loyalty to the caste. It has unwritten rules of self-protection ("*Omerta*") and I am implicated in its sins.

Dishonesty, cowardice, class loyalty, conformity and sexual sin in the clerical system are ancient and wide spread and I was party to them for close to three decades. The problem we face now is not about sex primarily, even deviant sex. Clericalism is what we have to worry about: namely, about being in rather than out, in power and in control of the property, loyal only to the boss and the rest of the boys—the material and cultural implications of the clerical *beneficium*.[119] Clericalism infests a caste and class, and has foisted itself upon what was in its origins and early life, and what it wishes to be even now, a genuine salvific human community. Clericalism is a worldly phenomenon and has nothing to do with the Christian gospel; in fact clericalism is antithetical to the gospel. Sexual aberration and sins of the flesh are epiphenomena (and a constant, no doubt) in the world and in the world of the church. The Catholic system of governance and ministry, however, is corrupting and has been since their outset. The emperor Constantine immeasurably increased the threat of a corrupt episcopacy by making the bishops of the church a new species of imperial civil servants. It's a wonder that the church survives The Church!

---

119   *Beneficium* is the land and/or income afforded a priest or a bishop when appointed to an office. For a definition and discussion of clerical culture see "The Clerical Culture" and "Clerical Culture Among Roman Catholic Clergy in the U.S." on the Voice of the Faithful website under "documents."

Gregory XVI (d. 1846), Pius IX (d.1878), X (d.1914) and XII (d. 1958), and for the past thirty years John Paul II (d.1978) and Benedict XVI are the prime examples of the distorted clericalist view of our church in modern culture, a culture which, admittedly, has its own even profounder distortions. The church is not in any way exempt from the effects of original and personal sin that inflict the capitalist or socialist worlds around us, or the 'modern world' of the Enlightenment that popes, bishops and some theologians ritually denounced. The Johannine "World," that sin-laden world, includes the church, and especially the Roman Catholic Church. As the church is in the world, so the "world" is in the church.

Those popes' clerical premise was wrong. Christendom was their premise and ideal– a world in which there is one just society linked to the one true church, the clergy setting the cultural, social and political standards, in which the cultural and much of the material property belonged to them, and from the heights of which they could pronounce on morality of others. Benedict XVI, succeeding on the rest of them and in accord with the belief of his predecessors, still thinks that Europe belongs to The Church, and he wants it back, at least in the constitution of the European Union.

The bend in the clerical moral life is not celibacy, and of this I am reasonably certain, for celibacy does not make pedophiles and ephebophiles. Dropping celibacy may help to dampen the instinct of priests and bishops toward philandering but it won't eliminate it—marriage doesn't eliminate it for married folk. Married pedophile priests would likely abuse their own sons as well as the sons or daughters of others. As long as hormones flow, The Church will have fornicators and adulterers as the church does. A theologian told me four decades ago that the man who does not have a problem with sex can only have an even bigger problem of some other sort. There was nothing in the priesthood absent a maturity I never reached to help me keep control of my affectional life—but nothing in it either to make me lose control of it.[120] So let's be clear about this: the celibacy rule is tough on priests but far from impossible. The rule may be dumb (I think it is) but most priests are able to live with it simply because they like and value what they do as priests. But neither the rule nor the practice of celibacy is *the*, or even *a*, cause of the children being raped.

Jimmy Breslin has taken his shot at the clerical "Roman" Church, made a claim, and suggested a response from ordinary Catholics, the people of the streets he loves. "Get out," he says to us. The Roman Catholic Church is too far-gone to be saved, to be

120   Greeley, *Priests.* Priests who are happy with their work stay in it; those who are unhappy fall in love and leave. That's me.

reformed. Start over again in Breslin's brand new Catholic church where he will be bishop and the poor will be served. It is right and just to be amazed, horrified, disgusted, and embarrassed by what we see, as Breslin is and as I am. Although his issue (corruption) is mine, is his solution mine? Alas, his is the solution of ancient anti-clericalism, and of those who are "enlightened" and convinced that the churches are filled with hypocrites, time-servers and bourgeois mediocrities.

True religion, Breslin says with Jonathan Edwards, is a matter of holy affection for God and one's neighbor.[121] That, he thinks, is rare indeed among the clerical leaders of the Roman Church for they have forgotten Christ. Unlike Jesus who said that we should attend to those who sit on the chair of Moses but not imitate them (Mt 23:2-3), Breslin tell us to go out from them to a new chair of Moses with Breslin sitting on it and listen to the gospel preached therein, a gospel meant for those who are willing to love the poor.

I must admit that at this point Breslin sounds a bit like Pope Francis. I would attend his church of the poor. When I read Breslin, I said to myself "God, that's just the way I feel!!" But to join him at the door is to solve nothing, except to exercise my disappointment and hurt but no more. From the point of view of a Catholic layman, to see something go this badly, something you love, is to feel as hopeless and helpless as Breslin did at the dying of his wife and the fatal sickness of his daughter. Two decades ago (1994) I watched the artery on my mother's neck stop beating. I couldn't weep her or my father back to life. He died in his sleep of congestive heart failure (1977). I was not with him when he died. I know what death is. After these deaths, I do know what hopelessness and helplessness are. Breslin is not alone in his sorrow, much less in his distress at the corrupt life of the Church. He is in a very long line of Christians who are sick over the state of the churches, a very long line of those Catholics who mourn the corruption of the Catholic Church. I recall that G. K. Chesterton once wrote that one of the "proofs" of divine favor toward the church is that it survives its leaders.

Now Breslin and I, in our dotage, watch the Catholic Church in America (and several other nations) bleed to death. Why not walk away rather than hold her till she dies or try to weep her back to a life she will never have? "Let the dead bury the dead," said Jesus. (Mt 8:22) The Catholic Church never has been, and never will be, the spotless Bride of Christ until it enters the Kingdom. With the likes of Cardinals Law, Burke, Egan, Mahoney, George, Wuerl, Rigali and Dolan sitting around "the throne of Peter" waiting for him

---

121   Jonathan Edwards, *Treatise on Religious Affections,* in the Complete Works vol. 2 (New Haven: Yale University Press, 2009).

to comfort them, his brethren, I want to weep myself. "It's too late," I am tempted to say with Breslin.

But Breslin is wrong. Breslin's answer to the problem is amputation: cut off the diseased flesh; save yourself and the poor! But Jesus says, "Pay attention to them for they sit on the chair of Moses..." (Mt. 23:1-4) and warns, "Watch the beam in your own eye." (Mt 7:5) This is enough scriptural warrant to call a halt to the exodus. The church of people like me and of the clergy high and low is not *only* or *completely* corrupt. Yes, it's corrupt enough to need house cleaning often, but the church as a whole hasn't forgotten Christ or the poor. It never has and never will, thanks to the grace of God. I am surprised that Breslin doesn't see this. Perhaps you can't appreciate the skyscraper when you walk on the sidewalk next to it. He is the street-wise man and during his professional life always managed to see the two-sidedness of the people, all people. How did he lose his "third eye," the one that sees through hypocrisy and phony religion to honesty and genuine religion, in this one case? How could he who knew people from the Mafia to the mayor forget that even bishops are human and two-faced?

He solves nothing by walking out. You salve your rage, nothing more, and turn your eyes from the dying church and, in doing so, even from yourself. By leaving with Breslin you hand the church over to the popes' ecclesiastical offspring (they think they own it, don't forget!) You hand it over to those new Bernard Laws who leap onto old apostolic thrones, who jump with ersatz humility and obedience from one hue of red to another, from chancery and seminary to diocese and archdiocese and, if they are lucky, to the big red hat faithfully carrying out the will of him who claims he sits on Peter's throne. As Nietzsche said of the clerical caste, unless there is a radical change, in another decade the stench will rise to Heaven. Well, Friedrich, there has been no change and the stench has been rising for a millennium and a half. God holds His divine nose, and so should we.

So we do have a big problem, presented in graphic terms by Breslin. But where shall we go? I can't join the ranks of the so-called Woityla Catholics, the "evangelical" Catholics, for he and they gave us the church we have today and will have tomorrow. While I do regard John Paul II as something of a genius in his display of his public persona, I can't stand the ideological papacy and episcopacy that he fostered, where there is allowed no voice but his own and his echoes. Rather than finding and acting on the genius of Catholicism he tried to make the church over in the very limited (if intense) vision of it that possessed him: obedience was his obsession. Too many years fighting Communists I suspect. For him the church was the pope plus parrots. Rather than stretching his mind and soul to meet the whole and the real church, he bent his energies toward contracting the church to those who sat around his throne. No, the hierarchy and especially the cult of the papacy fostered by the last two popes are part of the problem and not the solution.

Yet I cannot dismiss the papacy and the episcopacy out of hand as I think Breslin does. I want to see something done about them but I am not anxious to eliminate the offices, though I surely would eliminate a good number of the current leading figures in the church in America. The offices, after all, are just that, offices which the churches over centuries, close to millennia, have accepted. The great Reformers themselves, having rejected the leadership of bishops and popes, had to find substitute offices and officers to replace them, and were not notably successful in doing so. Lutheran synods and Calvinist presbyteries, indeed the Southern Baptist Convention, have not impressed me as improvements over the "Roman system."

Even if one is going to settle for the *status quo* in the shape of ecclesiastical government, do Catholics have to settle for the traditional obsequiousness toward the "sacred" holder of office and the notion that the pope and his administration of the church have somehow become "the will of God"? Can one be an anti-corruption, anti-clericalism Catholic? I hope so, but I regard it as highly unlikely that now or in the near future there will be truly reformist bishops. The "successors of Peter" have seen to that. Yes, there were and are genuine Catholic reformists. People, priests, nuns, monks and even some bishops have struggled over a thousand years to reform the Catholic Church. There are the Modernists who were crushed by Pius X and the theologians of the post-world war period who fell quiet when Pius XII compelled them to. There are the priest-theologians who have been ordered to silence and the sisters who have fallen under the modern Church inquisition. There are the Catholic lay persons, journalists and lawyers who are ignored. They are heroes and martyrs.

Why not reformers? Why not a latter day reformist movement in the Catholic Church? There are signs of it (Call to Action, Voice of the Faithful, Bishops Accountability, etc.) and the response of the hierarchy to them has been shocking, yet true to historical form: they reach for weed-killer. What these nervous and imperious bishops want is obedience. They do not ask whether there is a point to the protests and the reform movements. Their system is busy preserving itself. They don't go in search of the lost sheep; they eliminate them. (Jn. 10: 2ff.)

However, Breslin is unlike the reformers among the laity and priests. He seems entirely uninterested in genuine reform. He wants to take the path of Luther and Calvin and Knox. And how long did THAT reform last? Alas, not long. It seems that wherever two or three are gathered in His name there is another spirit present, an unholy spirit who waits to pounce on those who are convinced they are saved. Think of Elmer Gantry. Does Breslin think that the radical reformed communities such as he contemplates will have no pedophiles, no fornicating and adulterous clergy? No effete hierarchs? No crooks? No ambitious clerics? No liars? He hopes not, it seems, but history has already proven him wrong. Whether Luther's church or Breslin's, *Ecclesia semper reformanda est*. This implies that the church is always sinning. Sure, leave with Breslin but you can bet a pedophile or two will be in your procession, and the effete will line up behind Breslin, waiting for him to vacate his throne and within a decade or two there will be another *cappa magna*.

Our bishops have betrayed the church as the apostles in Jerusalem betrayed Jesus (I mean the Twelve]. Judas was one of them. As Breslin points out, there were only the women left at the foot of the cross (plus the Beloved Disciple whoever he or she may be) and at the tomb. Ten or perhaps eleven of the twelve took off. That's an 83% flee rate. Jimmy and I would betray the church as well were we to leave. If I were to get what Jimmy calls "mystical" about his proposed solution I would proclaim it to abandon the church, even the Roman Church, is to flee the cross. No desire for a pure and gospel-clean church justifies what Breslin calls for. Did Jesus himself flee Judaism and the high priesthood? Has Breslin forgotten what Jesus did? Jesus was a reformer, not a revolutionary or a schismatic. He was a rabbi, a teacher and an itinerant preacher.

My friend and seminary classmate John B. Sullivan told me a half century ago that the fledgling ecumenical dialogues of the 1960s would go just fine until the boys start to talk about who would hold the deeds to the property of an ecumenical church. The dialogues will collapse at that point, he maintained. The higher clergy rule the church in God's name, not in ours, and their "God" is notoriously sticky about the property that the high clergy hold, or so they tell us. Look at the fuss the popes kicked up when the Italians took over the Papal States in 1869. The popes thought God, through Constantine, had given them the center of the Italian peninsula! They claimed, and were convinced of it, that they could not lead the church spiritually unless they owned the center of Italy. Starting in 1870 the popes went into mourning until 1929 when Mussolini paid them for their loss and gave them Vatican City State as their redoubt.

Luther and Calvin saw this clearly: ownership is the root of power, and, in the One True Church that they quit, the higher clergy professedly owned nothing and yet controlled it all. Members of the Body have acquiesced in this since Constantine started out giving them building permits and land grants, and the Catholic system was blessed by the emperor. They, of course, would have us believe that ownership began at the Last Supper (in the case of Peter, even earlier). Ownership became the corruption of the caste. We in the laity have ratified the deeds in every generation by our acquiescence in this clerical flimflam, and are left in the shadows of the church, no land and no voice. We know who counts and the laity and the lower clergy are not among them. The fact of the matter is that we are not stakeholders much less stockholders so far as they are concerned. The kicker in all this is that the high clergy claim that this is just what Jesus intended!

In 1962-65, many reformist bishops and theologians in The Great Council of the eastern and western Catholic churches wanted to correct some of the papal and curial marginalization of bishops and laity. They tried to work it out so that at least bishops would have a say and that the laity would be included in the term "church." In both regards, the Council has been overruled by the last two popes. The bishops remain the honored altar boys of the Holy See, and the laity, unless they are monied, are ignored. Many Catholics know that the popes and the current episcopacy have betrayed the Council, their own predecessors, the ones they piously call "the Fathers of the Council."

I admit to teetering on the edge of Breslin's solution. The rage I would salve by ceasing with Breslin to care about "them" and refuse communion with "them" is in good part fueled by my failure as a Catholic to take my share in this moral mess seriously over the past five decades. I did not see the mess coming. I was too busy with my own life, whether as a priest or a married layman trying to make a living, turning away my eyes, simply accepting my assigned status as an ecclesial non-entity. There were reforming priests and laypersons in those days as there are now. I did not join them. The problem of caste has been staring me in the face since my seminary days 1953-1961. I wanted to be part of it, in fact. I thought it was a sanctified life. After all, there were no altar boys upstairs in the rectories in which I lived. I took it that the boys in red were doing the job but they weren't. It never occurred to me that there were men in red as well as black who lusted after bodies of children! It never occurred to me that other men in red would cover for them. It never occurred to me that the man in white would cover for them all. I was a self-absorbed fool. Like Breslin, I am an old man who lived with his eyes squeezed shut, for a while happy if one of them blessed me from a distance or even spoke to me.

I know now how the bishops have behaved toward predators and that the state institutions refused to take The Church on. I know now that there are wolves among the sheep, and that the false shepherds thought more of the wolves and their "priestly calling" than they did of the children. Now we know that among those false shepherds there are popes, bishops, archbishops, cardinals, founders of new religious orders and leaders of old ones, too. Even the sanctified ones (Fr. Bruce Ritter of New York) who saved children from the streets of New York have preyed on those very children. We cannot forget any of this. They must always be scrutinized.

This crisis reinforces the lesson of the Holocaust: the Catholic hierarchy is not to be trusted to do the right thing. It simply won't when its own interests are at stake. As Breslin reminds us, some of them even preside over churches in which priests rape nuns and they do nothing about it. John Paul II took an accused ephebophile, celibate fornicator and bigamist with him on one of his trips, honored him even after credible charges had been made against him, and refused to allow an investigation. The man's crimes were so blatant and the pope's self-deception so egregious that Benedict, his successor, had to act in spite of the damage that might be done to John Paul's saintly reputation. To canonize that pope no matter his many virtues is a new scandal. His canonization was compromised the very day he was told about Maciel, the founder of the Legionaries of Christ, a celibate priest who had two wives and families, and abused his own son as well as the seminarians under his charge, and still the pope embraced him and praised him and took him on his travelling road show. *Santo subito*, indeed! I am convinced that neither of the last two popes would have done anything about the pedophiles had not the breadth of the problem become public. The smell of corruption rose to the top. John Paul's canonization is a drop cloth.

We should give money to people of the street like Breslin does, like all good Catholics have done, give it to church people whom we have observed through the lens of suspicion and concluded to their trustworthiness. Give money to nuns and other women who show signs of independence from the male hierarchy from whom, history tells us, we can anticipate greater corruption to come. Be sure that the charities go to lay trustees and not to bishops and priests alone. Give generously to the hungry but starve the corruptors.

Perhaps my solution is as fanciful and as unlikely as Breslin's, but not quite as radical: I would demythologize the papacy, episcopate and the priesthood, and push them off the pedestal on which they have placed themselves (with our cooperation, it must be said). Help them take off their silly vestments and end their pompous ceremonies—these are no longer needed if indeed they ever were.[122] No matter how we lay persons love it, processions and vestments are the playthings of the effete and of showmen. Put independent lay boards (who answer to the church as well as to "The Church") in charge of the money. Let the bishops teach and oversee, but put some simple curbs on their power. Make sure that they are bound to tell the truth to the Catholic people and fire them when they don't. Listen to them, surely, for they sit on the chair of Moses but watch them and what they say very carefully, for there are and will always be many Judases as well many Peters among them. The Church needs suspicion in place of adulation. Help the bishops think and act like ordinary, responsible human beings with sharpened sympathies for other human beings, especially other people's children. Try hard to weed out the perverts and make accountability part of the bishops' job description (the last two popes didn't). Promote women and the sisters—there is nothing that the bishops and the pope fear more than women out of their "proper place." Reform, don't quit!

Gary Wills

Garry Wills presents us with a quite different solution to the problem of reform. Wills is an intellectual, a professor, a historian of international note, and a cultural critic who has been writing captivating books since I was a young man. Next to John Updike Wills is my favorite author. Three of his recent books are of particular interest to Catholics: *Papal Sin*, *Why I Am a Catholic*, and *Why Priests?: a Failed Tradition*.[123] The three would surely have been on the now abandoned Roman Index of Forbidden Books. They

---

122   Cardinal Burke's personal liturgical outfit as archbishop of St. Louis cost over $30,000. He had to add a set of cardinalatial vestments later when he was appointed head of the Roman Rota. Whatever the value of the work he did for the Vatican in recent years he is not worth a $30,000 set of vestments. I wonder where he got the money, and I wonder what his new cardinalatial vestments cost. I understand that he and Cardinal Law get a $10,000 retirement stipend every month and that their health insurance is covered by the Vatican. I am pleased that they are decently taken care of in their decline. See A.W.R. Sipe for photos and prices of vestments, and photos of His Eminence preening. http://www.awrsipe. com/Burke/TheCostofLookingGood2007.pdf.   Google *cappa magna* for more photos of Burke.

123   See the bibliography.

are closely connected. The first exposes the lies and self-deception practiced by popes and their men in the twentieth century. The second is a constructive account of what it is that keeps him a Catholic in the wake of the lies and self-deception. The third answers the further pertinent question of his critics. It must be considered a conclusion to the triad. They are on occasion querulous books that have stirred up quarrels among Catholics. The three directly or indirectly point to the needed reforms of the church. I find myself in agreement with much of his analysis, including both his criticisms of The Church and his expressions of faith and belief, expressions many bishops will find in contrast with what they expect of Catholics. I admire him as I do Breslin. Though I am tempted by Breslin's projection of "a church of the poor," I could not join it. I am not interested in new churches; there are far more than enough of them now. If you wish to leave, take your pick. I'm interested in a renewed, reformed Catholic church. So, too, is Wills. He doesn't announce a program for reform but what he does do is lay out the attitudinal and doctrinal groundwork for the church as he sees it, the church he believes in.[124]

The historical and theological meat of the book *Why Priests?* is a fascinating discussion of some doctrines that are central to the medieval and modern Catholic church which, he thinks, are inadequately founded in the early history of Christian belief and practice: the priesthood, the "Real Presence" of the body and blood of Christ under the elements of bread and wine in the Mass (transubstantiation), the notion that Jesus *was a priest* in his passion and death, offering a *sacrifice* to the Father, and that the consecration of the elements of bread and wine require a miracle on God's part and a duly ordained priest to "say the words" of the consecration. [125]

In fact, he says, only once in the New Testament texts is Christ himself named a "high priest," and never for that matter a low priest, and no one else is called a priest: not the 12 apostles, not any of their disciples, not the Epistle to the Hebrews where the term

---

124   He does it by telling the reader what he himself believes, especially in the conclusion to *Why Priests?* Of course, he had already done this in *Why I am a Catholic* at much greater length in a commentary on the Nicene creed, but some readers and reviewers still didn't get the point. They asked: if this is "all" he believes why is he a Catholic still and why doesn't he just admit to being a Protestant? This further question he answers in this last section of *Why Priests?*

125   One of the handful of great conundrums placed before seminarians of my generation was this: what happens when a renegade priest walks into a bakery and says "This is my Body." The same would go for Napa Valley winery. As I recall it this question was taken quite seriously.

"priest" is used of Christ. Christianity for the first two centuries is a priest-less, non-sacrificial set of communities that somehow fall under the control of bishops in the monarchical episcopate. The Jews had priests, the Romans had cults had priests, even the exotic cults of Asia Minor had priests, and Hindus had a priestly caste but not the Christian churches. Christianity was not a sacrificial cult and so had no need for priests. The Eucharist was an eschatological meal. Wills even names the gradual expansion of priestly authority and power a process of clerical "imperialism," which I take to be both a disease within and an invasion from without.

The argument he makes for his rejection of these doctrines and practices is primarily historical and reminiscent of the arguments advanced by the Reformers in the sixteenth century in the histories of Christianity written by the Centuriators of Magdeburg (1559-1574). The argument continues to the present in polemical works such as those of Ellen White, founder of the Seventh Day Adventist Church, and other sectarians. The claim is simple and much of it verifiable: The Catholic Church, increasingly under the leadership of the Roman bishops, added alien doctrines and practices to the scriptures and the practices of the early churches. All the doctrines discussed by Wills in the main body of the book fall under this, from the priesthood and the papacy to the sacramental system.[126]

However, Wills the Catholic and the historian, is not a Protestant polemicist. He is not attacking the Catholic Church. He aims at establishing what in the Catholic tradition of belief is in concert with the historical origins and growth of the church and what is not. Like an ideal bishop he is sorting out genuine from ersatz traditions hoping to arrive at The Tradition. His cut-off point for authentic Catholic Christian belief seems to be the fourth and fifth century Nicene Creed. In answer to his Catholic critics, he writes:

> But if I do not believe in popes and priests and sacraments, how can I call myself a Catholic? What do I believe? I get these questions all the time. Well, I will tell you what I believe. The things I believe are not incidental or peripheral, but central and essential. They are:

---

126   Catholic theologians and bishops continue to answer by saying that the monarchical episcopacy, the papacy and the sacraments are developments of the directions Jesus himself gave to his chosen apostles and are based on the words of Jesus in the gospels and of the apostles in their letters. All this is reasserted as essential belief for Catholics in the most recent Catholic council of bishops, Vatican II (1961-65). See works of Francis Sullivan S.J. on the teaching authority of pope and bishops (see bibliography).

God.
The Creation (which does not exclude evolution).
The Trinity.
Divine Providence.
The Incarnation.
The Resurrection.
The Gospels.
The Creed.
Baptism.
The Mystical Body of Christ (which is the real meaning of the Eucharist).
The Eucharist.
The Second Coming.
The Afterlife.
The Communion of Saints.
This seems a fair amount to believe.[127]

Yes, it is, and enough to qualify him as a Catholic in my book, and it lists what I believe as well. But the Nicene Creed, composed and accepted by the Catholic churches in the 4th and 5th centuries is not my own cut-off point. I would add for all the churches called Roman Catholic such doctrines and practices as the other five sacraments (even including some sort of ordination) not defined as such until the middle ages, and the early Marian doctrines. I would also add the teaching office of popes, patriarchs, bishops, and priests called the *Magisterium* (though I would place among the *magisters* theologians and even some charismatics, and perhaps some sort of representative lay body) but qualify that office as leading and serious, yet non-binding on doctrines which are not clearly traceable to the earliest sources in Christian history. The job of the *Magisterium* is to reiterate, apply and perhaps, in some cases, expand and explain, but not add.

For me the earliest sources are the New Testament, the chief figures in the Patristic period, and the practices of the earlier churches. Infallibility, universal jurisdiction of popes over the churches, apostolic succession, and the doctrines formulated in the nineteenth and twentieth centuries do not bind Catholics though they are claimed to be the spine of Catholicism. They are hyperbolic explosions of the Catholic theological "papist" wing imposed on the churches. In addition, I most certainly do not believe in the oppressive practices engaged upon by popes and bishops in the western churches by which they assert the papal and episcopal control over the minds and beliefs of Catholics. They do have traditions behind them for

127   *Why Priests?* 256-257.

this, but not a Christian Tradition. Like Kant, I think we should be wary of The Guardians!

So, finally, what kind of a reform of the church do I want? Not Breslin's schism, yet much of what Wills states and some of what he implies. What I want is a Church with a little bit of the humility practiced habitually by ordinary Catholics, some modesty on the part of Church leaders, some of the patience and synodism as practiced by the Eastern church patriarchs, and a great deal of the early churches' dedication to interchurch communication. The reformed Catholic Church should be a church that learns by listening and praying. I want a church whose priests choose celibacy or marriage. The reformed Catholic Church must be swept clean of episcopal careerists, perverts, and celibate fornicators and adulterers. I want a Catholic Church with a serious Roman connection, not a papal monarchy or an episcopal oligarchy. I don't want commands; I want invitations to communion in communities of faith and Eucharist that attend to the poor. I am emboldened by Breslin's critique and I am happy with Wills' invitation. I accept them both.

15. Preliminary Considerations on Reform

In this chapter and the next, I am up to something that is bold, and even immodest. I want to make proposals on how the Catholic church should reshape itself, and it is best that I clarify now, at the outset, why I think boldness and immodesty are required in the current ecclesial scene. First, I don't think those who disagree with me and those who might condemn my rules and reasons are wrong. Most of what I want to say departs by quite a distance from what has been "handed down" by the Church's *Magisterium*, from what is contained in its catechisms and theological teaching. Skating all too close to the Reformation criticisms of the "Romish system," I depart from the Catholic anti-Reformation convictions with trepidation. Second, I undoubtedly have a darker view of the leadership of the Catholic churches than many of my fellow Catholics have. This dark view colors my proposals. So this is no scientifically "objective" proposal. Third, my argument is only marginally historical and theological. I am tired of and bored by the "proofs" offered by Catholic theologians and historians, even the best of them, to justify the current shape of hierarchical Catholicism. I find it hard to believe that they themselves aren't bored, as their convictions have been undone by the actual performance of the hierarchy. The justifications, however impressive, fall when the hierarchy fails to lead morally. By their fruits, we shall know them, and we shall also know the system that breeds them!

In fact, my argument with the *Magisterium* and its teaching on church structure is moral. They (the *Magisters*) have failed and sinned in ways that call seriously into question both their political leadership of the church (their mistakes have piled up to a point that seems irreversible) and the sacrality in which they have decked themselves. Their leadership has been exposed in the past century as often devoid of the Holy Spirit, of courage and even basic decency. They have messed up the churches and need to be replaced. They, and the popes, live in a dream world of imperial Constantinian power and control. They must be rescued from the dream world if they are to live as Christians and lead churches. The whole effort of the following pages is to rid the church of clericalism, and put breaks on the claimed divinity of the hierarchy. Pope Francis is a decent starting point for reform but far from an adequate solution.

Now what do I mean when I charge irreparable failures? I cite a very few. A series of books would be needed to paint the whole picture, and such books already exist:

> The war on the modern world: They, the popes and their dedicated followers fought a three-century war on Modernity and the Enlightenment. They are still fighting it, now on secularization, relativism and the expansion of understandings of family. Their culture wars over the centuries distorted the proper role of Christian churches in the life of cultures. Their war is at bottom over who owns and runs the world, assuming that Satan rules when and where the pope and his bishops do not have the decisive word. The popes and bishops utterly failed for centuries to see that the Holy Spirit might act outside Catholic holy water, and failed to contribute to the construction of the "modern world." What a god-awful and deeply self-interested war! The theologians, Jesuits and others, became officers in that army. The few theologians who saw the war for what it was were thrown out into "exterior darkness." (Mt. 25:30)

> The Jews: The Church's and the churches' millennium long religious and social hatred of Jews and Judaism was transformed into the racial, political and social anti-Semitism of the Nazis, and lent rhetorical substance to the effort to kill all the Jews in Europe. To boot, the Church in Germany and elsewhere in Europe in nearly complete silence watched as millions of Jews disappeared. It is the sin against the Holy Spirit. (Mk 3:28)

> The children. "It would be better for anyone who leads astray one of these little ones who believe in me to be drowned by a millstone around his neck..." (Mt 18:1-9.) Thousands of American children, tens, perhaps hundreds of thousands of Catholic children and young people worldwide, have been abused by Catholic priests and bishops. Bishops have been abusers and many more kept a lid on the scandal for decades. If this is not the height of corruption, it would be hard to say what is.

The silence of the lower clergy in the face of perversion among some of their colleagues doesn't mystify me. I was trained to be one of them for eight years and was among them for almost two decades. However, I don't think you can call ignorance 'deliberate si-lence' unless the ignorance is willful. The high clergy, including the bishops of Rome, knew perfectly well what was going on with chil-dren, certainly for decades, probably always. That much is clear. Roger Mahoney, later the archbishop of Los Angeles, shared a rec-tory with a priest-pervert at one point. Maybe he didn't know what was going on with his rectory mate, but we can be sure Mahoney will never tell. He most certainly did know the extent and depth of the problem when he was archbishop of Los Angeles. He shifted the pedophiles hither and yon for a couple of decades, never fac-ing up to the problem until the Dallas meeting of bishops in 2002 when most bishops finally did so under public force. In his time, Mahoney became the Bernard Law of the west coast.

"Be not the first by whom the new is tried nor the last to lay the old aside" wrote Alexander Pope, The couplet forms a motto for Catholic bishops. This silence of those who knew, bishops espe-cially, was born of (a) a cultivated tendency to protect the brethren from exposure ("loyalty"), (b) the unwritten law demanding the avoidance of any scandal injuring the good name of the Church,[128] and (c) the conviction that pederasty is a sin rather than a crime or a psychological state, and so must be forgiven rather than reported and punished. Bing Crosby would never have turned Barry Fitzger-ald in to the cops. Neither would Des Spellacy (Robert de Nero) have made a fuss over his favorite pastor (Burgess Meredith), had the latter been an abuser. I would have gone to the appropriate bishop in New York and left it on his desk, returning to the rectory feeling that I had discharged my duty. Never would going to the police have been a live option. Secret sins, including my own, were to be kept secret lest scandal ensue.

The lower clergy, so far as I can see, were genuinely ignorant, perhaps in some cases willfully so. As a priest for twenty years (1961-1980) during the peak years of pederasty, I lacked any knowl-edge of it, with a few exceptions. One of these exceptions included a widely publicized news story in 1969 about the incarceration of a

128   Cardinal Ottaviani, *Crimen sollicitationis*. (1962). Gsearch.vatican. va and *Wikipedia*. This document, issued by the Holy Office of the Inqui-sition and approved by John XXIII, shows two things: the efforts of the pope and his cardinals to take abuse issues seriously enough ("crimes") to require all bishops to deal with it; and the fact that these "crimes" were well known and widespread enough to require the Pope's attention and a formal decree to all bishops everywhere, informing them of the legal steps to be taken in cases of this sort. However, the document required secrecy in these cases, and that may have fed the tendency of bishops to keep egre-gious cases of child abuse from exposure to public notice and prosecution.

young New York diocesan priest for serial rape of children. Another consisted of clerical rumors that a couple of seminary classmates of mine who were removed from their high school teaching positions for their abuse of teenage boys (see, I don't put their names down though they are in the public record!)[129] When I learned of the first I did not take it to be symptomatic of a wider problem. I spent four years in Cardinal Hayes High School as a student (1949-1953) and never heard a breath of scandal. I never met another kid who claimed to have been abused. Not until 2009 did I encounter online the list of New York priests who were suspended, laicized or on leave from the priesthood for abusing children. I had read that some priests had ongoing relationships with adult women, and I did not suspect at the time that even this was widespread in the U.S.[130] I imagined I was in a tiny minority of sinners not living up to ideal of chastity. I didn't even take the Father Gilbert Gauthe case (Louisiana, 1984) as a harbinger of a much larger and widespread condition until it had a second go round in the media in 2002 when the *Boston Globe* exposed abuse of children by a number of the Boston and Fall River Catholic clergy.[131] I paid no attention to the expanding literature on the problem aside from a few articles in the *National Catholic Reporter.* Culpable ignorance? Probably. To borrow John Dean's words to Richard Nixon, there was a cancer growing in the church and I paid it no heed as I struggled with my own problems.

But why would I have refused to learn more and why would I have kept my mouth shut had I? Surely, the training I received would have kept me from raising questions even when the provocations were staring me in the face: you never do or say what can damage the reputation of the church. My own sins in regard to chastity would have made me the last person in the clergy in a position to point a finger. My strong tendency to introversion would

---

129   See www.bishopsaccountability.com, under the archdiocese of New York and the diocese of Bridgeport.

130   This has not been investigated by anyone so far as I know, except for Andrew Greeley's summary of survey material in his book *Priests*, and the work of a few stalwart laypersons like Jason Berry, Michael D'Antonio, and the authors of *Betrayal*. See bibliography. There also ought to be an extensive and public investigation and a serious church-wide discussion of heterosexual violations of chastity and celibacy.... that is, unless bishops no longer take violations of chastity to be a serious matter. There won't be, of course, for such an investigation and discussion would doubtless end in the loss of more priests and bishops, and even promote debate over celibacy.

131   *Betrayal.* See the bibliography.

keep me from engaging in any public action. I am an extrovert only on special occasions. Finally, I had every reason to think that the bishops were doing the job they were appointed to do, looking after children and overseeing priests and religious.[132]

Strident attacks on the institutional and organizational side of the church is something I would be accused of, but my attacks are not on the institution or organization (I'm in favor of institutions and organizations) but on the office holders. This is not because they run them but because they have been morally at fault in the horrendous case of child abuse and a good number of other things, including despicable and cowardly abuse of theologians over the last four decades.[133] Leaders, even ordained leaders, are necessary, and much of the job description of a Catholic bishop meets real needs of the Catholic people. In the case of abuse (and at many other points in Catholic history) they didn't do the right thing, and this is but a confirmation of the corruptions of *clericalism*. Christopher Hitchens stands for those many critics who are outraged at there being a church at all, bishops at all, priests at all. I think the church needs serious reform and re-making but I don't think of it as Hitchens does. The society needs the church and the church needs a Patriarch of the West (or some such), dressed down and shorn of the adulatory blather heaped upon him by himself and other Catholics. Catholics need a coordinator and a mediator. Every diocese needs a bishop, or some such. Papolatry must end, not the bishop of Rome. Episcopal pretentions to divine authority need to end, not bishops. Clericalism must end, not the priestly ministry. Christendom and the clerical Church must end not the church or churches.

The church is what it is and thus it has been and will be forever more, a church of the redeemed sinner in a community always sinning, always reaching for holiness, always loving God and its neighbors, always flopping on its face. *Ecclesia semper reformanda est.* And, with Brother Martin Luther (John Paul II called him "brother" on the 500th anniversary of his birth), Christians must say we are all *simul justus et peccator*. So also the church. The just man sins seven times daily as the Scriptures have it, and the pope and

---

132   A seminary classmate of mine who married shortly after our ordination in 1961 told me in 1986 at lunch in the District of Columbia that the cost of settling the cases of abuse would be about four billion dollars. I didn't believe him. I didn't even know the Church had four billion dollars! It did and billions more.

133   Bradford Hinze, "A Decade of Disciplining Theologians," *Horizons: The Journal of the College Theology Society* 37 (Spring 2010): 92-126. Benedict XVI was more interested in shutting up dissenting theologians than protecting children.

bishops probably seven times seventy. (Prov 24:16)

I am not a theological Protestant, though some would take me to be so. Theologically I think like a Catholic, with two basic assumptions. (1) that God is present to all of creation and to all human beings immediately, directly, silently, always, and that that Presence is experienced by us even when we don't know it; (2) that the meaning of that immediate Presence is mediated to us through our experience in nature, history and culture, especially through the church (revelation)—even through Dawkins, Hitchens and their tribe. This is the sacramental principle that forms the substance of Catholic religious experience, especially displayed in worship and sacrament. But neither the Church nor the church has a monopoly on God's grace. I have a greyhound, Bridget by name, who mediates God's grace to me morning and evening and in between, and she is not even a Catholic much less a bishop. When I watch her sleep (she sleeps about twenty hours a day) I meditate on the glory of God shinning in her. She, too, is a gift of God meant to bring before my soul the giftedness of human and animal living and the beauty of what is not seen, and before her there were Isis, Hincmar, Moses and Susie.

For all its flaws, vicious as some of them are, the Catholic Church is the source of my thought and hopes, and remains my spiritual home. "Where shall I go?" To the well from which I have drawn for seventy years, with growing conviction that I find there the wisdom not only of Jesus but of the authentic disciples, pearls too often buried in a pile of ecclesiastical horse pucky. On Sunday, I listen to the Scriptures, hear a sermon and receive the Eucharist. I do not forget the saints, or my parents and grandparents as far back as anyone could wish, my friends, my teachers, my parish, the hundreds of admirable priests I have met. To be truthful, I sometimes worry that I am more of a Catholic than I am a Christian. The church remains the source of the standards and values I cling to even when I do not meet and act on them. The church has not let me down but popes and bishops have, without ceasing. I wish I could say that the difference between them and me is a minor matter of policy or practice but it runs much deeper. They believe they are special instruments of God and I don't think they are special in the least. Surely, they are no more special than Bridget, my greyhound. Perhaps had I the opportunity to watch a bishop nap…

In the case at hand, the abuse of children and the responsibilities of leaders who know of it, I regard some things as settled and they underlie the recommendations in the next chapter:

Crimes have been committed by some priests and bishops,

crimes have NOT been committed by all or most priests, but by enough of them to be shocking (est. 4,000+ out of about 50,000 between 1960 and 2000 in the United States).

Most priests, including myself, were unaware of the perversion of young people going on around them, and so, with a few notable exceptions such as Thomas Doyle and Gerald Fitzgerald, did nothing to stop it, is mind-boggling but true.[134] Ostriches perhaps.

Most bishops knew and did not come forward to inform their people and the civil community of the facts of which they were well aware. The Roman leaders of the church did not want any public knowledge of the facts and were convinced that they could handle the problem *inter muros*.[135] They did not have the interests of the Catholic people, of society, of families and of children at heart. In fact it has been documented that bishops knew for several decades that a plague had struck the clergy and families, and yet spent their time, energy and church resources keeping the facts from the public authorities and the Catholic people in order to protect the clergy's public reputation and the Church's property and financial resources. Above all they wanted to avoid scandal, and in doing so caused the second greatest church scandal of the twentieth century.[136]

Pedophilia and warnings of its danger have been a matter of public record for nearly three decades [e.g. Fr. Gilbert Gauthe's trial for sex crimes in Louisiana in 1984 and the footprints of clerical pedophilia in church law from the early church to today].[137] There were atrocities similar to Gauthe's taking place at the same time

---

134   Fr. Gerald Fitzgerald, founder of *The Servants of the Paraclete*, a religious order dedicated to ministry to troubled priests, spent decades warning bishops about the church-wide problem of abusive priests, but was ignored. He even got to the pope and to the head of the Sacred Congregation for the Defense of the Faith. Nothing happened. The popes were specifically warned by Fitzgerald and Doyle of almost certain recidivism of pedophiles.

135   Alfredo Ottaviani, *Crimen sollicitationis* (1962). Gsearch.vatican.va. I surmise that Ottaviani's heavy emphasis on the need for secrecy in cases of solicitation contributed to the episcopal suppression of complaints since.

136   The greatest in my view was the "diplomatic" handing of the Nazi threat.

137   Thomas   Doyle   deposition.   http://www.richardsipe.com/ Doyle/2008/2008-06-14-Jane_Doe_vs_OMI_of_Texas.pdf.

in Boston and Rhode Island, well known to the diocesan bishops and their close subordinates at the time. In spite of already existing church law on the subject of abuse, the bishops were so intent on secrecy and quashing "scandal," they paid no attention to Fr. Gerald Fitzgerald's warnings in the 1960s or to Fr. Thomas Doyle's prescient report to the bishops in 1985. As a group the bishops were unable to bring themselves to respond to the matter even after reading the Doyle Report.[138]

- The media is not the enemy (as several cardinals, Bernard Law of Boston prominent among them, made them out to be), nor are the public prosecutors. The former have been, in my view, restrained and balanced in their reporting. If anything the latter were and remain loath to prosecute churchmen, and not for the best reasons I am sure. Nor is there much evidence of historic American anti-Catholicism at work in the publicity.[139] The predators and their episcopal superiors are the enemy. They created the scandal. Even Pope Ratzinger recognized this. The evil, he said, is within the Church itself, though he did not point the finger at the bishops who were responsible for the cover-up.

- No bishops have been removed from office for this moral lapse.[140] A handful of resignations have been accepted by the pope, but only when public exposure and pressure intruded into the "special relationship" between pope and his bishops. National bishops' conferences refuse responsibility for correction of lapses on the part of their colleagues. In addition, as far as we know, they did not report their colleagues to the Higher Authorities. The individual bishop is responsible to the pope alone, not to his colleagues, not to his church, not to his people, not to families, not to children and certainly not to civil authorities—in spite of the

---

138   Doyle report. We have no public record of those deliberations. What we know is that the bishops, with few exceptions, knew and did nothing.

139   *Mediareport.org* for a different judgment of the media.

140   Archbishop Wesoslowski and his criminal use of children was the object of considerable attention in the media in the summer of 2014 (*NY Times* and the *National Catholic Reporter* circa July 1, 2014). He died in Rome under house arrest in the Vatican just as his church trial had begun in August 2015.

bishops' expressed intentions to have it otherwise.[141] The recently resigned pontiff apparently had no intention of removing or correcting bishops, which shows us where his own loyalties lie.[142]

• Is true and sweeping reform possible under the current government structure? I assume not. Under the present generation of bishops? No. As a consequence of the crimes and the episcopal cover-up, the church in the United States has been immensely damaged in reputation, in resources and in membership. The damage hasn't ceased due to the failure of church leaders.

• Despite some efforts, bishops have been unable to provide communal support for priests that might sustain their efforts at moral probity and deep spiritual life. Some of this may rest on the lack of spiritual depth and maturity on the part of bishops themselves. It would seem that they do not regard themselves as ministering to priests in spite of official Church rhetoric.

• This tragedy is not American alone, but is shared by the Irish church as well, and the churches in Canada, Poland, Germany, the Netherlands, Australia and quite possibly the churches worldwide, over the same sins of priests and the same episcopal irresponsibility. The problems are systemic.[143] They must be met systemically. The situation is not merely a sin here and a sin there but an institution wide moral collapse on every level of leadership. Nor is it just a matter of the sins of this or that priest or bishop but of general moral laxity in the Church and an atmosphere of corporate corruption.

141   See the NCCB statement on their website.

142   He did remove Maciel Degollado, the founding father and head of the Legionaries of Christ. Pope Francis, thank God, had the good sense to remove pedophile and ephebophile Archbishop Josef Wesoslowski, his envoy to the Dominican Republic, and the German spend thrift bishop Franz von Elst of Limburg.

143   Years of reading steamy Protestant accounts, often by ex-priests, of "the sins of the confessional" failed to convince me that there was much to it but the last decade has convinced me otherwise. See W. M. Shea, *The Lion and the Lamb: Evangelicals and Catholics in America* (NY: Oxford University Press, 2004).

I had along with the rest of my seminary mates gotten some advice from the authorities in charge of our education. One *bon mot* was from the spiritual director, Monsignor Robert Brown, who warned us all to "Watch out for the pious ones." "Better the bottle than the bosom, worthy brothers!" he said to two hundred and fifty seminarians in one of his weekly spiritual nosegays. You can always dry out, he meant, but once you're on the bosom or the bosom is on you, there's no drying out to be done. Monsignor Francis Reh (RIP), a New York seminary rector who inexplicably became a bishop instructed us in our last year before ordination, "If you can't be good at least look good. If you have to do it, don't do it in your own parish." No mystery about the "it," I hope. What he took to be realism we took to be cynicism. When we were told by another spiritual director, "There is no vacation from your vocation" we all seemed to know what he meant: have a good summer, don't mess with the ladies, and come back. But what in heaven's name did the other two mean? It is better to be a drunken priest than a married priest? Or: For the church's sake be discrete? In both cases it is bad advice, bad for the soul of the future priest and bad for the church. Reh didn't say "If you're having problems with celibacy, if you are having heterosexual or homosexual relations with adults, if you want to abuse children, for God's sake and your own, turn yourself in to the bishop and ask him for help." That may have happened here and there but we will never know. Whether high or low the clergy have secrets to keep.

We have plenty of "spiritual direction" in the seminary but even then, there is nothing about children. Why was there nothing said about the desire to have sex with children? There was nothing serious or cynical, just nothing. The only thing said, as I remember it, were jokes we told about Episcopalian priests and their altar boys, not about Catholic (i.e., "real") priests and theirs. Was I asleep during that part of the sex and sin lecture? Not a chance. I never went to sleep when any of my seminary superiors were talking about sex. I can only conclude that my superiors, like me, knew nothing about it or thought that it was so much a marginal phenomenon it was hardly worth mentioning.

Ecclesiological claims. Before I get on with the few recommendations in the area of church reform, may I say that two things are noteworthy about this chapter. (1) It proves my claim that I am not a theologian, and so in accord with my long run prejudice I will not argue theologically—I am unable as well as unwilling to do so, and (2) it makes evident that I am a heretic according to the doctrinal standards of the Church and my understanding of the leader-ship class of the church and of the doctrines that have been built up around it is contradictory to those doctrines (papal jurisdiction over all the churches, papal infallibility, and the apostolic succes-sion of popes and bishops). I would deny their right to rule the churches *as they do*. Since it is clear to me that the last two popes and their bishops have repudiated the Great Council and show no inter-est in church reform, lay Catholics need to take the lead and press the ordained leaders. What has been called by the previous two popes' men "the Reform of the Reform," namely the aim of the last two popes and their men to roll back the slight gains of the Council in the name of a hyper-hierarchical model of church life, is an act of disloyalty to the church as a whole that should be repudiated by ev-ery Catholic Christian, a disloyalty that decisively undercuts their pretentions to divine appointment. Few if any bishops have stood up, or are standing up to the historic papal onslaught; few priests have done so against their bishops. Oddly, it is now the bishops themselves who seem to have jumped back on board the papolatry train and given up on the reassertion of episcopal "dignity" of their fellow bishops at Vatican II.

So, I add to the decades and probably centuries long surrender of the bodies of our children to the lusts of priests and bishops, a very grave sin indeed, another and perhaps as serious a charge: the bishops are dishonest in other things as well. This includes their surrender of their churches to a renewed papal monarchy. They not only have no spine, they do not believe that the Holy Spirit re-sides in the church primarily, and only secondarily, if at all, in the papacy and in themselves. Recall the old story of the Holy Trinity's vacation plans: They met in heaven to plan this year's vacation. The Father wanted to take a round-the-world tour to check on His cre-ation; the Son proposed to visit Judea where He hadn't been in two thousand years; the Holy Spirit suggested visiting Rome since She had never been there. The leadership class, the Church, betrayed the church.

Don't ask whether my suggested reform can or will happen. Some of it can't and most of it is unlikely ever to happen. Can the Catholic Church undergo a significant reformation? I doubt it, but I don't at all doubt that it will change… and perhaps for the better (at least for a while, at least here and there). My impossible dream is that the College of Cardinals will sooner or later elect to the papacy a monarch who doesn't believe in monarchy, and who wants Chris-tian reform. Perhaps Pope Francis is that man. The bishops need to have their feet held to the fire with charity and persistence by the laity, by religious orders, and by women religious until they summon up the courage to abandon papolatry. They are desperately stuck in a tar pit of their own making, apparently loving it, and they need to be pulled out of it by their sisters and brothers who love them and the church enough to put their backs to the wheel of history, to *reverse the wheel*. Neither the bishops nor the pope, I fear, are capable of reforming a Church they themselves have made. The church must reform The Church. The Church has no motive for reform but the laity and the lower clergy do. The responsibility lies with us since popes and bishops have refused it.

Historical-theological supposition: In the face of their immorality I am driven to the conclusion that the papacy and the episcopacy are a natural development of leadership, and have nothing whatsoever to do with Christ's institution or the positive will of God—at least no more or less than the development of the Mormon apostles and president or the board of trustees of the Southern Baptist Convention. I've reached this conclusion based on my moral judgment of the bishops and the Vatican's behavior over the past thirty years (and doubtless more) of betrayal of children and parents. No one could possibly be God's will for the church who behaves like this. You might as well argue that kings rule by divine right and will no matter what they do. The divine aura that the hierarchy exudes must be the result of human hubris and sleight of hand, not of divine providence. Papal and episcopal pretentions are exposed as the action and inaction of a corrupt class and by the never ending list of their victims. "By their fruits shall you know them," said the Lord. (Mt. 7:16-20) Jesus had something else to say about this situation: "You know how among the gentiles those who seem to exercise authority lord it over them; their great ones make their importance felt. It cannot be that way with you." (Mark 10:41f) Well, dear Lord, it is that way with us now and so the case is proved.

I work under a simple and, for me, new rule: never believe what anyone says about their own importance and power, especially so when they drag God and Christ into it. Such men cannot possibly have been anointed by the Holy Spirit. No decent pagan would have acted as they have. When they define themselves as the successors to the Twelve they are wailing for the perpetuation of their own office and their own spiritual superiority. But they have surrendered the latter and should lose the former. Jesus named their predecessors "whitened sepulchers" and the description fits them. "You will know them by the love they have for one another"…and so we do. (Jn.13) Remember: Judas was an apostle and a bishop, according to their own interpretation of the Johannine account of the

Last Supper as the first ordination and consecration. His spirit lives on, and none of this is new. It has been going on for ages in various forms laid down by the particular shape of papal power in each age. Nevertheless, let's begin the struggle to clean up the mess by refusing our trust except where they prove themselves worthy of it. There is no authority where authority is not recognized. Let us not abandon the church, as Jimmy Breslin would, but let us abandon its corrupt leadership. Remember: they have and will abandon our children to the perverts rather than create a ripple on the Tiber.[144]

In what follows, I suppose these propositions to be true:

> Whenever the leadership of the churches makes claims about itself, its power and authority, it leaves its proper field that is to proclaim the gospel in witness to Jesus, the Son of God. In such cases, their claims are to be ignored by Catholics.
>
> Whenever the leadership of the church acts to silence Catholics and other Christians it exceeds its mandate. It has the authority to witness, not to dominate, not to command, but to open the gates and not to close them.
>
> Whenever the leadership of The Church acts as if it owns, controls, or dominates the Catholic people and the *church's* property and resources, it exceeds its mandate and its acts should be ignored by the people and confronted legally and even physically when necessary.
>
> Whenever the leadership of the church acts irresponsibly and immorally, violating the gospel, the Catholic people are within their rights to demand a change of leadership. As President Nixon can be forced out of the White House, as Cardinal Law can be forced from his archdiocese, so any

144   The bishops did not turn the Jesus movement of the first three centuries into a church monarchy. Taking Ireneaus of Lyons as a prime example, they in fact saved the churches from dissolution in the second and third centuries by preserving a version of the apostolic tradition of teaching about Jesus opposed to Gnostic and other esoteric traditions of teaching. Their success kicked off the idea that they in fact were the "successors of the Apostles," a bit of a stretch for a disparate crowd of administrators who gradually crowded out the other prominent (charismatic?) ministries in the second and third century churches. See the *Didache* for a picture of a Christian community at the turn of the first century when the Jesus movement was still a movement and not the Catholic, much less the "Roman" Catholic Church, and Clement's *First Letter to the Corinthians* for the still deflated episcopal/presbyteral roles. Apostolic Succession as a doctrine is as "meaningful" in our age as the medieval claims that the bread of the Eucharist bleeds. And it is of a piece with papal jurisdiction and infallibility, and makes no more sense than either of them.

bishop can be driven from his job when he doesn't do the job.

The authority of Christ and the action of the Holy Spirit reside primarily in the church and only in The Church insofar as and as long as the church delegates authority to them.

The Catholic Church is not by divine right a monarchy. It is a community of communities, freely established by the choice of churches. Governance is not a matter of revelation or an imposition of Jesus. Yes, it is, in the case of the Roman Catholic Church, a long-standing tradition; sometimes it works and sometimes it does not. But the form of church leadership is not in "the deposit of faith." It is an accident of history rather than an inspiration of the Holy Spirit.

Clericalism and Reform

The aim of reform in this age is to put a definitive end to clericalism, that culture of Christian people with regard to governance that has reigned since The Church aligned itself with the imperial power and structure of the age of Constantine. The papacy is the epitome and font of the culture of clericalism. Clerical culture manifests itself in episcopal and priestly monopoly rule over the churches and all other ministries and activities of the churches. The reign of the clerics must be ended because (a) it divides the church illegitimately into clergy and lay, and (b) the ordained ministers have shown themselves to be untrustworthy, and (c) it inevitably renders lay Catholics passive in evangelical terms.

Even the churches of the Reformation are afflicted by clericalism, though for the most part in a less virulent form. The culture of clericalism is ubiquitous in the Catholic churches and is marked somewhat differently in the Eastern Orthodox and Western churches by hierarchical structure, celibacy, and intensity of misogynism. True, clerical culture lasting as it has over fifteen hundred years was a major contributor to the cultures of the West and the East, and it allowed for at least a mediocre spiritual and material ministry to the Christian people. However, it degenerated into monarchism, totalitarianism and corruption both spiritual and material. Every reform movement in the Church has been assimilated by the clerical culture with varying degrees of success, including the early monastic movement East and West, the Western reform movement of the medieval religious orders, the Reformation of the sixteenth century West and even the reforms decreed by Vatican II. The reform impulses of the second Vatican Council were thoroughly clerical. In fact, after Vatican II the High Priests put an end to the reforms timorously announced by their predecessors in the Great Council itself.

Clerical culture is protean and omnivorous. Some would say with reason as well as conviction that the clerical caste system is essential to Catholicism and that without it there would be no Catholic church. They say that the episcopacy and the priesthood are God's doing, and that without them the Roman Catholic Church would be just another Protestant "sect." That may be true, but I think that the Roman Catholic ecclesiastical structure is not normative and the only legitimate form of Christian governance. "Essential to Catholicism" is one thing; essential to the church catholic is another.

The papacy should not be seen as the will of God for the church in any special way, any more or any less than the Stated Clerk of a Reformed Presbytery or the Southern Baptist Convention or the Dalai Lama. Leadership is generated by the churches in different ways and forms. God does not respect some ecclesiastical arrangements over others. The Mormons have theirs and we Catholics have ours. The papacy is a natural growth (and too frequently a deformation) of the leadership of the Christian communities that began after the capital of the Roman Empire was moved to the east. The bishops of Rome began to claim hegemony over the churches of the East and West, supporting this gradual but never-ending seizure of spiritual and material power by a variety of claims to divine institution and authority. True, the authority of the bishops of Rome provided a needed check to the attempts of the secular authority to control the bishops and local churches. However, the papacy turned the ministry of the bishops of Rome to an institutionally self-centered crushing or subjection of other gifts of the Holy Spirit to the administrative power of a papal monarchy and the subordination of divine grace to the higher clergy. It seems that most if not all of the poor souls who are elected to this office are seized immediately by an obsession driving them to assert the rights and privileges of the divine monarchy. If the whole church structure is to be reformed the papacy must be the prime site of the transformation, not only causing reform but undergoing it. However, it is no use waiting on a pope to reform the church. A pope may be counted upon to reform this or that, but not his own divine office and its prerogatives. When John Paul II wrote in *Ut unum sint* (1995) that he hoped the Protestants and Orthodox would help reshape the petrine office in a way that it would be of greater service to church unity, I don't think anyone took him seriously, not even himself.

My father's friend, Pat Howley, an IRA man in the old country was refused absolution by a priest when he was in jail for revolutionary activities, often said to me when he was in his cups, "The

Irish are a priest-ridden people, Billy." So they were. Pat kept on saying that to me when I was a seminarian and a priest. He didn't want me to forget. Catholics are priest, bishop, and pope-ridden people to this day.

16. Objective of Reform:

Stripping Away Sacrality

Sad to say, I wouldn't know how to reform my local supermarket and this makes me hesitate to say what I think about reform in the church. But I know that the church needs reform and I have a view of what that reform needs to head for. So, I will share with you my views of the goals of reform based on my perception of what the church looks like now and what it should be, as well as the values at stake. The fact that these proposals would be dismissed out of hand by the hierarchy if they even bothered to look at them is no excuse to refrain from stating them as proposals. For too long, I and many Catholics have kept quiet when the existence and meaning of the Catholic church we love have been endangered by the very people charged with leading it.

At the very least, these few proposals are useful for turning the flashlight of common concern on areas in which the church has fallen short of the gospel ideals. The model of the need for reform is the New Testament picture of the High Priests and Pharisees who are the Catholic hierarchy's predecessors and models, and its recounting of Jesus' criticism of them. The popes and bishops themselves gradually adopted facets and meanings of the Jewish priestly caste, as well as of the pagan priesthoods of Rome, as the models for their own high priesthood. They look and act like High Priests.

As a statement of the basic ecclesiology that underlies my reform suggestions, I propose the following:

- Jesus is the Savior and Son of God through faith in whom human beings are brought to communal maturity and promised eternal life. We believe with St. Paul that Jesus' death and resurrection have given us hope of this salvation here and beyond.
- Mercifully, the grace of God reaches us all, even the most recalcitrant sinners, through nature and history. God's plan and God's grace are meant for the entire human race which is predestined to the kingdom of God. All forms of Christian life and all forms of religious life, and even a life with-

out God in mind, are touched by the grace and providence of God.

- All Christians are catholic Christians. They are all members of the same church. The church is already one (it always has been) in the unity of faith, hope and love just as the human race is already one in spite of its divisions and deadly tensions. All the churches are the sacrament of God as is Jesus himself. In origin and destiny, we are one even if in the meantime we behave badly toward one another.

- Christians are meant for life in communities as it was in the beginning. The churches are crucial for maturing in faith, hope and love. The Eucharist and hearing the scriptures and preaching are focal points of Christian worship and belief.

- The divisions among Christians, and indeed among human beings, are artificial and sinful especially those caused by the seemingly universal conviction that "we" are right and "they" are wrong. "They" may be, but then so may we and we all need to grow up.

- Precise governmental and ritual structures are adventitious to the process of revelation, salvation and community life. Jesus did not establish a 'Church' which is 'true' as distinct from churches which are more or less true or which He did not establish. Every church in which the gospel is preached and life is lived according to that gospel is more or less true. They are all equally bound to unity of faith, hope and love. The One True Church, the pure church, is an eschatological reality rather than a historical reality, an ideal image subject to various ideological manipulations rather than a thing.

- The hierarchism and clericalism that characterize the Roman Catholic Church are not matters of the positive will of God or the command of Jesus, and have done enough damage to the church to lead me to the conclusion that they are blocks to the life of Christian communities under their thrall. They should be eliminated, and the social shape of the Catholic communities should be restructured.

The goal of reform today is to live as a universal church that is a communion of local churches, a community of communities, not a papal monarchy which rules by divine right and controls bishops and churches, producing a formal unity of units rather than a vital community of communities. Some of the Eastern Orthodox and Uniate churches along with the Anglican communion might, in some small ways, serve as starting points for reflection though

they, too, are possessed by the vice of hierarchy and clericalism.
The spread of national conferences of bishops following the second
Vatican Council was a small step in this direction but with a nervous "Peter" in the background worried that the conferences might
act in matters of faith and practice without checking in with "Peter." Only "Peter," the monarch, can act and speak for the universal church, so they think! The growing horizontal relationship of
bishops was carefully and increasingly hedged in by the ever present and more important vertical relationship of individual bishops
with the pope. Even when bishops met in Rome in recent synods,
the synods could not speak to the churches! They had to submit
their findings to the pope and his curia who would in turn decide
what might be said and omit what they pleased.

The steps that ought to be taken to make the ideal of the community of communities concrete include:

Ending Careerism. It must be ordinary practice to keep the
bishops where they are, in the dioceses to which they were appointed. Attach the episcopate to men and women outstanding for
wisdom and holiness, not ambition and a "correct" religious and
theological ideology, and their own drive to hold center stage in
the drama of salvation. Keep pastors in their parishes. The wish
to better their own situation by "going up higher" has become a
curse. The curse of "translation" of bishops from see to see was recognized at the Council of Trent and condemned there, and recently
Cardinal Gantin wrote a powerful memo condemning it in the contemporary church.[145] The father should stay with the family and not
go flitting off to another family. In a Catholic marriage, this would
be called adultery. Any diocese that does not have suitable candidates for the episcopacy among its laity and clergy ought to be put
in receivership; something is profoundly wrong with that church.

Ending clericalism. Retain the office, or perhaps the *function* of bishop and priest, and perhaps find other names for them.
However, there should be no distinction in the church between the
clergy and laity, except in *functions* assigned to some Christians for
some time. As for a class or caste of ordained Catholics now called
priests, bishops and popes, Christian teaching and practices on
which this division is based should be eliminated and should be replaced by the Christian teaching that accords with the saying of St.
Paul, "there is no distinction between Jews and Gentile, slave and
free, male and female" in the Christian churches or in the variety of

---

145   Cardinal Bernard Gantin, http://www.dailycatholic.org/issue/ar
chives/1999Jul/135jul21,vol.10,no.135txt/jul21nv2.htm.

church ministries and functions. (Gal. 3:27-28) Such divisions were forced upon the body of Christ by decisions made in the social history of the church and by the sins of office holders, and preserved in and by ecclesiastical bureaucracies. [146]

Getting rid of the "ontological sign." The unwanted divisions and clericalism are reinforced by the doctrine that the sacrament of orders causes a 'sign' to be placed on the soul of the recipient marking them eternally as clergy with a special status in the church, in the Kingdom of God, and even in Hell should they go there. The sacrament in fact designates the recipients for specific functions temporarily, not ontologically. The ministers are simply Christians who share, like all Christians, in the priesthood, the prophetic office and the rule of Christ and who are called and accepted by the community to a specific service such as presiding at the Eucharistic table. Baptism/Confirmation is the only sign of Christian conversion and dedication that the church needs. No one needs a special sign beyond Baptism to pray the Eucharistic prayer or to minister to the community. What he or she needs is the favor of God recognized by a community, and accepted by the community. No one is forever a minister, an overseer, a prophet, a teacher. Keep ontology out of this discussion.[147] The prophets of Israel didn't need the "ontological character"; the kings and priests did, one of the things we inherited and now must escape. "The order of Melchizedec," to which every Catholic priest is ordained, was a mistake.

Getting rid of the accoutrements of sacred office. All of the distinctive marks of the lower and higher clergy which serve to distinguish them from the Christian people and one another are to be abandoned, except insofar as they serve the function to which some Christians are called by the community to perform. Thus, the functions of presiding at the Eucharistic table and preaching to and teaching the Christian people (all necessary communal functions) are not to be marked by accoutrements, special dress, peculiar hats, and rings made of precious metal. Vestments are out! Priests and bishops are to dress no differently than worshipping and work-

---

146   I am not talking about the Pauline distinctions between ministries.

147   This is an odd position for me to take in view of the fact that after thirty five years of marriage and life outside the clerical world my wife still tells me regularly that I think and like a cleric. Maybe there is something to this ontology stuff after all! I prefer to think of it as a psychology: there surely is a clerical mentality that, however, is not at all restricted to the Christian caste. Religions often if not always have castes.

ing Christian men and women. I am not calling for the restoration of a simple and mythic early Christianity, much less the Puritan forms of dress and piety; I am arguing that culturally founded and bounded ways of marking the ministers of the church have divided the people of God into classes, and that ought to be reversed. In addition, the liturgical dress looks silly, especially in the case of bishops and popes. "Ludicrous" is the word to describe men dressed in ersatz fourth century costumes marching down the cathedral isle in a display of pompous religiosity. Pope Francis seems to have grasped the anomaly of servants wearing the symbols of masters, and to a small degree so did Pope Paul VI when he abandoned the tri-level crown of the sacred emperor. Francis and his successors need to take this much further than they have thus far.

Teaching the various candidates for Christian service how to be human beings and Christians. It is the responsibility of the whole church to educate and designate Christians to their temporary functions, and do so in ways that will affirm their humanity and never in ways that set them apart from or superior to the Christian people. Their "ontological identity" is that of Christians, not clergy; they are not to be inducted into a caste. As I recall it, in my seminary education, too much energy is spent marking priests and bishops distinct from and superior to the laity. I'm hoping that we can have shepherds without them turning the rest of us into sheep.

Ending Christendom. All church law is applicable to all Christians in the same way. All Christians are equally subject to the civil laws proper to their culture. Ministers of the gospel are in no way distinct before the law, civil or ecclesiastical. When they commit crimes they are to be treated as criminals. In addition, church law should not be written by clergy alone but should be an expression of the practices of the life of a church.

Eliminating all ecclesiastical titles and distinctions. We have only one Father and He is in heaven. "Successors of the apostles" and "the Vicar of Christ," "Your Holiness" and "Your Grace," "Monsignor," and other such titles of occupancy and supernatural origin and favor should not be used. They, like the robes of office, are the products of an imperial age which has come to an end long since, albeit much more slowly in The Church. The Church seems to cling desperately to such marks of distinction. Christians have only one Lord, one "Monsignor."

Appointing bishops in a predictable and horizontal fashion.

They are replaceable—no tenure. They are renewable but not without the approval of their people. They are to be transparent—no secrets kept to make them look good. When a diocese or a pastorate is vacant, candidates are to be presented by representatives of the local churches and ranked publicly by the bishops of the province. People of the diocese or their representatives approve in a manner that is convenient, public and informed. The laity should also be able, by specific processes, to recall any minister. For example, the Catholics of Rome ought to be able to recall their bishop and to replace him or her. Bishops are 'married' to their sees for specific periods of time with no 'divorce' and remarriage. They are locals, they remain local, and they retire locally. They should be buried locally, in the midst of the people whom they served. This is possible only if the appointment of bishops is taken out of the hands of the bishop of Rome and the Vatican Congregation of Bishops and placed in the hands of the people and the lower clergy, and the bishops (or some such) of a national church province. The current appointment process is deeply flawed and politicized, and even personalized. Many of the episcopal appointments of the last two popes were scandalously ideological.

Investigating and publicly discussing episcopal candidates, with moral criteria foremost. They have to be men and women of learning, character and courage, enough to withstand their inclination to serve their own interests or those of the caste, rather than the Christian people of their dioceses. Any person, who like Archbishop John Myers of Newark NJ, plans to spend a million dollars of his people's money to build an estate for his retirement, should be retired from the episcopal role and from the priesthood. Retired bishops, archbishops, cardinals and popes belong in their dioceses, living like their people, on the economic and social level of their people.

Requiring bishops to report to their people on the state of their churches. Lay moral and financial oversight must be required for bishops. Bishops do not own the church or the churches. At most they are custodians, not monarchs.

Consulting the people on matters of doctrine as well as church policy. The *Magisterium* is primarily the church and only secondarily its officers and servants who must speak for the churches' faith, not for or about themselves. Christians need to be heard. The gospel and its implications are theirs, too. Insofar as they could the bishops have closed off all other voices.

Broadening and deepening Ecumenism. The Holy Spirit gives life to the church, yes, but to all the churches. End all "one true church" talk. The church catholic is all the churches, Protestant as well as Catholic. Drop the Vatican II declaration that "fullness of the church subsists in the Roman Catholic Church..." The fullness of the church dwells where two or three are gathered in His name. There is nothing about the Roman Catholic Church that sets it above (or below) any other concrete community of Christians. The one true church is an assembly of equals in Christ, not a monarchy or a hierarchy established by heavenly decree.

Removing bishops who abetted or abet sexual predators, or any other criminals who do so in the future. They should be stripped of their rank, including cardinals Mahoney, Law, Rigali, etc., and undergo legal review both ecclesiastical and civil. On the supposition that they have violated church and civil law they should suffer the penalties of the law. The offending bishops should be removed from office just like offending priests, and the penance of bishops should be public, civil and ecclesiastical. Do not allow the Vatican to become a safe house for bishops who commit crimes, as John Paul II and Benedict XVI did in the case of Bernard Law.

Calling women and married men to preside over the Eucharist and become pastors, bishops and popes. Their exclusion is the most glaring bit of false traditionalism in the episcopal and papal playbook. The highly selective clerical memory called "Tradition" in this case masks misogynism and archaic views of purity.[148]

Requiring national synods composed of leaders and representatives of the local churches to meet every five years, and ecumenical councils every ten years, something that is in line with the reforms mandated by the Council of Trent. It would have been put into effect were it not for the paranoid fear of councils that has gripped the souls of popes since the Constantine called and presided over the Council of Nicaea (325). Councils should have legislative authority for the national and universal church, and consider issues pertinent to the believing and practicing life of the church. These synods are to be open to representatives of all Christian communities, not only to the ones called Catholic. The leaders of one Christian church are

---

148   A seminary song in my day went: "It's Tradition, it's Tradition, it's a very, very, very old Tradition. You can ask the Roman Rota; it won't help you one iota. For no amount of wishin', no, no amount of wishin' can ever change or hope to change a very old Tradition."

not to assume superiority to the leaders of other communities for all have been called by the Spirit and their respective communities into positions of service.

Allowing all Christians to enunciate their faith in beliefs and practices proper to the gospel, especially bishops who should lead in affirming Christian truth. All Christians are bound to listen to other Christians respectfully. No one is to be denied this freedom to speak and to hear. All Christians are equally bound to seek and affirm the truth and the truths of the gospel. No one Christian or set of Christians should command other Christians what to believe or do. The mad schismatic energies of Christians must be contained by other ways than monarchical and oligarchic power.

Dropping the oath of office and its demands for secrecy wherein church leaders (bishops and cardinals) are bound to cover up corruption among the clergy and other acts which may expose the church to negative judgment. A basic rule of the current Catholic episcopacy is "Never allow scandal," but the rule has made Catholic Church itself a scandal. The Christian people of a parish or a diocese have the right to know what's wrong, and bishops and pastors have the responsibility to tell them.[149]

These seventeen items are crucial to the reform of the contemporary Catholic Church. If the underlying issues are to be dealt with honestly and fully an ecumenical synod is required, a council including laypersons who shall have speaking and voting rights. If the Council is to be successful, the meaning and extent of what the higher clergy are pleased to call "The Tradition" and the "Sacred Magisterium" which now hedge us in need to be reconsidered and redefined. The Church and the church need a reformed constitution (rewrite the Code of Canon Law). The mantle of the "Sacred" and the "Holy" should be ripped off the human and natural growth of church government and bureaucracy. The church needs to be freed of its formal "sacrality" since its un-holiness can no longer be denied.

My proposals, I admit, may add up to suicide for the Catholic Church. They may gut the essentials of what has been known as Catholicism. They seem to fall somewhere between low-church

---

149   When Governor Frank Keating, as head of the national Catholic commission on sexual abuse, claimed that dealing with bishops was like dealing with the Mafia, the bishops who had begged him to lead the probe and oversight fired him. One can see why they fired him but his analogy has not been refuted.

Protestantism and Christian anarchism. I have already explained why I am driven to offer them. If I am correct, the present crisis of abuse and its cover-up by the Catholic bishops and the Vatican will continue unless the church can void monarchism. I believe that the fertile ground from which the abuse sprung is the lethal combination of hierarchy and clericalism. If this ground is also essential to Catholicism, then we are faced with a stark choice: re-form or die. Moses tells us to choose life: "This day I call heaven and earth as witnesses against you that I have set before you life and death, blessings and curses. Choose life." (Deut. 30:19)

17. After Francis

Pope Francis seems to be of another mind than his two predecessors in many respects and this provides us with a bit of hope for genuine reform in church governance. Recognizing his gifts of temperament and intelligence, I have hope that Francis and perhaps his successor can lead in the transformation of Roman Catholic Church governance but I am quite sure that he (they) will not be able to do what seems to me required. Things will go better under Francis in practical governance but whether they can solve the big problems remains unlikely. The synod on the family (2015) will be the test of Francis' and the delegate bishops' conception of collegiality and their willingness to take the possible changes seriously.

There are barriers to reform, including the vast historical drift toward centralization of power and decision-making in Rome and the church doctrines of universal sovereignty and infallibility of the pope. Many Catholics, most especially the high clergy it seems, are convinced that the papacy in its present configuration is God's will for the church, and they behave accordingly. The problems Francis has to deal with are intractable in that they infest the inherited definition of Roman Catholicism.

The first problem is that the last two popes, John Paul II and Benedict XVI, reverted to the notion that the Catholic Church is an absolute monarchy. In spite of the good intentions of the bishops and theologians of the Great Council to condition papal monarchy with a bit of episcopal power sharing, *Lumen gentium* and *Gaudium et spes* happily carried on the tradition of absolute papal authority. One cannot end an absolute monarchy by declaring that there are two thousand lesser monarchs, and then asking the absolute monarch if that's OK with him. He may say yes or he may say no. Paul VI said a qualified yes and his successors said no. To effect the change the monarch has to be down in the pit with the others, speaking and writing and voting, thus surrendering his monarchical status.

This fact, this doctrinal conundrum, grounds both the achievement and failure evident in the reigns of John Paul and Benedict. Their achievement is because both men thought the divine spotlight ought to fall on them and they worked at it indefatigably until, at last, Benedict couldn't take it anymore. The failure occurred in that with such monarchical conviction any modification of their rule by bishops, even in Council, was quite unthinkable. The Catholic Church is not a conciliar church; it isn't even a conversational church. The Council's irresolution on this matter set up collegiality for contradiction by John Paul and Benedict. After them, no one questions who is in charge and if there is to be any change in monarchical status it is the monarch himself who will have to promulgate it. Not likely even for a well-disposed monarch (Francis).

The intensity of the monarchical rule depends on factors ranging from secular political context and available media of control to the psychological character of the monarch himself and the willingness of Catholics and other Christians to live with him. This leads to the variations in exercise of control by all the popes [e.g., Pius XII vs. John XXIII]. The historical inertia for the past millennium and a half has been in the direction of centralization of power in the pope and his curial servants and advisors. Yes, there are limits to the power of papal monarchy; for example, in spite of their honest intentions to serve in this regard, John Paul and Benedict were not able to perform the most basic of "petrine" tasks: unify the churches and mediate differences. They were able to "strengthen the brethren" perhaps but neither of them was, by nature, a unifier or a mediator. They were commanders. They sat atop a church divided to its core and left it every bit as much divided internally and externally as when they assumed power, perhaps even more so. Instead of "thinking with the church" (i.e. us) they spent their energies thinking *for* the church and telling the rest of us what to think. Not only is absolute monarchy absurd conceptually; it doesn't work even in the hands of the best and the brightest.

Though many Catholics regard this centralization of power in popes as having a supernatural root in the intentions of Jesus, I do not and neither do a significant number of Catholics.[150] To me it has been, and remains, an often unfortunate "natural" development resting on the papal-inspired and disseminated myth of Peter, on the decisions of a Roman emperor or two in the fourth century, and on the gradual and willful accretion of political and ecclesiastical power by the bishops of Rome. That "natural" growth has displayed itself recently in the much encouraged popular revival of papolatry in John Paul's reign. The enthusiasm of some theologians for a form of Catholic piety they call "Evangelical Catholicism" is another revival of the late nineteenth century heresy "ultramontanism" that led to the definition of papal infallibility (1870) and the

---

150   D'Antonio et al., *American Catholics Today: New Realities of Their Faith and Their Church* (NY: Rowman and Littlefield, 2007) p. 98, figure 6:2.

persecution of the Catholic modernists.[151] Disaster lies on any path strengthening the grip of papacy on Catholic Christianity, even the grip of so genial a monarch as Pope Francis.

I doubt that anyone will be elected to the papal office or appointed to the episcopacy who does not subscribe fully to that sanctified gathering and use of power. I also do not believe that anyone holding the papacy can reverse that inertia in significant ways aside from an impossible proclamation that the pope no longer wants to be a monarch. The greatest council in the history of the Western Catholic Church tried and failed to moderate the absolute monarchy. The most that can be hoped for is conviction on the part of Francis and the next office holder, in concert with the convictions of their electors and fellow bishops, that inclusion, respect and restraint should be the practice of the Roman bishop and his curia when it comes to dealing with other bishops and other churches. The idea that popes and bishops should be interested in what priests and lay Catholics think and believe is too much to be hoped for. There is no mechanism; there are no persons capable of calling the top Catholic leadership to task or even informing them of the church's problem. When Paul VI died, internal dialogue in the Catholic Church died with him, and the great papal monologue continued.

Certainly some of the machinery for distribution of power and free speech is in place, thanks to John Paul's two predecessors and the Council itself. However, even now it is evident that the holder of the chair of Peter is quite capable of voiding that distribution whenever he chooses and, when he does so, he can count on the compliance of his brother bishops. In spite of this, decentralization should be given another try. I am not sanguine about the chances, however. If the mature Christian faith and trust of a man like John XXIII and many of the fathers of the Council could be succeeded by a restoration of divine monarchy under John Paul II and his episcopal epigones, our future as a community of equals is not bright.

The second problem Francis and the next pope will face is replacing the docile episcopate created by his immediate predecessors. The work of John Paul and Benedict to effect church unity

---

151   See William Portier, "Here Come the Evangelical Catholics," *Communio* 31 (Spring 2004) 35-66, and George Weigel *Evangelical Catholicism: Deep Reform in the 21st-Century Church* (NY: Basic Books, 2014). Ultramontanism ("beyond the mountains") is "a religious belief within the Catholic Church that places strong emphasis on the prerogatives and powers of the Pope." *Wikipedia*. The term is medieval in origin, and since then its precise referent has varied with the political context. The mountains referred to are the Alps, which separate Italy from the rest of Europe.

by loyalty oaths and episcopal ideological uniformity must be undone. The fact that Pope Francis could congratulate retired Archbishop John Quinn on the publication of his books on reform is a
good sign.[152] The fact that Catholic bishops, like Catholic popes, are
men of orthodox catholic faith (as they should be), as exhibited in
the classical creeds, conciliar teaching, and doctrines of the churches of Christ seems to me evident. But there is no need for Catholic bishops to be hermeneutical parrots. Bishops, archbishops and
cardinals seem devoted to repeating, without nuance, the cascad-
ing stream of papal and curial pronouncements under John Paul
and Benedict. We need bishops with brains and the courage to use
them, and with the notion that their job is to witness to the gospel
in their own circumstances without wary and pious eyes cast over
their shoulders to "the Holy Father," waiting on him for enlightenment and promotion. After all, the popes are Christians like us
and in need of conversion of mind as well as heart. Bishops are appointed to witness Christ's resurrection and to serve the churches,
not to witness the papacy and serve it.

I am not sanguine about this possibility either, although under powerful men like Pius XII and John XXIII such intelligent and
brave men were raised to the episcopacy and the cardinalate, and
revealed themselves at the Council.[153] The full blown renewal of
the imperial papacy is in place now for over a quarter of a century,
the episcopacy has been reduced to mediocrity and codependen-
cy, and one must ask whether reversal is any longer possible and
whether the bishops are capable of honest and decent leadership of
the churches. Surely they are not up to another Council. John Paul
and Benedict, as secure as they seem to have been, could not have
abided one. In a Council there are just too many voices that *might*
need to be heard by popes who do not want to hear them. After all,
that is exactly what happened at Vatican II.

The primary impact of the last two papacies, of the supine posture of the bishops, and of the abuse scandal has been a disastrous
alienation of the laity. While the laity in the church have long been
accustomed to listen to the clerical witness, and support the clerical
procession (and it is a unique show, let's face it), the absence of a
many sided public conversation among church leaders has grown
intolerable. The notion of communion in the church has been distorted and reduced to a rhetorical mechanism for stifling conversa-

---

152   Archbishop John Quinn, *Reform of the Papacy* (NY: Herder and
Herder, 1999) and *Ever Ancient, Ever New: Structures of Communion in the
Church* (New Jersey: Paulist Press, 2013).

153   Cf. John W O'Malley, *What Happened at Vatican II?* (Cambridge
MA: Harvard University Press, 2008).

tion between clergy and laity, and among the clergy themselves, covering the ecclesial rift. Pope Francis in his address to the 2014 Synod of Bishops, acknowledged this when he called on the bishops to express their views on the knotty family issues before them without fear. Only a deliberate, radical, long-term and widely supported effort can overcome the distortion and reduction, and end the monarchy. If the bishops cannot talk to the pope as equals, if the people cannot talk with the bishops and priests as equals, if the one does not listen to the other, what hope have we of a decent community life? None. Where there is no many-sided communication, there is no community. We can see the results of this "failure to communicate" in the disaster of Paul VI's *Humanae vitae* (1968). He and his successors refused to recognize the voice of the faithful expressed in the committee he himself appointed. Poor Pope Paul VI couldn't bring himself to correct his predecessors. They had to be right; they were popes after all!

The outcome of the next turn of the papal wheel is particularly fateful for the church and for me if I'm around for it. I sincerely hope I do not outlive Pope Francis. He is only a couple of years younger than I and in far better health. He is such a breath of the Spirit that I tremble over the choice of a successor. Monarchy breeds my trembling. For forty-five years of my Catholic life, between the ages of twenty and sixty-five years, the problem of Catholicism for me had been the more typically academic one. For example, what is the hermeneutic capable of leading us through the minefield of data we now have on the actual practice and beliefs of the early churches? But now, during the last decade or so, and much to my surprise at first, what I thought was "the problem" has been demoted and replaced.

Now the "problem of Catholicism" is moral: Can these men be trusted? Are they morally decent? I no longer believe they can be trusted and are morally decent, and that is the basis of my pessimism. I wait on the them as well as the Holy Spirit to show me, my wife and my sons that we can trust them again, and that they can behave themselves as Christians rather than a-moral managers and two-bit politicians. We also hope for a genuine communion in place of the rhetorical communion now suffocating the church. Alas, they believe what they teach about themselves: that they are special, indeed unique instruments of God in the rule of the churches, true Successors to the Apostles." I believe, and many Catholics with me, that they are poor souls bent on doing a job that is overwhelming, and that God has no more *or less* to do with them than God has with the local Baptist pastor and his deacons or with the Mormon Church's President, Twelve Apostles and bishops. They are as a whole little people in jobs too big for them. The papacy and the episcopacy need to be subject to demythologization. Historians and theologians must lead in this transformation.

Of course there is room for hope, supernaturally grounded (it's a gift), that the Catholic Church can be healed of its current malaise and thrall. I cling to this hope in prayer for the church. I pray, with equal conviction, "God help the next pope!" and "God help the church which must live under his rule!" This has likely been the prayer of many Catholics during conclaves. I recall with the clarity of color and depth the first time that John Paul II appeared after his election. My mother sat in the blue armchair with its *fleur de lis* pattern standing below the framed blessing of John XXIII which she received on her thirty-fifth wedding anniversary, and watched intently and silently as the new pope gave his blessing. At the end, and to my shock, she said: "He has mean eyes. God help the priests." It was a flash of insight which history has validated. That pope proved her true. Yet we can hope with Charles J. Reid in the *National Catholic Reporter*:[154]

> The logic of the papal monarchy died in Garibaldi's cannonades back in 1870. Ever since, the papacy has been transitioning to something quite different. And Pope Francis is accelerating that transition, making it complete. On his watch the papacy is rapidly becoming what it should be—a great voice and witness for world Christianity in the spirit of the Gospels.

I join Reid, but still I wonder if the circle can be squared, for alongside the witness for which I am grateful, there is monarchy which I abhor. My sincere hope is that God who has gifted us with the former has nothing to do with the latter.

---

154   *National Catholic Reporter*, 1/17/2014.

18. Interreligious Dialogue:

What's the Point?

I was set up for a lifelong interest in Judaism through my childhood experience growing up in a Bronx apartment complex two floors above a Jewish family whose two sons were close in age to my brother and me. The buildings on Frisby Avenue were otherwise populated by Christians of one stripe or another, many of them Catholic. The Karps were certainly not important influences at the time on our family (occasionally my father drank beer with Sol Karp in the Frisby Tavern, and Tim and I played street games with Morty and Kenny). They helped create in a young Catholic mind and conscience some important questions: what are they and why aren't they Catholic? Why don't they accept the fact that the Messiah has come? Why do some Catholics (my relatives and parish priests among them) make snide remarks about them? Above all else, why did the Nazis want to kill them all? I had, at the time, no answers. To my ten-year old mind, Jews were a mystery and their destiny monstrous.

When I was an assistant pastor in the Pelham Manor Catholic church, I was one day called to the office to meet a woman who asked to see a priest. I was on duty that day and so it fell to me to talk with her. Irena Cabot, the wife of a prominent Bronx doctor who lived in Pelham Manor a couple of blocks south of the rectory, introduced herself and said immediately that she is Jewish, she needed to talk, and please don't try to convert her for she has enough guilt in her life without becoming a Christian. She told me that her mother had recently died and Irena needed reassurance that her mother is in heaven. She came to the Catholic rectory for reassurance rather than to the Rabbi "because he is a Reformed Jew and who knows what he believes!" She said she was confident that I believed in eternal life because the Pope does and so I must. I spent an hour listening to her tales about her mother, reassuring her, and thus began a half-century relationship with an extraordinary woman who educated me about Judaism and about her many troubles! I became a spiritual support over long distances to a woman of great intelligence and deep spirituality. I'm sure I got at least as much benefit as she did from the decades long conversation.

Some quarter of a century later, I was on the faculty of religious studies at the University of South Florida and had been for ten years. The first Catholic president of the university invited the most prominent scholar of Judaism in the country to join our faculty, Jacob Neusner, a man of high recognition across the profession of academic religionists, known not only for his hugely productive scholarship but also for his volatile temperament. The man was a powerhouse of intellect and conviction, and since I needed education in Jewish tradition, I quickly realized I had met the master. He taught "Introduction to Judaism" and I sat in on the semester long class. He became a great friend and an older and wiser brother, something I needed badly at the time. He set an example for me in the most important area of my life: his fidelity to Judaism made me a better, more loyal and critical Catholic in an academic environment in which the Catholic Church remained an object of suspicion. I asked him once why he had such high interest in the Catholic Church among the many Christian denominations. He said: "It's the biggest and best show in town. It's where the action is." He hit that one on the nose. Neusner added that among the many Christian denominations the Catholic Church had an intellectual structure closest to Judaism. He meant that the Catholic emphasis on a living tradition of teaching as well as the sacred scripture paralleled the Jewish Talmudic tradition and the Torah.

I was able to move from Catholic University to the University of South Florida because an Episcopal priest, an adjunct faculty member and chaplain there, noticed my application and called it to the attention of the chairman and the hiring committee. Robert Giannini, a former Catholic and later to become the dean of the Episcopal cathedral in St. Petersburg and then of the Episcopal cathedral in Indianapolis, and his wife met us and our truck and spent the day setting up our rented row house in Temple Terrace. Talk about generosity! I even got his invitation to preach at an Episcopal liturgy that I accepted and it turned out to be the last time I ever stood at a pulpit. It was primarily he who introduced me to the academic world of a state university and to Episcopalian Christianity. An act of kindness opened another door for my mind and heart.

In 1968, I attended a conference given by Bernard Lonergan, S.J., on his soon-to-be completed and long anticipated book, *Method in Theology*. Great conference, mind-bending in fact, and I even got to chat with the Great Man himself a couple of times. There was, of all things, a Presbyterian minister in attendance along with a hundred or so Catholics and several former students at the Gregorian University where Lonergan taught, and a gaggle of Jesuits. A handful of my friends got quite chummy with the Reverend Ross MacKenzie, making an effort to find out why this offspring of John Calvin and John Knox would turn up at a Jesuit sponsored event focused on the theology of (to the public and even ecumenical mind) an obscure Jesuit theologian. I forget now his reasons but I do remember well how delightful and funny a person he was. A couple of us Catholic clerics even wrote a comic letter to his wife, Flora, informing her that Ross had decided to become a celibate priest and that as a consequence she would have to become a nun. She wrote back and told us we could have him and she'd be glad to become a nun and celibate herself. Ross and Flora allowed me another peek into what previously seemed to me a dark and strongly anti-Catholic corner of Christian church life.

On one hand, following up on these fortuitous experiences, I never became a professional, active ecumenist or an ecumenical theologian. I had excellent models among my co-religionists, including Cardinal Walter Kasper, Brother Jeffrey Gros, Sister Susan Wood and Francis X. Clooney, S. J. whose expertise and charity I could never match.[155] On the other hand my amateur and personal interest in the relations between Christian churches and between religions never slackened. For example, I spent two decades learning about fundamentalism and evangelicalism, and wrote a book on the latter.[156] My conviction regarding the relations between Christianities is simple (too simple many would say): the churches are already one in faith, hope and charity, and Christians of all sorts are already brothers and sisters in Christ. My equally simple conviction about the relations between religions is that we had better get past the ignorance, the antagonisms and the competition, and enter into the profound dialogue and educational effort by which the world religions can be at peace within and among themselves. We are all human. It's time for the leadership to recognize and act on the already existing unity—something they have been struggling with since the second Vatican Council. This is not my conviction alone; it is the Catholic position—or close to it.

What has been going on with ecumenical and inter-religious dialogue? A fifty-year attempt to arrive at a fair understanding

155   Walter Kasper, *Harvesting the Fruits: Basic Aspects of Christian Faith in Ecumenical Dialogue* (NY: Continuum Group, 2009); Jeffrey Gros, FSC, Eamon McManus and Ann Riggs, *Introduction to Ecumenism* (NY: Paulist Press, 1998); Susan Wood. SCL, *Sacramental Orders* (Collegeville MIN: Liturgical Press, 2000); Francis X Clooney, *Comparative Theology: Deep Learning Across Religious Borders* (Summerset NJ: Wiley-Blackwell, 2010).

156   *The Lion and the Lamb: Evangelicals and Catholics in America* (NY: Oxford University Press, 2004).

among religions, a "just love" as Sr. Margaret Farley might call it. Actually, we could trace the roots of this attempt back one hundred and fifty years to the American Protestant ecumenical movement of the 19th century, a movement aimed at a union of Protestant Christians who were worried about Protestant splintering into hundreds (by now thousands) of denominations. Catholics weren't invited to participate, in principle because Catholics weren't Christians in the view of 19th century Protestants. For their part, Catholics wouldn't have joined the movement anyway because they already were the One True Church and didn't want to talk to people who didn't recognize that fact. The only ecumenism Catholics would recognize at the time was conversion to the one, true Church and submission to the Holy Father and his local representatives.

The movement started at a particular time and place to deal with a particular problem, namely rampaging schism among Protestants. It failed to halt schism and failed to create the one, holy, universal and apostolic church spoken of in the creeds, but it did keep the American mainline Protestant churches in touch with one another on key issues such as cooperation on missions. The 19th century movement later blossomed into the founding of the National Council of Churches and eventually the World Council of Churches.

Serious and public dialogue among Christian churches, now including the Roman Catholic Church and the Eastern Orthodox Churches, began after the Second World War, some sixty year ago. Simultaneously, Christians began talking with Jews and leading figures of other religions such as Hinduism and Buddhism. Why then?

Let me offer a conventional hypothesis. World War II caused an immense psychological and spiritual shock. Hundreds upon hundreds of millions of people saw evil incarnate and felt the effects of it. Hollywood is still producing fine films about that war, but rarely does it capture its impact on the social order of which religion is a part. We do remember the military and civilian casualties but we sometimes forget that the human minds and hearts of the survivors of the war were sometimes changed for the good. My generation and my father's (the latter called by Tom Brokaw 'the greatest generation') were shaken not only by the physical devastation of most of Europe and the Soviet Union but by the extent, the effects and the depth of nationalist, racial and class prejudices, prejudices buried deep in our Western cultural psyche. We saw what happened when hate-filled images and inherited beliefs were adopted and manipulated by fascists and communists. They led to 50 million deaths in the war and perhaps 50 million more in the class wars in the Soviet Union and Communist China, and that is a conservative estimate. During the war, six million Jews and five million Poles were destroyed simply because they were Jews and Poles. Think of the 20 million Soviet civilians killed by the *Wehrmacht* and the million and a half *Wehrmacht* soldiers killed in the drive for Berlin in 1945, and the hundreds of thousands of German and Japanese civilians obliterated by deliberate allied bombings of cities. Think of Hiroshima and Nagasaki. Compared to this calculated slaughter of 100,000,000 over thirty or so years, people like Attila the Hun and Genghis Kahn were Sisters of Mercy. Any fool could see that the old ways just didn't work. Catholic leaders especially were stunned by all this for at least three good empirical (as distinct from ideal or spiritual) reasons.

First, Catholic leaders realized that if Hitler had eliminated the Jews, the churches were next, especially the Roman Catholic church because of its internationalist, "cosmopolitan," racially mongrel profile. Hitler's manipulation and persecution of Catholics in Germany and elsewhere would have become a permanent and prominent feature of a European Nazi Reich.

Second, before and during the war large numbers of German Catholics, and Catholics and Orthodox in eastern European countries, became willing and indeed sometimes fanatical instruments of Nazi tyranny and racism. Hitler himself was a Catholic, along with Himmler, Heydrich and Goebbels. In 1938, 22.7 percent of the SS were practicing Catholics and possibly as large a number practicing Lutherans.[157] How could church leaders have allowed this to happen and how could church leaders make it unlikely to happen ever again?

Third, many Catholic leaders realized that the historical Catholic religious hatred of Jews had fed the wide and deep underground river of European xenophobia and anti-Semitism that surfaced in Nazi secular racism. As Hitler told one of the German Catholic bishops in 1933 "As for the Jews I am just carrying on the same policy which the Catholic church had adopted for 1500 years."[158]

The shock from the murder of millions forced the realization on Catholics, Protestants and Jews that they need to start talking to one another. It started at first over the back fence and then in a fifty-year public religious block party of conversation and argument that has been going on since. For Catholics, the conversation came to a head at the second Vatican Council with the passage of a short <u>document called</u> *Nostra aetate* ("In our time") in which the bishops

157   Paul Johnson, *A History of Christianity* (NY: Simon and Schuster, 1976), 490.

158   *Ibid.*

and the pope renounced the traditional Catholic/Christian teaching that "the Jews killed Christ" and called for respectful relations of Catholics with Jews and members of the major world religions including Islam. This was the most controversial and hard-fought document at the Council. Hatred dies hard, and so does devotion to what we thought and taught in the past.

That, in a nut shell, is what I think is behind the ecumenical movement among Christians in Europe and the US, and what is behind the intense inter-religious dialogue between Christians and Jews which still grabs headlines. Let me give you a recent example of the change in relations.

Rabbi Jacob Neusner, mentioned above, is the outstanding translator and interpreter of Talmudic Jewish religious sources during the last fifty-year period. He now holds an endowed chair in Jewish theology at Bard College having taught for decades at Dartmouth, Brown and the University of South Florida where I met him. In 1994, he penned what I think is a classic modern text on Jesus and Judaism entitled *A Rabbi Talks with Jesus*.[159] It is still in print and deserves to be read by those who wonder why the Jews who knew Him and knew of Him did not regard Him as Messiah.

In the book, Rabbi Neusner enters into an imaginative dialogue with Jesus after the Sermon on the Mount as is shaped by St. Matthew. While he listens to Jesus deliver his program of renewal of Judaism, Neusner realizes that Jesus' sermon is in fact an abandonment of the revelation through Moses in the written Torah and in the oral traditions encapsulated later in the two Talmuds. Neusner asks himself: "Would I have followed Jesus?" and answers, "No, I would not have, for he is mistaken about Judaism and rejects the teachings of Moses." At the end he pleads with Jesus not to go down to Jerusalem to his certain death. Jesus answers, "I must go, my Father is calling me." Neusner replies that he will not follow Jesus but will return to his family and to his home as Moses said he should. There are two things central to Judaism in Neusner's view that Jesus largely ignored: the family and the people of Israel. To put it in other terms, the reform fashioned by Jesus was universalist while Judaism is particularist.

I'm not citing the book because I think my friend Rabbi Neusner is right and Jesus was wrong, or vice versa, but because what happened to the author as a result of the book reveals the profound change of the past fifty years. The book made it into the hands of Cardinal Ratzinger, the redoubtable guardian of Catholic orthodoxy, who wrote a commendatory blurb for the book. As Pope

159   Jacob Neusner, *A Rabbi Talks with Jesus* (Winsor Canada: McGill-Queens University Press, 2000).

Benedict, Ratzinger published his own book entitled *Jesus of Nazareth*.[160] In it, he reserved an entire chapter to the Sermon on the Mount and to Neusner's view of Jesus and respectfully disagreed with him. When Pope Benedict XVI arrived in Washington in 2008, he arranged to have Rabbi Neusner and his wife Suzanne there for a meeting with representatives of other religions and called him forward to greet him warmly and to praise his work. Later the Pope visited the Grand Synagogue in Rome and on the day after, at his own initiative, he met privately in his study with Rabbi Neusner and his wife Suzanne and again praised his book.

Now I ask you, especially you who, like me, remember the bad old days, could you have conceived of such a meeting and exchange at any time in the thousand years before World War II. Could you see a pope holding the hand of a Jew who wrote in unhesitating terms that Jesus was mistaken?[161] Yes, it is pretty neat of Neusner and the Pope to pull this unusual event off, but that is not the point. Their reward will come, as Jesus said, in heaven. The point is that things have changed in the past fifty years so radically that Neusner could write such a book and a Pope would thank him for it! These two men are hard-nosed religious conservatives, who disagree radically about the things that mean most to them and say it at the very moment when their hands are joined for the sake of justice and mercy and in respect and affection.

Finally, let me return to the initial question: what is the point of inter-religious dialogue? There are three points that I can state simply and directly:

The first is this: a web of understanding and kindness is being spun, a web that includes Christians and Jews, but also Muslims as well as Buddhists and Hindus. "Never again," cried Pope Paul VI to the U.N. General Assembly twenty years after the war. "Never again war!" He meant that war should never happen again, nor should such madness be permitted for any human community on the earth. It is love, human inter-connectedness, which drives the demons out.

The second is the health of our civic community and the freedom and character of its culture. Without religious dialogue our nation's civic life is Balkanized, and churches, mosques, synagogues and temples are fortresses rather than passageways. If so, our civic, political and cultural life will be inevitably blind-sided and the demons will reemerge.

160   *Jesus of Nazareth: From the Baptism in the Jordan to the Transfiguration* (NY: Doubleday, 2007).

161   The document had its root in a meeting of Jules Isaac and John XXIII before the Council. See O'Malley, *What Happened at Vatican II*, 219.

The third point of dialogue is the health of the religious communities themselves. Religious communities, whatever else they are about, are about love, hope and faith. They are NOT about xenophobia and turf struggles—or at least they shouldn't be, no matter how often historically religions have been twisted into them. Xenophobia and tribalism are the demons to be exorcized in all our religious communities. Religions are at their best when they take the hard and high road to mutual understanding and respect rather than the easy road to mutual ignorance and rejection. Too often, our religious communities have taken that easy road. Too often, they have served nations and peoples rather than justice and mercy. Jesus himself, echoing other religious teachers, spoke of narrow and rising roads that lead to the Kingdom, and the wide and sloping roads that lead to destruction. (Mt.7: 13-14).

Catastrophe is not the easy way for human beings to learn but in some cases, it may be the only way. We were so divided and scarred in our miserably balkanized past that we were pulled into self-destructive madness. When that happens, as it did in the second World War, we see all at once what hatred and indifference have led us to: the murder of millions. This is what happened to our fathers and mothers in faith. In response to that catastrophe we must do well together, we must learn to care about each other and to lean on each other, we must learn to understand and trust one another. This is among the most difficult tasks to have ever confronted the religions. We can never again stand on the sidelines when hatred threatens to destroy human beings. We can never claim ignorance again. If we do not continue vigorously on the path to mutual understanding, our world will end.

19. Why I Am Not a Theologian II

While I have great respect for the vocation of Catholic theologian, I don't have that vocation as I pointed out in chapter thirteen. I am not one because Cardinal Ratzinger speaking for Pope John Paul II sketched limit rules for theologians that I will not accept. While several of my close friends are theologians, I myself must beg off the title taken in its strictly defined Catholic sense for it demands far more than I can supply. One might suppose that I was once a theologian (after all, I held a joint appointment to the theology and religion departments of the Catholic University of America in the 1970s and I was chairman of the theology department at Saint Louis University in the 1900s) and it appeared to some that I left my practice of theology when I left the priesthood, resigned my position at Catholic University and joined the faculty of religious studies at the University of South Florida in 1980. While I do confess to a good bit of conceptual and rhetorical maneuvering on the issue over the years, nonetheless I have never been a theologian and only rarely aspired to be one.

I felt theology from the outset of my education and throughout my academic career to be an uncomfortable world. I dropped my membership in The Catholic Theological Society of America decades ago because, after suffering through a few annual meetings, that same discomfort surfaced sharply there. I retained an active membership in the College Theology Society because the atmosphere at the annual meetings was lighter, breathable and far less ecclesiastical. The refrain often rings in my mind, "Love many, trust few. Always paddle your own canoe," a fit motto for a loner, not for a Catholic theologian.

Although some of the issues theologians address are vital concerns of mine as well, I could never bring myself to accept in advance whatever the episcopal and papal *Magisterium* may decide upon. The *Magisters* have made very plain what they think their role in the lives of Catholic Christian communities is and what sway they should have over my mind and the minds of Catholics. I don't accept that understanding as in any way divine in inspiration, or in any way definitive of Christian belief. Historically they have often been correct in answering the tough religious and theological questions but they have been wrong perhaps as often, especially wrong about themselves, and especially frightful about the implications of justice and mercy for their own practice. I have no intention now to honor their call for religious assent to their decisions in advance, something they think is essential to Christian faith and Catholic self-definition. I think I am responsible for what I find believable, and must determine for myself what I believe. Yes, yes, cafeteria Catholicism! Yes, cursed autonomy! If this is an unacceptable stance for a Catholic, so be it. I will have to answer for it soon enough.

As I look back over the decades, I spy another reason why I am not a theologian: contemporary Catholic theology, for very good reason, requires one to live in the world of theory or scholarship, and I am not equipped intellectually or psychologically to do either. I am not brainless but I am no theoretician or scholar. I don't think deeply and broadly enough to be a theologian. While theologians have been my good friends over the decades, I want no mission and I have no theory. I am a teacher as I was once a preacher. I enjoyed being both, each in its time.

In the several years (1957-1961) in the New York archdiocesan seminary I was curious as to how my peers and my co-religionists talk about God. I noted that the textbook footnotes were filled with the names and dates of heretics and their heresies. All of them were anathematized by the *Magisterium* and, when possible, killed by the *Magisterium* (or by the "secular arm" as they would put it!) The Latin textbook theology of those days was built in part on opposition, refutation and punishment. Think of what would have happened to Martin Luther had Pope Leo X been able to get his hands round his neck. He would have gone the way of Jan Huss. Doctrines, I concluded, were dangerous even in the relatively enlightened years of the 1950s. I was a witness from afar to the excommunication in those years of the stubborn Jesuit Father Leonard Feeney for taking seriously and literally a doctrine Catholics had been taught for well over a millennium, namely "Outside the Church there is no salvation." How could that be? But read the words of Pope Pius XI:[162]

> For if, as they continually state, they [Protestants] long to
> be united with Us and ours, why do they not hasten to
> enter the Church, "the Mother and mistress of all Christ's
> faithful"? Let them hear Lactantius crying out: "The
> Catholic Church is alone in keeping the true worship. This

---

162   Pope Pius XI, *Mortalium animos*, 1928. #26. The words are an example of the cramped minds of good and very bright men. Papal documents of the past two centuries are dotted with similar foolishness. Not much thinking outside the box by the successors of St. Peter it seems.

is the fount of truth, this the house of Faith, this the temple
of God: if any man enter not here, or if any man go forth
from it, he is a stranger to the hope of life and salvation."
Let none delude himself with obstinate wrangling. For life
and salvation are here concerned..."

Sounds like Feeneyism to me, and it was common doctrine in
the church. I was being taught that very same "Feeneyism" in my
Catholic sixth grade class at the time and my father asked me what
I thought of "Outside the church there is no salvation." My father
had tipped me off to the doctrine's falsehood by the time I was ten
years old (he said it was nonsense). A few years later Rome caught
up with my father and fired Fr. Feeney when he became an embarrassment at his Center near Harvard University.[163] To him the old
saying meant that most of the Harvard faculty and student body
were damned. He was formally expelled from the Jesuits when he
refused his superiors' command that he move to Holy Cross College perched atop one of the seven hills of Worcester from his established base in Cambridge, the center of the academic landscape.
Admittedly no Catholic hierarchy would have killed me or my father at that late date but I remain convinced they would if there
were, God forbid, a return to Christendom. Pius IX, John Paul and
Benedict, Cardinal Spellman, Cardinal Mcintyre, and Cardinal
Law, in different circumstance than our own would be lighting the
faggots. I do not at all doubt the sincerity of the current church
leaders who oppose the death penalty, and neither do I doubt the
sincerity of the leaders of the past who were devoted enough to
Catholic orthodoxy to take a few lives here and there. The classic
anti-Catholic tirade, *Fox's' Book of Martyrs*, was not entirely mistak-
en about Catholic blood lust.[164] In the sixteenth century, Hans Kung
would be toast and I would be hiding in the Alpine forest.

So why did I think that doctrines were dangerous? In part, time
and place. In the 1950's seminary of the archdiocese of New York
I learned that Catholic scripture scholars were attempting to forge
for the second time in half a century some room for themselves in
the interpretation of the bible on historical and literary, rather than
doctrinal, grounds. The first time was at the end of the 19th century.

---

163   The immediate problem was Feeney's disobedience; the deeper
problem was his theological rejection of any possibility of salvation *extra
ecclesiam*. This exposed a sectarian doctrine of the church that even Rome
and his own bishop couldn't abide but couldn't reject.

164   John Foxe, *Fox's Book of Martyrs or A History of the Lives, Sufferings,
and Triumphant Deaths of the Primitive Protestant Martyrs*. (Amazon Kindle
Edition).

That movement went nowhere on account of the vigorous opposition of Rome; Pius X pronounced the excommunication (1907) of half a dozen foremost European Catholic "Modernists" and the dismissal and intimidation of many more priest-scholars.[165] With even my feeble grasp on basic Christian principles, I could see that the documents of Pope Pius X condemning the "Modernists" had little to do with Christian faith and had more than a pinch of tribal madness to them. In those years, as in the years of Nazism, as in the abuse crisis of 1985 and following, the Church revealed to the church and the world the shocking evil that gripped it. Yet both Pius X and John Paul II were canonized.

After the Modernists had been crushed, the second attempt to bring historical methods into theology came after the Second World War. This French "new theology" was condemned in a papal encyclical and its adherents effectively silenced by Roman authorities.[166] Anyone could see that, on both occasions, when the scripture scholars' and the historical theologians' textual work came close to the borders of the established Roman scholastic theology and doctrine, the reactions of Roman theologians and hierarchs could get very nasty. In 1907 and following, some biblical scholars had their careers ended or threatened, and in some cases, their lives ruined because of their views on matters of historical methods and doctrine.[167] A story was told in the midst of all this that a French scripture scholar insisted in these inquisitional circumstances that a scholar "must always distinguish between what one publishes, what one teaches in the classroom, what one writes in one's notes but doesn't say, and what one really thinks and dare not say or write down." The mid-century wave of ecclesiastical obscurantism nearly engulfed a new generation of Catholic intellectuals. Several were formally silenced for the years leading up to Vatican II. They were forbidden to write or teach.

The tsunami of papal suppression of modernism after 1907 had weakened by 1950 but was still in evidence when I was in train-

---

165   *Lamentabili* and *Pascendi dominici gregis* in English translation are kept in print by Sisters of St. Paul. For the story of the Modernists and the popes, see Paul Kurtz, *Politics of Heresy: Modernist Crisis in Roman Catholicism* (Berkeley CA: University of California Press, 1986).

166   Pius XII, *Humani generis*. Vatican website.

167   My teacher of biblical studies, Myles M. Bourke, and my classmate Richard Dillon were both subject to attack on their orthodoxy as a result of their published essays on the New Testament infancy narratives. As usual the basic issue was: "Who's in charge here?" rather than "What does the text mean?" Scholars ask the second question; the Congregation of the Doctrine of the Faith asks the first.

ing. Ethicists and systematic theologians who strayed off the established doctrinal reservation were condemned or called to heel by the Holy Office of the Inquisition—as they still are by its successor, the Congregation for the Doctrine of the Faith, perhaps the dumbest and most wicked venture of the Roman Church into thought control by bureaucracy.[168]

For example, take the old question of the messianic and divine consciousness of Jesus as well as the historicity of the biblical accounts, both issues much debated over the past century, and the potent magisterial teachings on birth control, the indissolubility of marriage and homosexual practice.[169] The tension and suffering that Roman magisterial oversight has caused for the past century will undoubtedly continue till the end of time, always for "the good of the church." Shepherds and their dogs care for sheep by slaying wolves, after all. There was a brief hiatus after the Second Vatican Council. Paul VI certainly regarded himself as the guardian of doctrines but he didn't seem to be as bloodthirsty about it. The tide of repression returned in the papacy of John Paul II and flourished under his successor Benedict XVI.[170] Alas, it seems the nature of a hierarchical system to do damage to people in fulfilling its responsibility for the Truth and whatever it is the popes and their Code of Canon Law mean by "the common good."

In my twenties, my reaction to the Catholic "thought police" was to distance myself from the interpretation of doctrines. I de-

168   Bradford Hinze, "A Decade of Disciplining Theologians" in *Horizons, the Journal of the College Theology Society*, 37 (Spring 2010): 92-126.

169   Father Lonergan was attacked in print on one occasion by an imprudent and impudent Roman theologian for his work on the consciousness of Jesus. Lonergan's devastating response can be found in "Christ as Subject: A Reply" in *Collection: Papers by Bernard Lonergan, S. J* (NY: Herder and Herder, 1967), 164-197.

170   Diarmaid MacCulloch, "The Popes," *The Guardian* (April 2, 2011). The Oxford historian writes: "we can't be certain that the apostle Peter ever went there—the most we can say is that in the mid-second century, Christians in Rome passionately believed that he had died in their city. Out of their clerical leadership, there emerged (a century and a half after Peter's lifetime) one cleric styled a bishop. That meant revising Rome's Christian past: only in the fourth century did Peter come to be seen not merely as the chief founder of the Christian church in Rome, but also as its first bishop... The dominance of the church of the Bishop of Rome was a freak in human experience, albeit a freak with profound consequences today. Its break-up in the 16th-century Reformation was a return to the normality of religious history, not some unexpected or even undesirable accident."

cided to have as little as possible to do with moral and doctrinal
theology beyond learning what I had to in order to pass examinations and to preach and teach within acceptable Catholic limits.
This was a step off the plateau of Catholic theology though I didn't
know it at the time. I determined in my thirties that I would engage in the study of pre-theological questions and in the study of
Fr. Lonergan's methodological work, in American philosophy and,
finally, to dip lightly into something I would now call the history of
ideas. I style myself a Catholic intellectual rather than a theologian.
I write "op-ed" pieces, not theology. The thought police don't care
about such unimportant fields.

The experience of seminary education, yielding messages picked
up in the classroom as well as seminary life generally, pulled me
away from theology (not from the classical doctrines themselves,
please note!) I wanted nothing to do with a field of study, no matter
how attractive and worthy, that would a potential bother to church
authorities and thus to myself. Frankly, the authorities scared me
and still do! Theologians, in addition to ability and knowledge and
love of the church, need a special blend of courage and calm to face
the Guardians. I do not have it: they throw me into a tizzy and a
rage.

I was, and still remain after five decades, a Roman Catholic, a
firm believer in the doctrines of the creeds and intent upon participation in the church's worship and its intellectual life. I became an
even happier Catholic after the Great Council in 1962-1965, but I
think that the past fifty years have borne out my hesitations about
theology in the Catholic Church. What many theologians must experience as an illuminating path through life, I have found to be a
minefield for decades. Still, even today, the Roman Catholic Church
with all its flaws and perhaps in part because of them remains "the
Greatest Show on Earth."

Whatever I may have written or said over the years at Catholic
University that led anyone to think that I imagined myself to be a
theologian, I recant and repent. There, in the 1970s, I sat in on classes given by Avery Dulles, S.J. and William Hill, O.P., and rubbed
collegial elbows with the likes of Joseph Komonchak, William
Loewe, Stephen Happel and Charles Curran, serious theologians
all. I found out from them what real theologians are, and knew I
was not one of them. I am a Catholic who makes a living reading
and writing (even teaching, but in this case always *ad mentem ecce-
siae* mind you!) about matters that are of interest to the church, and
about the church and God. I am not a theologian. By quite a stretch,
I might be called a "theologianlite." A theologian in the Catholic
tradition is missioned by the Church to read, teach and write about

the mysteries of salvation. I try not to do that—though I admit to an occasional slip when cornered. I am, after all, a Christian and happy to speak as one even if I don't belong to the theological Guild.

As I explained in chapter thirteen, I agree with Cardinal Ratzinger that theology is an ecclesial vocation and that theologians are to be mandated by church leaders; I discovered and then decided with his help over the course of those years that I am not one.[171] For nineteen years I had been missioned to preach and did it with joy, but I could not imagine myself missioned to think *ad mentem ecclesiae*.[172] My occasional lapses into theology were brought on by my preachy temperament rather than by a commission, Catholic or evangelical. My guiding rule over the past half-century has been to stay out of the way of hierarchs. They run a game that I do not want to play because I am quite sure I would lose.[173]

Although I often spoke about the church and to members of it, I don't want to speak *for* The Church. I only speak for myself. My skittishness about theology was intensified over the years by a few theologians.[174] Each in his own way suggested that I am so impressed by the work of Enlightenment thinkers I studied at Columbia University that they regard me as favorable to Enlightenment ideas of which they cannot, as Catholic theologians, approve. They were correct and still I rejoice in those Enlightenment ideas and ideals. In my view, the leaders of the Roman Catholic Church and those theologians could do with a bit of Enlightenment themselves.

While still put off by the Catholic authorities and their modes of operation *vis a vis* Catholic theologians (and lay people in general),

---

171   I must confess as well that over the years I have become less interested in systematic theology and more in history. This may have something to do with a slow deterioration of my theoretic abilities, such as they were. Dennis Doyle's book on *Communion Ecclesiology: Vision and Versions* (NY: Orbis, 2000) may be the last book in Catholic theology I have read. The sort of book that interests me most is John O'Malley's on Vatican II. As far as "Catholic intellectual" is concerned I have my heroes and examples in the like of Peter and Margaret Steinfels, Garry Wills and Terry Eagleton, all of whom since they are lay persons are of no interest to The Church while of great value to the church.

172   *Ecclesiae* means the higher clergy and especially the popes, i.e., The Church.

173   The anti-modernist oath that I had to sign in 1978 at Catholic University upset me. I had to do so in order to obtain tenure. I practiced a bit of Jesuitical "mental reservation."

174   Professors Matthew Lamb, Terrence Tekippe, Robert Imbelli, William Portier and Dennis Doyle all of whom deserve the title Catholic theologian though they are theologians of quite different sorts.

while still shy of "Rome" and of bishops, and while still unnerved by the term "theologian" as my job description, I nonetheless retain my union card as a Catholic intellectual who wants no share in a Church mission that would include any magisterial component. [175] In other words, I cannot be trusted to "teach as true what the Church teaches," except descriptively. I am convinced (believe) that the Holy Spirit guides the church, and sometimes even The Church, in the long run but it is the short run that I worry about. The history of the church leads me to think that the leaders too rarely listen to the Holy Spirit.

I can't kid myself into thinking that this shyness of theology was a matter of humility. In fact, humility has little to do with it. Rather, it was a matter of self-interest and of an ephemeral peace of mind, a need to avoid controversy and contestation with religious authorities that, given my temperament, were sure to arise. I confess to an intense dislike of the dogmatic temperament and a marked distrust of those who hold power in the church or anywhere else.[176] And so, though a Catholic in mind and practice, I have steered clear of subjects of concern to bishops and the Vatican offices. Now that I am a quasi-layman I am even less worthy of their attention, and in this, I find additional reassurance. The bishops do not care what meandering laypersons, especially former priests, think or write. Now that I am an old man, however, and as a result of the recent pressing corruption of the Catholic hierarchy, I think I should speak out on behalf of a decent Christian church.

---

175   The Roman Rescript (1982) allowing me to marry in the church and legitimizing my children also forbade me to teach theology at any level of the education system and has caused me some gyrations at points in the past three decades. It also forbids me any liturgical role in the public worship of the church. I am not allowed even to read the Scriptural texts at Mass or perform the duties of an altar boy/girl. See Appendix #9.

176   By dogmatic temperament I mean the tendency to proclaim beliefs that do not admit of question and which understands serious reservations as heresy and the fruit of the Evil One (or some such).

20. Is Believing Knowing?

Aknotty problem arises when one catches oneself talking about believing and beliefs. This is at least true for a person like me who spent fifty years in classrooms explaining to approximately ten thousand students the difference between knowing and believing generally and especially in the case of religious faith. I didn't get to an irrefutable theory. As I said, I don't have theories but I did manage to adopt a few views or opinions. For me, the distinction between knowing and believing was not a game of classroom ideological Ping-Pong; it was a life and death decision. The atheist literature of recent years and Western high culture at large for centuries displays an unease (to say the least!) with religious belief. In fact, the atheists have seemed to be not much in favor of believing, especially those religious beliefs which to them are obviously unbelievable. Science, since it is known for its delicate and systematic handling of evidence, passes their criteria for knowledge in spite of the fact that prodigious amounts of believing go on in science, but religious believing and beliefs fail on all counts. While science and common sense involve believing, those beliefs can come under empirical examination, be transmogrified into knowledge as, to adopt John Dewey's phrase, "warrantedly assertable," or dropped. For the scientifically inclined atheist, the problem with religious belief is that it is not knowledge and cannot be turned into knowledge.[177]

In what sense are the church's beliefs about God knowledge? Take the Trinity, for example, or the Real Presence of Christ in the Eucharistic elements of bread and wine. I don't think these beliefs are knowledge though they mean what they say. While knowing and believing are intertwined in common usage, it is a mistake to talk as if what you believe, you in fact know. Believing is *cognitive* in the strict sense but it is not *knowledge* [i.e., immanently generated]. Nor does it meet Fr. Lonergan's definition of knowing as the

---

177   Bernard Lonergan's comments on belief and its relation to knowledge are, to my mind, quite straightforward, and not terribly hard to understand. They are, in many respects, a deepening of the Thomist theory. But they are also imbedded in a highly complex cognitional theory, epistemology, metaphysics and a theory of religion that are more difficult to comprehend. See *Insight* and *Method in Theology*.

achievement of a "virtually unconditioned judgment of fact." Let me turn to examples.

To pick up again the work of St. Thomas on this subject, I answer St. Thomas' question, *An Deus sit?* affirmatively: Yes, God is! In brief, I know that God exists because my desire for God is a fact and is unlimited. My desire is not for this or for that or any collection of this or that's. The unrestricted desire is the basic datum in any question about the existence of God. I loved God before I read Lonergan's *Insight*. In fact, reading Lonergan gave me intellectual problems with the *existence* of God that took me close to two decades to resolve in dialogue with *Insight*, perhaps the most important wrestle of my intellectual and affectional life.[178] For those years I didn't understand Lonergan's proof/syllogism:[179]

> If being is completely intelligible, then God exists.
> But being is completely intelligible.
> Therefore God exists.

However, I answer another question, *Quid Deus sit?* with justifiable hesitation: "I really don't know *what* God is" except that I desire whatever He, She or It is. If God is really God, I *can't* know *what* God is, for God is no *thing* among other things! And I am built to understand and know *things* in relation to me and to other things. Others (chiefly but not solely Roman Catholics) have told me that God is good and I believe them. I can see in my experience why they tell me that God is good. I can see it when my greyhound sleeps and runs and stares soulfully into my eyes. But I also see in my experience of the world, and of myself and of humanity, plenty of reason to worry that God may not be so good after all and is not to be trusted to follow the modest standards of justice and mercy to which we human beings have clouded access. God transcends every*thing* entirely, including our standards and ideals. God's ways are not ours, the Scriptures say. This is not so hard to know. As Hillarie Belloc wrote, "How odd of God to choose the Jews...."[180] How odd indeed is God!

I stand with the former proposition, namely that God is good, because I am religious and Christian, meaning that I *believe* that God is the source of the good in the world and in me. But I also do not

178   Deciding to resign from the priesthood and to love Helene was very big! It was so for her as well.

179   *Insight*, 672. I could go into my difficulties and their resolution, but there is too much theory involved and the process is obscure.

180   Belloc is quoting an earlier poem. See "William Ewer" in *Wikipedia*.

know that God is good. I do not even *know* that the category applies to God. Fr. Lonergan seems to know it as evidenced in Chapter XIX of *Insight,* but I do not.[181] I believe it and I hope it is true as I believe and hope that God has saved us and continues to save us through Jesus Christ and the church. But I don't *know* that, I *believe* it.

To make the distinction between knowledge and belief in the most direct, commonsensical and traditional way I can, let me say that knowledge is what we have after careful and completed inquiry. As Lonergan says in *Insight* and *Method,* we know when we have reached a virtually unconditioned judgment of fact.[182] Lonergan calls this immanently generated knowledge. I know, for example, that Amtrak will take me from Boston to Washington D.C. but I do not know whether Amtrak will take me to Dayton, Ohio. I can know it easily enough, but I don't know it yet. Again, I *know* that the American naturalist philosophers of the first half of the 20th century made a serious mistake in their theory of God and religion, and I *know* what that mistake is. I also *know* that the key difference between evangelicals and Catholics is over the nature and functions of the church and not over the classic Christian doctrines of the Creeds. These differences are examples of the few things that I *know* by imminently generated knowledge. I spent years of research coming to know them.

Ordinarily, knowledge is knowing a fact or value and it is expressed in a proposition or a series of propositions. Beliefs are also expressed in propositions and so are cognitive, that is, they regard matters of fact and value. Believing is what you do when you accept someone else's knowledge and you don't have immanently generated knowledge of it yourself. For example, I don't know whether Amtrak will take me from Boston to Dayton but I'm ready to believe a travel agent on the matter. We presume in the other person or the community the knowledge we lack. We presume in the other person or community the integrity that inspires our trust. We *choose* to believe what we do not know because we discern in the believer and his or her community the value of believing. We choose to believe when what is proclaimed to us stirs within us both our conscience and our best hopes. Therefore, I don't believe Hitler, Stalin and Mao. I do believe St. Paul and my parents. I don't think I'm being technical here—we do this every day. Lonergan says in several places that "98% of what a genius knows he believes." [183] For me, the percentage is probably closer to 99.8. To

181   657-668. Extraordinary pages!

182   A judgment of value is also the result of a virtually unconditioned but it's content is not a judgment of fact but of the value of believing.

183   Lonergan, *A Second Collection* (Philadelphia: Westminster Press,

sum the process up in personal terms, I am not a Catholic Christian because I believe as I do; rather, I believe as I do because I am a Catholic Christian. When I was a child, I *knew* in Catholic Christians the good of being a Catholic Christian and so I came to *believe* what Catholic Christians believe (for the most part!)

To put the distinction between knowing and believing in another way, I *know* that God exists but I *believe* that Jesus was raised from the dead. Both propositions state facts, both are in that sense cognitive, both can in a wide sense be called "knowledge," but there is a telling, deep and for our earthly time impassible difference as I utter them. I understand this difference after a decades-long struggle with the first nineteen chapters of *Insight*. No amount of intellectual struggle about the Resurrection or prayer is going to change the status of my belief and transform it into imminently generated knowledge, at least not until I meet God face to face rather than in a glass darkly. (1Cor.13: 12-13) I *believe* I will do so. To put the matter briefly, I don't *know* that which I *believe*, and I *believe* some things that I can't now *know*.

Do I locate religious belief in another realm than the cognitive, that is, is believing unrelated to knowing? Many see the danger that believing may easily be situated, as some modernists and postmodernists do, in another realm than the cognitive, perhaps emotive, perhaps fancy, perhaps wishful thinking, perhaps poetry, or perhaps even simple nonsense. Some think that believers know something that I think that believers believe and do not know. Some think they know that Jesus is risen and I think they believe it. In short, I do not separate knowledge and belief; I distinguish them from one another. I distinguish between the judgments of fact and of value on the one hand and, on the other, the belief (about facts in some cases) that the judgment of value leads me to choose. I believe because I have found it good to believe.

To sharpen the matter up, let me tell you a story. When entering this murky field of thought I wish I could be more theoretic in my proposal and not so commonsensical and narrative-laden, but we all do what we can. At my age and mindset, stories interest me and so I shall proceed with stories to make my simple point. The point has to do with religious belief as much as belief-in-general.

In 1973, Professor Charles Frankel, a highly reputed Columbia University philosopher, was a member of my dissertation examining board.[184] After an initial round of Lonerganian and Naturalist gibber-jabber with the other examiners during which he remained

1975), 219.

184   Frankel and his wife were murdered in their home in 1979 during a robbery. See *Wikipedia* under his name.

quiet and seemed to be following the conversation closely, Frankel broke in at a point which interested him: "Do you mean," he asked me with obvious incredulity, "that you *know* that God exists?" After a moment's silence in which I contemplated the abyss opening before me, I said with my accustomed firmness, "Yes, I do." [185] As pity joined his incredulity, he turned his eyes down and exempted himself from the rest of the conversation. I can imagine (I imagine and do not know or believe!) that he ruminated: "Good grief, are we going to give a Columbia philosophy doctorate to this relic?" Well, they did, and passed me with what they *believed* to be "distinction," while I *know* that I am (and my dissertation was) undistinguished. "Distinction" was a matter of grade inflation I suspect.

A similar instance occurred several years before in a Union Theological Seminary seminar on the doctrine of God. Before us was an influential book in which the author claimed that the gospel narratives of the resurrection of Jesus were religious poetry that had very little if anything to do with a dead body or the empty tomb. I had been assigned to respond. I received hoots from my seminar mates when I finished saying that I thought the gospels and Paul meant in the first place that the Jesus who died was no longer dead and that the tomb was empty. It is Christian *belief* that He is. I added that I don't think the resurrection narratives and Paul's proclamation are poetry first and foremost; this is a matter of hermeneutical *knowledge.* As the hooting died down I felt as a fundamentalist must feel when he or she mentions Verbal Plenary Inspiration and the Inerrancy of the Scriptures in an academic environment. My seminar mates were genuinely amused. Thank God I didn't mention the Virgin Birth! Had I, my mates would have had apoplexy. Again, I imagine the question among my liberal Protestant seminar mates, "Who let this fool in?"

Now suppose Professor Frankel had asked me this: "You mean you *know* that Jesus is risen from the dead?" What should I have answered? I would have said, "No, I don't *know* it, I *believe* it." And had he asked why I believe it I would have said, "Because my mother and father told me He did." That seemingly flippant response stands in for the apostolic witness, the scriptures, and the tradition of the church, all handed over to me by my parents. Believe me, I know how preposterous my statement about knowing that God exists must have sounded to Frankel and just how irresponsible and reprehensible this confession is to our current crop of atheist authors. I feel badly that they take it this way, but there it is. For what I apprehend as the value of believing my community's

---

185   Perhaps I should have added "And so do you!" but that would have been snippy no matter how true.

witness I am willing to be dismissed by my cultured peers. *But I have no immanently generated knowledge that Jesus is risen from the dead.* Moreover, I doubt that the pope does. The pope doesn't *know* that Jesus is risen; he *believes* it because we, the Christian people do, and the pope is a Christian.

This, to my mind, is a sharp, clear and adequate, if not theoretically satisfactory distinction between knowing and believing. To take it a step further, though I know that God exists and I know that God isn't anything else, I don't know *what* God is and I don't even know what God is up to. However, I try to live by what my parents "handed over to me" about how to live. I taught my own children the same—although they may no longer believe as I do. They may not know the value of being a Catholic Christian and therefore believing what Catholic Christians believe... yet.

21. Common Sense and God

I noticed, long ago, that the first person tends to disappear, or perhaps better to be hidden, in academic and professional discourse. Of course, academics are usually talking about data, facts, theories and the opinions of others, and academics are nearly always concerned with truth, truths, or the probably and possibly true, in a field in which what *we* personally feel or think about it all is largely irrelevant. What counts is what is there, what the case is, what explains and what results, and how to arrive at each. With all that included, it should make little or no difference whether *we* are the ones who discover, prove, assert, suggest, or someone else is.

I remember, as if it were yesterday, when I was in eighth grade in St. Raymond's Church school in the east Bronx, Brother Aloysius, F.S.C. called me to his office to reprimand me for signing my name to a class paper in other than the prescribed Palmer Method script in which the nuns and brothers drilled us for eight years. I was making a first stab at developing my own signature style after the example of my father whose script very much impressed me. "Well," said Brother Aloysius, "don't get personal around here, young man! I don't care what style your father has or you want!" and slapped me hard enough to bend my back. The slap was unusual. He must have been having a bad day. Ordinarily he would have used the ruler on my hand or the pointer on my backside.

However, this was part of the lesson of my education that the ideal was set by others for my imitation: it was not only the best, it was the only ideal worth consideration. In concert with my education in English composition, the personal pronoun was to disappear, and so any signature style to rival Ms. Palmer's was banned. No "I" in composition, no "My" in handwriting. The teachers wanted the facts, and the facts transcended in importance any "I" or "We" that tried to tag along into language. (Well, maybe in literature on occasion where the genre permitted, but watch that, too; certainly never in whatever falls under title "the sciences."). For fifty years, I have gotten the question from fresh-persons: "Professor, am I allowed to use the personal pronoun in my paper?" So the school teachers are still Aristotelian and Thomists, insisting on "Just the facts, Ma'am." They still, in habit or conviction, believe that there are facts, the statement of which transcends the human subject, all subjects, any subject at all, every subject and even language itself. A fact, after all, is just that: a fact. It is bracing, isn't it, to see something has such a hold on common sense that even post-modern personalization of knowledge can't break it?

Why is the human subject written out? For good reasons, of course, in certain kinds of expression. For one thing, it would be boring to repeat it. For another, we can safely take it for granted, for everyone should know that when you say, "Barak Obama doesn't get it," you mean, "*I think* Barak Obama doesn't get it." Or when you say, "Joe Biden isn't a good enough Catholic to receive communion," you mean, "*I don't think* he is, at any rate..." And when you say, "the moon is blue," you mean that's the way it looks to you and it well might look green to someone else. But then, again, you can't very well leave yourself out when you want to say you're here, or you're pregnant. In these cases, indirect discourse makes little or no sense.

Even when the human subject quite properly disappears in many propositions, we know it is only hiding. Facts may transcend subjectivity, but fact finders remain subjects rather than objects, and when the finder tells us *what* he or she has found, we know that the fact didn't find or utter itself. In the utterance, the subject may hide but the subject doesn't evaporate. When the question is answered, the questioner is still with us no matter whether he or she is correct. The human subject, the questioner, the question itself, doesn't disappear into the answer. It just modestly covers itself for a few moments from the blinding light of the truth it imparts, as Adam and Eve covered themselves from the dangerous gaze of God. (Gen 3:7)

About propositions, always the answers to questions, St. Thomas made a distinction. Propositions are either *quoad nos* or *quoad se*. They are either about things in relation to one another (*ad se*) or things in relation to us (*ad nos*). So far as the things related to us are concerned, propositions can be taken as descriptions; the propositions in which things are related to one another can be taken as explanatory, at least in aim. The proposition "the moon is blue" is *quoad nos*: it means, "It looks blue to me." A proposition asserting that the moon is in a certain position relative to the other bodies in the solar system is *quoad se*. Both mean to be statements of fact, but the second is a fact mediated through a number of mathematical calculations in which the subject disappears. The second is either true or it isn't, and it makes no difference whether we or anyone else watches and describes. The propositions *quoad nos* belong in the category of common sense. They are about objects related to us. The propositions *quoad se* fall under the category of science or philosophy, or theory of some sort. They are about objects related to one another; that, at bottom, is why "I" disappears.

As I mentioned above, in his *Pars prima* to the *Summa theologiae* St. Thomas asks a question: *An deus sit?* Does God exist? What a curious question. Is it a question that leads us to propositions *quoad nos* or *quoad se?* Yes, God exists, Thomas answers, in spite of the several objections he lists and then refutes. He proceeds to offer his famous five ways of knowing that God exists. His nice simple question is turning out to be complicated, for he begins each "way" with a reference to the manner in which we experience the world, drops in a universal principle, and informs us that this is a way in which we all know "*ut deus sit.*" We are drawn in a very rapid progression from the way the world is experienced by us, to a general proposition, to a conclusion of fact: this Existent is what all of us call God. In other words, we already knew God exists, we just didn't know *how* we knew, and St. Thomas meant to give us a helping hand. Philosophers, as some have slyly suggested, propose arguments to prove the truth of what they already know to be true. This seems to be the case with Aquinas and his audience. I do not think that this is a circular chain of reasoning, as it would seem to dullards.

Are "the five ways" valid proofs? Well, yes and no. They are valid for people like myself who think his presuppositions are valid and they are invalid for those who don't share his presuppositions (for example, that the universe is intelligible, that it "makes sense" through and through). The five ways are valid for me but not at all for David Hume. I and others like me straddle the world of thought and conviction of the Aristotelian heritage of the church and of its realist philosophy on the one hand and, on the other hand, the world of post-modern recognition that there are a numberless number of churches, traditions, philosophies and arguments. Therefore, it is both correct and incorrect at the same time, in defiance of the long established principle that no proposition can be true and untrue at the same time in the same respect. St. Thomas' answer to his question helps me to know what I already knew and how I already knew it before I read the *Pars Prima*, as well as baffles and confounds me because my poor mind has such hard time thinking about the same proposition in two quite different contexts. If you want a refresher on just how hard it is to know *how* we know that God exists, read through the 667 pages of Bernard Lonergan's *Insight: A Study of Human Understanding* which is devoted to unpacking the suppositions of an affirmation that God is—an affirmation which takes place on p. 672. Lonergan thought that knowing God exists is not difficult; knowing *how* we know is very difficult indeed. And just what *do* I think about the existence of God? Well, let's just bury that for a while, and allow this human subject to hide in the argument!

Now, why do I talk about this? Surely not because I want to fix the reader's mind's eye on the problem of the existence of God, but rather because I want to fix your eye on the origin and aim and transit of the question *An deus sit?* St. Thomas' question was answered in the realm of philosophical theory, but it didn't start there. His answer involves five seemingly simple arguments that would persuade any moderately intelligent medieval person, but it is in fact complex, an argument that buckles under its presuppositions and runs over the banks of theory into the marshland of common sense. In other words, the five ways are vulnerable.

The answer, *Deus est,* fits a specific theoretic context (*quoad se*); nevertheless it is related to how we live our lives. The question grows out of life as it is lived and falls back into it again, though in the *Summa theologiae* it is a fact embedded in a theory. From *quoad nos* through *quoad se* to *quoad nos* again, from commonsense concern to philosophy to commonsense concern. Within the next few pages Aquinas is writing about whether God reveals, whether God is one or three, whether God creates. By then St. Thomas is no longer talking about what all of us humans call God, but about what Christians call God, and the way to *that* God is not by the reason common to all but by the faith common to some. By the very fact St. Thomas lists the various objections to his proposal, he admits that the question, the process and its conclusion are challengeable. He was a very modest man and ready to talk to those who disagreed.

I must caution the reader that I am an instance of the dominance of common sense over theory. After fifty years in the academic world the realm of theory is more elusive and strained, and less and less penetrable, and the swamp of commonsense is more engulfing and comforting. Like Guy Noir, the fabled private detective of St. Paul MN, I got into academia to find answers to life's enduring questions and like Guy Noir I'm still looking for one, just one.[186] As I recall, studying in the Columbia University School of Philosophy (1964-1973) was a personal quest that had mostly to do with my roiling unsettlement with the answers to life's enduring questions that had been handed to me in my tradition, and an intense desire to find out what other people thought about the Big Questions of meaning and truth. The Columbia faculty in those days looked favorably on the Big Questions and did not disappoint me on that score. I wanted to know whether their answers were any more interesting and trustworthy than the ones handed on to me. My unsettlement is akin to what St. Paul or his disciple referred to

---

186   See the stories of Guy Noir by Garrison Keeler, *Prairie Home Companion,* National Public Radio.

as the "itching ears" unworthy of a believer (1 Tim, 4:3). I seriously doubt at this late date that I was moved to study by an impulse to a life of theory. I was studying because I wanted to know what to believe.

To simplify just a bit, I found that the answers generated by folks from other tribes, specifically American Naturalist philosophers and linguistic analysts of the twentieth century, weren't any better or clearer, and that the answers given to me by my tribe were more interesting, and trustworthy enough to command the investment of a life. That investment could be understood as being driven by the desire to live a dedicated life of theory, science, reason, and argument, of absorption of data and their interpretation. This is the desire of every budding intellectual, whether he or she can stand the tension of theory or not. Emanuel Kant and Bernard Lonergan could; I couldn't. The desire for the life of theory drives those who are icons of the pure desire to know. My desire to know is usually quite impure and barely lifts my head above the weeds of common sense. To stretch the point a bit, the *quoad nos* is my homeland; so far as *quoad se* is concerned I've lucky to get a couple of days' vacation there once in a great while. Theory, both philosophy and theology, is to me something like a gymnasium: a construct to be admired from a distance and rarely, if ever, engaged.

At Columbia, released from my Roman Catholic clerical hothouse for a few hours every week, I fell in love with the American philosophers of the so-called Golden Age (1880-1940) who contradicted some of what I believed and affirmed, and yet understood and illuminated almost all of the other things I believed and gave me even more to believe. I spent a dozen years of my life reading Santayana, Dewey, Woodbridge, Randall, Lamprecht, Hook, Pierce, Royce, James and Hocking. The last four I threw in to get a taste of American theists who claimed to be every bit as "empirical" and "experiential" as the Naturalists. Though it was intellectually an awful strain staying in the realm of theory with them, and ultimately a failure, I kept at it because I was in love. Here, I said to myself, are a crowd of men and women asking questions that are real questions, not just ones that have already been answered to the satisfaction of another crowd of heroes.

I produced a dissertation and then a book in which I tried to show that the Naturalists/atheists were wrong about certain basic issues—the existence of God for one and the dumbing down of metaphysics for another—but the dissertation and the book were love songs nonetheless. What I admired most was their mind and spirit and their ways of thinking and living, their wonderful flights into theory and their personal ticks, and their humanism. My work on them was guided by the intellectual achievement of Bernard Lonergan, the Jesuit methodologist. After many years of dalliance in graduate school, I discovered that my affection for the Americans was real enough, but the deeper affection and affinity was for this curious and challenging Canadian Jesuit. He packaged and distributed something called "generalized empirical method" and insisted that the foundations of practical and reflective life are uncovered in an intricate cognitional theory, in the acts and possibility of our questioning anything and everything, of understanding, of judging and deciding; the cognitional theory was thoroughly St. Thomas and in part Kant, but both on steroids. What the American Naturalists did for Aristotle and Plato, Lonergan did for Aquinas and Kant; he pulled them from the past and gave them a future together. Since I had read a bit of Aristotle, of St. Thomas, of David Hume and of Kant, I had some idea of what Lonergan was up to, so reading *Insight* was a thrilling intellectual and frequently mind-numbing experience.

My second large interest began to develop as I was finishing the book on the American Naturalists and awaited its publication (1984). I had left the Catholic University of America after seven years and, by the greatest good fortune, secured an appointment to the department of religious studies at the vast southern campus of the Florida state university system in Tampa. In classrooms there, I ran into my first biblical fundamentalists. They were much harder for me to love than the Naturalists, but they so astounded me by their odd behavior and belief that I threw myself into a circumstantially restrained research program (I had a lot of other things to learn in those years—including how to be married, another of those "life's enduring questions" to which there are myriad answers, none of them definitive). Twenty years later, this resulted in my book titled *The Lion and the Lamb: Evangelicals and Catholics in America* (2004). My doctoral dissertation was a dialectical analysis of Naturalist positions in cognitional theory, epistemology and metaphysics. The first book, *The Naturalists and the Supernatural* (1984), had to do with the intellectual foundations of American atheism and its view of religion. They had some very interesting and valuable things to say about religion, mainly because they actually thought about it, unlike the so-called "New Atheists" of our own time.

The second book, The *Lion and the Lamb*, discussed the evangelical and Catholic religions, the rejection of each by the other, and the possibility of a new and constructive relationship. All of my research and writing has been driven by a desire to test for common ground by outlining and contrasting differences and tracing their roots; all of it is soaked in affection and respect for the other tribes, and aimed at the human world we inhabit in common. I hope they are not entirely without value to theoreticians far more able than I.

***

Now, let us get to the crux: I claim to *know* that God is; in fact, I've always known that God exists. But *how* do I know? How could I suggest, as I do, that the 95% of those now living on the planet, who are not intellectuals or philosophers, *know* that God (or some such) exists? How do they know, how do I know what Dawkins and Hitchens don't get? The academic class is in a much better position to know that God exists than the lower orders of society who haven't the leisure or the resources to spend time thinking about it. However, about sixty percent of the academics think that God doesn't exist or that the existence of God always remains a question to which there is no answer and, since one can't answer that question, why tie one's underwear in a knot over it?

Maybe there is a way to know that God exists that philosophers are unaware of. If not, the 95% of the masses are kidding themselves, living in a primitive dream world. It seems especially cheeky of me, the least among the academics, to say that in spite of the claim to atheism or agnosticism, Naturalists are in fact theists (or some such) and don't know that they are or, perhaps a bit more accurately, they don't know that they know that God exists. They expend a great deal of intellectual effort denying that God exists because they don't know *how* they and everybody else knows that He does. As I am forced to wonder how I know that God exists, there is an equal puzzle to the atheist position that there is no God when they are in the very same world with the very same intellectual and psychological faculties as I, although I admit that they are far brighter and perhaps more psychologically stable (and "clear") than I. The puzzles deepen when I reflect that I have been reading atheists since the 1970's (Jacques Monod was the first, and very disturbing he was), wondering what planet they live on for it seemed to me that they are mistaken.[187] They didn't notice something I came upon with decisive help, perhaps. Or I was fortunate enough to be born into an atmosphere drenched with God-talk. Anyway, their atheism forced me to face the issue: one of us is mistaken in fact or in language.

One way of looking at my case and the case of the billions is that we were taught that God exists and were given a language to speak to and about Him. We then spend our lives talking into the void,

187   Jacques Monod. *Chance and Necessity: An Essay on the Natural Philosophy of Modern Biology* (NY: Vintage, 1972).

hoping for an answer and, when we don't get one, imagining reasons for the lack of communication from the other side. Once I gave up praying for a long time because there was "no one picking up the phone over there." Isn't this supposed to be a two way street? Another way to imagine my situation is to call it "wish fulfillment," that is, I need God and make Him up to satisfy my needs. Ludwig Feuerbach, the nineteenth century projection theorist, is perhaps my favorite atheist though George Santayana is a very close second: Feuerbach thought we needed a Heavenly Family and made one up. Sigmund Freud, who made use of Feuerbach's projection theory, isn't among my favorites; I don't like his original "family" at all! He didn't show much of Feuerbach's compassion.[188]

The key to atheist denial is the problem of evil, some think, even though many of them now want to claim the key is science which can't know God but potentially knows everything else. The key to what I think about the matter is the answer to the question: do we experience our experiencing? Do we experience our understanding, our judgments, our decisions? Yes, we do. Check it out yourself. We are all reflectively conscious, even the atheist, and so we can experience our experiencing, our understanding, our judgments, our decisions. For a decade or so I took my first level experiencing to be the obvious source of my knowledge that God exists, that what I was experiencing (along with everything else *in my experiencing*) was God. But no, that is not the case. Our knowing is fitted to matter, to the finite, to "things out there" and "things in here," to objects and their relationships to us and other objects.

Perhaps, I decided, it is better said that God was *surrounding* me and my experience, as the horizon surrounds us when we stand on a hill. At least my experiencing was *accompanied* by what I call God, and who is always present to my experiencing even in its worst and most painful moments—such as being burnt at nine years old when I was crying out to Him to act in alleviating my pain. He didn't (the problem of evil!), but the "Presence" never ceased. I didn't like the fact that He didn't heal me instantly. The pain and His failure to act as I wanted was enough to turn a nine year old into an atheist. But no, all I did was complain to Him. I remember those many long months of severe depression when I wept in the seminary chapel asking why He wouldn't act to save me from depression. He didn't and, worse, He didn't tell me why. Or those years when I was sunk in anxiety over the celibate priesthood I couldn't stand; it took Him

---

188   Ludwig Feuerbach, *The Essence of Christianity* (Buffalo NY: Prometheus Press, 1989); George Santayana, *The Life of Reason: Reason in Religion* (Classic Books, 2010); Sigmund Freud. *The Future of an Illusion* (NY: W.W. Norton & Co., 1989).

(and me) fifteen years to set me free.

However, the absence of God's action to help me did not undercut the fact of His "Presence", the "Light" (yes, more metaphors!) within that never went out. It was the Presence, the "Light" within that enabled me to answer Professor Frankel's question, "Do you mean to tell me you *know* that God exists?" with such firmness and conviction. I might shilly-shally in my many moment of philosophical reverie when I wasn't on the spot, but Frankel put me on the spot. I was conscious of God's presence to my experiencing, understanding, judging and deciding, but the odd thing was that God was not anything else, and He wasn't *gegenstand*: God wasn't *in* the "field of my experience." The new atheists like Richard Dawkins and Christopher Hitchens are "in my field of experience," I know that in all probability they exist (there are the videos!), but God is not in the "field" and there is no video. How could I "experience" God when God wasn't a thing *in* my experience? If God wasn't a thing *in* experiencing, how could I know that He exists? Experiencing God ("Light") isn't like experiencing anything else, for God isn't *in* experience. Once again, how could I know what scientists, philosophers and I couldn't see? It would seem that Dawkins and Hitchens have the best of the argument. They are so convinced that they mock me and my people as poor delusional folk: How can you possibly know what you (we) can't experience? Something that is a no-thing? But we religious people can understand the atheist mistake: they think that if God isn't an entity He can't exist!

Of course some would claim that what I was experiencing was my own experience, my own consciousness, my own sense of "being" and of acting. True. No argument here, for like atheists I am reflectively conscious. Bridget, my greyhound, "knows" she exists, as I know that she and I exist, but she doesn't run into David Hume or Sam Harris on her daily walk. Therefore, she is not forced to stop and think about it. She doesn't read or speak or hear others speak about this deep mystery. She just takes existence for granted, and does what she does. She's equipped for that and carries it out with moderate intelligence (she's no Australian sheep-dog or honey badger when it comes to brains!) She knows that her dish is filled with hamburger and rice and doesn't stand there wondering as we might were we confronted with Manna in the desert. (Exodus 16: 4ff.) She wonders, however, when she sees a rapidly moving fury animal thirty yards ahead, her ears rise to the occasion and her nostrils quiver like mad, and she wants with desperation to check it out to decide what to do. If she experiences God, she doesn't know it because she doesn't reflect on her own experience, but I do and so do other people who know God exists. She learns but she doesn't reflect, which she has to do if she is to know how she knows. And that's the catch. She sees the fat grey rabbit in the brush but doesn't sit and wonder about it.

Our atheist friends would say that I don't know that God exists; they would say I know that I exist. I am my own "companion," not God. Maybe, but not likely. *It* (the Presence) just doesn't feel like me at all. They would say that I'm surely experiencing but not God. When I experience me I do not experience God, they would say. I began to think that I was experiencing God, as if I had a sixth sense, a third eye that could "see" God. But this grew less and less likely a solution as I began to "feel" (= was conscious of) God's Presence more as an experienced companion and an Absence as an object. I wasn't "sensing" God in any of the five senses and, even if I had some sort of sixth sense, God is not an object to be grasped by any number of senses (i.e., God is "Absent"). God is what I am reaching for. I am not projecting; I am chasing what must be "there" to be chased. As the mystics might put it, God chases me, too. We're both rabbits and greyhounds, but full of wonder.

Whatever I would "grasp" couldn't be God. When I "grasp" I grasp the world of things or I "grasp" me because I can be a thing to myself. God is some "Other" that simply eludes me as an object and isn't me and isn't anything else. Again, God is not an object. Once I turn myself to myself, I am an object to myself. God isn't an object to any of my senses. God is a Presence. My greyhound Bridget experiences, understands, judges and decides but (a) she doesn't seem to experience her experiencing, understanding, judging and deciding, that is, she's not *reflectively* conscious, just conscious; and (b) she is evidently interested in me in her limited way for I am an object in her experience but I see no evidence that she has any interest in God. When I talk to her about going OUT or ask if she is HUNGRY, she cannot sleep. She gets excited. Whenever I try to talk to her about my experience she goes to sleep, and that, would say my atheist friends, is exactly what I should do when I start talking about a God who cannot be sensed! Remember John Wisdom's wonderful parable of the invisible Gardener who couldn't be detected in the garden in any way. Therefore, God was not existent in any reasonable sense? To exist, for Wisdom, is to be an object.

So, have I talked myself into a conundrum? A cul-de-sac? A dead end? Almost, but not quite. When I question (i.e. reflect upon) my commonsense experience, understanding, judging, deciding and acting, I simply cannot deny that there is not just me but a Presence to me, the "other side" of my finitude, and an Absence from my field of knowing but a Presence to all my knowing and loving that is haunting and *here*. No ghost this, no dream, no wish, just a heading for, an intention of, what's beyond and behind all else that I know and love. And by reflecting, I know what I already knew by my experiencing, understanding, judging, deciding and acting. Pay attention, brothers and sisters, not to me but to yourselves. Reflect. Bend back on yourself! You, too, will know what you already knew. You will also understand why some people think that God doesn't exist, in fact *can't* exist: God isn't in any way in front of them. God isn't a thing.

The "Inner" and the "Outer Word" are terms proposed by two Jesuits, Bernard Lonergan and Karl Rahner. The first is the Word "spoken within," as Christians would have it, by the Holy Spirit and the Outer Word spoken in the history of the Jews and in their scripture, and in the revelation of God in Christ. They are both free gifts, according to Catholic tradition, the one working on all human beings to orient them toward God and the other working through the church's preaching and living the Gospel and through the witness of Jews. Since I assume that the Inner Word is given to all who do not refuse it and that the Outer Word is *meant* for all, I am going to assume that it is given to atheists as well as to all believers and potential believers, and, realize it or not, we are all in the same "language game." Atheists don't take the same stand that I do but I am going to assume that the Inner Word is working in them and Revelation beckons to them. It is the same with me. They are sisters and brothers of mine in the Presence even though they haven't realized it yet. They are taken by the Absence. It's a difficult thing to *think* the problem of God through, though we, all of us, *know* already that God exists. God doesn't *appear* and so doesn't *appear to exist*. All I can say to those who, like me, are caused to wonder about this complex practical and philosophical issue is, "re-flect!" Drop the materialist mistake, namely, "the real is what you can feel." I'm not proving anything here; I'm indicating a line of self-reflection that I am sure other self-reflective beings can explore. My mother and father weren't philosophers, nor am I, and they would surely be disturbed by the atheist's argument but they'd end up following the Light they have "seen" rather than the darkness proposed by Monod among others. They were not tricked nor did they trick themselves. My parents knew and let life flow from there. The mystery here isn't that my parents experienced God's presence; the mystery is that atheists and agnostics don't get it. As for who's right and who's wrong, we can do no more than struggle under the burden and limits of our human existence, waiting for the ice to break, "waiting for Godot."

***

So, in the end I ask myself: what are you doing, Bill? My answer is this: I am trying to put into words the origins in practice, in the world of commonsense, of my feeble and failing attempts at a life of sanctity and of theory which are, as it turns out, a search for a sanctity given with life itself, and for reasons for what I already knew by common sense to be the case. To sum it up, in this book I mean to be a religious man, a Catholic Christian who has been worrying the old bone of faith and reason for half a century, who learns a bit here and there, who cannot leave off arguing internally with himself, with those whose form of life and language differs from and sometimes contradicts that of my own community, and whose understanding of my community differs from my own. This effort is worthwhile if it conveys, even in a small way, Catholic convictions about reason, faith, church and culture. Like musicians, we have to make a living but we play on even when we're not being paid. The fact is that we *love* the music. Cacophonous as the music too often sounds, I hope to go on playing forever. Laying down the pen, turning off the Apple Mini will be a sorrowful moment. The joyful side of this moment is that I will no longer need the pen or the Apple. The music is eternal, I believe, and the band is already playing.

Appendices

Appendix 1.

Early Thoughts on Leaving the Priesthood—August 1969

The following essay was written during the summer of 1969 and published in the alumnae journal of the College of New Rochelle. Although it is presented as an analysis of reasons for the sky-rocketing number of defections from the priesthood at that time including the chaplain of the college just the year before, the essay reflects the personal struggle of the author. Toward the end, it be-comes whiney. I wouldn't write that part today.

To think with accuracy and moderation about the decision facing priests today is no easy task. Most priests and a rapidly increasing number of laymen have friends who have left the practice of the ministry. It is an upsetting experience for the friends as well as for the priests themselves. However, beyond the priests and their friends and others who may have had some direct share in this painful business, there are others who are variously mystified, hurt or angered by it. There are also, unfortunately, the scoffers who can find in such things a playground for cynicism and verbal cruelty.

This article is a comment on the experience of leaving the priest-hood. I am a priest, although not a very good one by many stan-dards. Among the many personal failings that have injured my ministry there is a marked lack of dedication and stability of in-tention. Some might even call it a lack of faith. At any rate, that instability is heightened when a friend or acquaintance leaves the priesthood. I am affected and frightened by it, confused and threat-ened by it. I was ordained what seems to be many years ago into a life that, for all its difficulties, was secure and stable and completely without second thoughts. It is no longer so with the priesthood. To think and write now about the matter of leaving the priesthood is not, then, merely to write and think about others. We all come to the subject with personal feelings and questions.

It may be well to point out at the outset that the abandonment of the ministry on a large scale is not, in my opinion, a first-level problem. By this I mean that it is a symptom of a disturbance rather than a cause. It is the result of factors that are not to be explained in terms of human frailty or unfaithfulness or even lust. The men who are leaving the priesthood are not particularly frail; they are as faithful as most of their confreres who remain; they can be no more accused of any of the seven deadly sins than their predecessors.

Before seeking out their sin, it might be well to ask another range of questions such as the life they have lived, the families they have come from, the kind of men they are, the kind of men they have worked with and under, the kind of communities they have served, what they expected of the priesthood, and what, in fact, they experienced in it. To come to any satisfactory and reasonably objective understanding of the matter requires sociological, psychological and unobtainable spiritual data on the Catholic community as well as on the men themselves. At any rate, simplistic explanations are to be avoided as assiduously as moral judgments. It cannot be the purpose of this article to attempt an explanation or render divine judgment, but to make some few remarks on three aspects of the problem that occur to me as important, namely:

1. The suffering involved for the man;
2. Celibacy and its relation to the decision;
3. The need of the church and the meaning of the priesthood.

What I advance are personal views, or, better, ruminations which I hope will be of help in clarifying the readers' own views on the subject. My views arise from some degree of personal experience and highly emotional questioning and conviction. I beg the reader to read *cum grano saltis.*

1. The suffering experienced and caused by a man who decides to leave the ministry can be imaginatively represented in a series of three concentric circles: parish, family and self. He suffers in making his decision because others suffer. He does not, with ill will, wish to abandon his ministry or his people, yet in fact he does and this causes his people pain, doubt, confusion, anger. Even

those friends in the community who most fully accept and even understand why he decides as he does feel a definite loss, and that feeling is more profound in relation to the excellence of his ministry.

It would be reasonable to say that in most cases a great deal of pain is inflicted on family, parents and close relatives. This is not only because they are Catholics and perhaps opposed to the choice on religious grounds, although this certainly has its place. One would have to experience the pride of Catholics in their priest son and their high regard for the priesthood to appreciate how deep a disturbance this causes. But the pain goes far beyond disturbed pride and religious conviction. It reaches to the simple suffering of parents with a son whose life in not peaceful and joyous, whose hopes have not been met, who has attempted seriously to give his life in one way and now faces the prospect of a radical change. If one has experienced the level of suffering in a family in which a divorce has taken place one has some idea of the dislocation which results in the family of a priest who decides to change his life's course.

And then there is the personal upheaval endemic to the change. One begins at fourteen or eighteen or twenty hoping and believing and praying and studying. Perhaps eight to ten years of seminary are followed by more years of ministry. One does not walk away from this without undergoing great struggle and without leaving a good piece of one's life behind. Leaving the priesthood is a form of death—followed, let it be hoped, by a rebirth—but death nonetheless. I know a number of men who have left the priesthood. None have left it easily or lightly or without the most anxious consideration. None have left without literally years of intense personal conflict. These are not shallow, superficial or uncaring men; in my experience the opposite is true.

The point of this all too brief mention of the agony of a man, or his family and friends, or those who were served by him, is to forestall any suggestion that leaving the priesthood is an easy matter for any man. To suggest that it is lightly accomplished or done without agony is to suggest that the men involved are less than sensitive human beings. On the contrary, their pain may be assumed to have been and, in all probability, continues to be great. The discussion, then, can take place only in an atmosphere of compassion, as a search for understanding and with a desire to help, wherever possible. The compassion called for overcomes the question of moral judgment, for such judgment is singularly out of place here. How does one go about making a moral judgment on the meaning or direction of a man's life?

2. I suppose some words should be written on the connection between the legal obligation of celibacy and the present situation of the priesthood. The subject of celibacy is a bore. How much a bore it has become is indicated in the recent New York Times report of the marriage of Bishop James Shannon was reported on page thirty-three, along with a bomb scare at a local Y.M.C.A. The matter is of little interest any longer. From the theological point of view the arguments for the retention of the western custom are presented in Pope Paul's recent letter on the subject, while the chief arguments against continuance were well put four hundred and fifty years ago by Martin Luther in his *Babylonian Captivity of the Church*. It may be doubted that much more in the way of theological insight will be made available before the law is changed or the situation settles as it is (the latter being a distinct possibility given the temper of the bishops on the matter).

The question here is not the law of celibacy, its evangelical quality, or its contribution to the holiness of the western clergy, but rather the connection between celibacy and the abandonment of the ministry. That there is some connection is evident: the men who leave the priesthood do not remain celibate. In all probability they leave in order to marry or at least open to the possibility. It would be foolish to deny that celibacy is a factor, but it is difficult to be precise as to the exact role it plays in the decision.

Why is it a factor at all? Didn't these men know what they were doing when they made their irrevocable commitment? The answer to this question is not so simple as it might seem or as some would like it. One could claim that they did and then denounce their unfaithfulness to their mature declaration; or claim that they didn't, that they were "too young" to make such a commitment (one wonders at what age one could make such a commitment at all then), thereby negating the value and meaning of the faithful celibacy of thousands who obviously meant what they said and have lived what they meant. Perhaps a personal comment might at least clarify one possible answer.

Yes, I did know what I was doing. I knew I could never marry. No, I didn't know what I was doing, for I had little idea what not being married would mean to a man of thirty three. This kind of answer is obvious, and it has probably gone through the mind of every married person as well as many priests. But I think there is a more influential factor at work in this matter than the growing knowledge of the implications of loneliness and sexual abstention.

I became a priest because I love the priesthood. I promised to remain celibate so that I could become a priest. I did not love celibacy then, and I don't love it now. When I promised to remain unmarried in order to become a priest, the link between celibacy and the priesthood was unquestioned. The thought that such a link was only man-made (as Luther put it) and so unnecessary and reversible did not enter my mind before the subject was raised on the Council floor by bishops. It suddenly dawned on thousands of priests that what was earlier a burden to be bourn (often with joy so great is the love of the priesthood) for the sake of the priestly *diaconia* was actually a decidedly unnecessary burden bourn because one man (Pope Paul VI) would not make one simple decision. That the decision would involve incalculable political and economic results for the Church is beside the point.

It is psychologically inevitable that once celibacy is not seen as God's will for Roman Catholic priests but rather as the popes' and bishops' will, many men begin to reconsider. That men should change their minds in such a situation is to be expected. It is doubly to be expected when changing one's mind can be understood as the heroic thing to do, when the 'prophets' begin to announce that they must, in conscience, oppose the Church by marrying, and this for the sake of the gospel. The latter may be the case with some few men if public statements are to be believed, but only with a few. The men who have made a decision to leave the priesthood have left quietly, with regret and with singularly un-heroic tread. We must assume that, after anguished consideration, they saw marriage as the more valuable option for themselves.

3.   Frequently enough the question is raised: would any of these men remain in the ministry if they were allowed to marry? This question moves us closer to the fundamental issue at stake in the priesthood today. My suspicion is that many would not. My further suspicion is that some men are leaving the priesthood because they are unhappy exercising the ministry and see no point in continuing, at great personal cost, a relatively meaningless and inconsequential task. I suggest that many do not leave a happy priesthood in order to marry more happily, or leave the priesthood because they are unhappy because they are celibate. We leave and marry after considerable disaffection in an unhappy ministry. We marry in hope of meaning and joy in a life which has precious little of either. Sexual love is notorious for its infusions of both meaning and joy on at least a temporary basis. For all of us hoped that the priesthood would be a meaningful and joyous, even if difficult, life. For many reasons and for many men, it has become flat and pointless.

This third part of this essay is an attempt to explore the point that the ministry is pointless in the minds of some priests and to suggest why that might be so. We set to one side, in other words, circumstances that might urge a change in the direction of one's life in any case. It is conceivable that a man might personally contribute far more to society and to the Christian community in some other ministry than the priestly one. That a change of direction under such circumstances should disturb anyone is ridiculous. Also set aside the psychological or relational problems that, in an individual case, might make the ministry exceedingly difficult. For example, the ministry might not be the place for a man who has severe problems dealing with authority figures. We set these aside in order to concentrate attention on a more significant aspect of the problem. Some men leave the priesthood because they no longer think it is valuable enough to continue.

At some point in their consideration, the priesthood as a life worth affirming at high cost is rejected. Something takes its place as worth a life and worth the considerable amount of suffering attached to abandoning it. I am suggesting that involved in the widespread flight from the priesthood is a crisis of meaning. I do not think that sex, neurosis, authority problems, and so forth, explain what is happening. The fact is that many men find no point in continuing. That this crisis is also a crisis of faith or belief, as some have suggested, is also possible. At any rate, if the problem is to be approached intelligently, it must be approached at least in part from this aspect. No number of surveys or psychological studies, nor any defensive episcopal denunciation will halt the flow of decent and healthy men from what they increasingly find to be a less meaningful occupation.

We priests have found so many safe, useful and tiring things to do with our time and energy that we have hardly begun to realize what the gospel demands of us and of our ministry. The laity, as is its own special wont, has been careful to avoid giving the impression that it wants or needs the gospel preached, has given its rewards to those who preach a semblance of it eloquently, softly and without sting, and has deftly cooperated in the turn off of those who may have preached it without favor. As ever they would rather be bored rather than challenged. I think that the priest is supposed to preach the gospel and break the bread. He is the servant of the church only in being a servant of the Word. I think this is all he is supposed to do by virtue of his office. I also think that this only *sounds* trite. The question, then, is: what is the priesthood all about? For it to be worth affirming, choosing and living at high cost it must meet a real and pressing need of the church and so possess possibilities of meaning which will attract and hold men in the present mess in Roman Catholicism. A number of the aspects of the ministry that attracted us to it initially, and the social and religious power that kept us and our predecessors happily employed are no longer operative.

A series of social, cultural and religious transformations have left the priesthood in a peculiar position. The theological notions that lay at the basis of the vocation in the past have vanished while, in many cases, the secondary roles become primary as numbers of priests trained and experienced in theology, the arts and the social sciences discover that the priesthood is of doubtful value to them. After all, one can teach, be a theologian, dedicate one's life to individual and social transformation or help reconstruct family life without offering Mass every day. One can even, in most cases, do any of these things more effectively outside the priesthood than in it. Why remain? Well, if there is nothing to be said for the ministry, if the ministry contributes nothing of unique value to the community, then, indeed, why remain?

If the ministry appears so valueless that men leave it in large numbers unwilling to bear the suffering involved in that ministry in what are admittedly the often absurd conditions of the American church, we cannot point only at the men and cry "derelict" with our bishops. We must face the fact that no segment of the American church can avoid responsibility for the situation: we have not valued the ministry as it should have been valued. We have malformed it; mistaken it, abused it. The episcopate has been so interested in filling work-slots with dedicated and chaste servants that it failed to educate its candidates for orders with anything approaching the qualities required for Christian witness. In fact, it appears that the American bishops are often willing to put up with anything from their clergy and even from one another except free witness to the gospel.

We priests have found so many safe, useful and tiring things to do with our time and energy that we have hardly begun to realize what the gospel demands of us and our ministry. And the laity, as is its own special wont, has been careful to avoid giving the impression that it wants or needs the gospel preached, has given its rewards to those who preach a semblance of it eloquently, softly and without sting, and has deftly turned off those who may have preached it without favor. As ever, they would rather be bored than challenged.

I think that the priest is supposed to preach the gospel and break the bread. He is a servant of the church only in being a servant of the Word. I think that is about all he is supposed to do by virtue of his office. I also think that this only *sounds* trite. He has not been trained to do either. He often enough doesn't really enjoy or want to do either, and if he happens to do both well and honestly, he suffers for it at the hands of his superiors and his people.

With this as background and with the present breakdown of the social and religious strictures formerly placed on "ex-priests," it is little wonder that men choose to find another thing to do. The things we used to hide in, pour our energy into, justify our existence with in place of preaching and praying no longer make sense. We can no longer even make them make sense! Bingo, day camps, Boy Scouts, Holy Name Societies, daily Mass in empty churches, sliding confessional doors, etc., simply do not fill the void. Many will find another way of life more valuable, productive and satisfying. Many are not happy in doing what they no longer believe valuable enough to hold them in the priesthood. It is in such a context that I would maintain that celibacy is an excuse rather than a cause for leaving the ministry.

The good of the priesthood, the meaning that makes its exercise so important to the Christian community, has been successfully clouded over. What one is brought to wonder if the clouding might have been more effectively managed if deliberately done. The priest is to be a mediator of the gospel, in his word and in his life. His special role in the community is a dedicated study of the Word of God in Scripture and the church's understanding of that Word. Secondly, he is to preach that Word where and when it is needed, in season and out of season, without fear or favor. He is to preach it as challenge, as rebuke, as exhortation, as judgment and consolation. Where witness to that gospel is to be bourn, he bears it in his flesh—whether his bishop or congregation approves of it or not. He is responsible to the Word, to the church's historical interpretation of the Word, and only then to a social order that we customarily call the Roman Catholic Church, to bishops and to the people.

Whether or not we can agree that Daniel Berrigan or Joseph Groppi are correct on the positions they have taken in their application, I think we can agree that they have taken their priestly ministry quite seriously precisely because they have taken the meaning of the gospel seriously.

A good number of theologians have taken the meaning seriously over the past couple of decades and have suffered for that. What they have in common is not their reflective understanding of the gospel in all its implication, but rather an admirable devotion to truth of God's Word in Jesus, to their decision to preach and live that truth. It is the task of the priest to know, preach and live the Word. We priests (your humble servant being first among the number) are not often known for our courageous preaching of and profound love for the gospel of Jesus Christ. When some bit of social or personal pressure is applied, we collapse rather readily.

Nor have we shown considerable interest over the years in prayer. By this I mean private prayer but I especially mean our lack of interest in community prayer. The most often heard complaint on this college campus is that liturgy is dull, lifeless and meaningless. We are prayers who are uninterested in praying, who resent any suggestion that prayer is our livelihood.

If this is correct, if preaching the Word and breaking the bread for the Christian people is the meaning of the priesthood, what is to be expected when these central aspects are ignored, circumscribed and perhaps even covered over? When substitute interests fail or become socially valueless, when one begins to doubt that they are so important to the life of the church that one must spend one's life on them, one won't spend one's life on them.

In some cases this crisis in meaning is also a crisis in

belief as well. Charles Davis pointed out last year in a brief article on the priesthood that the old myths are failing — we Catholics no longer believe in the myth of the church, he said. Be that as it may, there are some who claim, and perhaps rightly, that what is failing is our belief that the sacraments are important enough to spend our lives on. What is fading is our conviction that the Christian people need them both desperately, that they need us to do these things for them, that they need us, in other words, for far more than maintenance of the ecclesiastical machinery. In my opinion it is consider-ations such as these that will illuminate the decision of some men to leave the priesthood. In their minds the priesthood is simply not important enough to be both-ered about.

What has been attempted here is a clarification of some aspects of a problem that is second level and symptom-atic rather than radical and causative. Men are not leav-ing the priesthood in a flighty, irresponsible fashion but after long and frequently harrowing personal suffering. They are not being led out by lust—few of us are led anywhere by lust, it seems to me. The motives prompt-ing them are as complex as the motives that led them to the priesthood in the first place, as complex as those which hold us where we are now. The tendency on the one hand to explain "defection" as a result of surren-der to sexual need or on the other as rebellion against church structures, represent simplifications dangerous to the church, dangerous because, once accepted, they will block further and accurate understanding. Nor would either suggestion be acceptable to anyone ac-quainted with the men who have left the ministry.

There is an advantage to the present situation. Priests are faced with alternatives. They are called upon to grasp more profoundly or realize afresh the meaning of their task among Catholics; they may continue to live lives of frustration and anger; or they might quite sensibly leave the ministry. In the past only the first two were socially and religious acceptable. Now there is a third, and some are availing themselves of it. In my opinion the number in the second category should decrease, and the need to face the issue should confirm and increase the number who are attempting the first. The phenomenon, then, is a moment of grace for the church.

Appendix 2

Letter from a Priest

Reverend John B. Sullivan
Church of the Visitation
160 Van Courtland Park South
Bronx, New York 10463

May 30, 1967

Dear Bill,

It seems to be unusually quiet around here today, probably because of the holiday many people have gone away for the day.

But I can't help thinking about the many discussions I've been somewhat involved in with priest friends lately. They are certainly not the usual gripe-and-joke sessions that seem to have been the trend for the last few years. And, overall, I think we are better off for getting more serious.

I am particularly moved, for example, by your own statements about *leaving the priesthood if things don't change.* I have always admired your honesty and ability to draw logical conclusions even when the process of arriving at your conclusions costs great expense of your intellectual and spiritual energies.

I know I must be temperamentally different from yourself. And in addition I must be somewhat blind or naïve intellectually. But I do think I too am being honest.

I know that there are many things that need improvement in every area of our lives. If I could do anything that would certainly change things for the better, I would do that no matter how difficult it became for me personally. Since I can't be that certain about anything I might do having that effect, I choose to continue trying to do the small insignificant things, usually on a personal basis, that might help to give people encouragement to live with their difficulties for another day. I'm sure this was a factor in my decision to accept the priesthood. And I'm sure that the consolation and help that have come to many people through me is at the basis of my general satisfaction with the priesthood. I can't imagine doing nearly as much good in any other way than as a priest.

One thing I want to take back is what I said to you the other night about becoming a pastor sooner if a lot of priests decide to leave. You are right—nobody wants it, and really, I don't either. I believe a pastor is no more a priest than someone like ourselves—except that he can write checks and build; but he has no more real influence over people because of his "administrative" functions. I really didn't mean what I said even when I said it. I meant it as a kind of joke but it didn't come off that way I'm sure.

I certainly don't mean to be counseling you. I shall always respect you and your decisions regardless of where they take you. It's just that from my way of looking at the Church and the priesthood, *I don't know how you or anybody can make it better by leaving.*

And this is what prompted me to begin this letter that I figured not to be so long. You know, John Fitzgerald was here in my room only a few weeks ago. I deliberately said nothing while, for the first hour or so he spoke out with all his honesty and enthusiasm about what had to be done to make the Church meaningful.

When I did finally get a chance, I tried to remind him that unless he learned how to relate to his superiors, he was going to find himself out on a limb like DuBay. But he reminded me that DuBay, whatever we may think of his ideas, is still a priest even though suspended. *He is not quitting because things are not going his way.* Fitz would never have left either, I'm sure. And yet rather suddenly he is not with us anymore anyhow. Which to me is another real lesson that I am not very important, nor [is] anything I have to say about making things better or more meaningful. The Church and the Priesthood, too, is a lot bigger than any one of us. I prefer, perhaps naively, to let the Holy Spirit direct the structure as we now have it, and let changes develop without getting people upset.

Bill, keep well; I'll call you soon.

Celibately,

John

Appendix 3

Letters between a father and son July 1970

College of New Rochelle Summer Campus
Vinalhaven, Maine
July 14 1970

Dear Mom and Dad,

The second week begins today. Miss you. I can't, however, believe how easily I slip into the quiet routine here and how much I love it. Sometimes I think I was born at the wrong time and in the wrong place. Maybe an 18th century millionaire I should have been. This year we've got a working motorboat and have spent hours riding around the cove and the outlying islands, and even a couple of hours fishing, during which I caught a dogfish (small shark) which pulled the hook right off the line. Beautiful. Also getting a good deal of work done. Had an idea today on a thesis topic that sounds pretty good. The Naturalists have done a good deal of writing on the subject of the development of knowledge in Catholic-Christian thought from its beginning. I think they are mistaken, but I might try to do a study of what they think is our "mistake." The advantage of this topic is that it's on a subject that interests me and the topic is sufficiently limited that I won't have to spend the rest of my life working on it. So—I'll think it over gradually as I read and see if there is enough material to work on.

Sisters Mary Alice Gallin and Nancy Malone and I are alone here until Sr. Rose and Sister Anne (the last dinner companions at home) join us on July 25. We've been talking quite seriously each night for two or three hours about the state of Christian life on campus and about ways of meeting the religious problems of the campus population. The discussions have been very fruitful because they have been personal rather than organizational or abstract. We've really been talking about ourselves and our own mission at the college, criticizing and reconstructing our own approaches to our Christian life. They are fine women.

And, of course, I've been doing a lot of ruminating about the future
and about my own decisions with regard to it. As usual (but with
much less upset than usual), I swing back and forth, depending
on my mood. I still don't know which way to move. I'm 'hung up'
as they say now. I'm strongly moved in about six different directions at once. I want very much to teach full time. But I can't quite
get over the pull to do something for and in the diocese. Hung up
there. I suppose I won't know what to do—I'll just have to decide
and take my chances. But there is time yet for that. There is the
problem lurking in the background—the desire to chuck the whole
thing, to go off and do my own thing, to work and maybe marry
and become just an ordinary human being struggling with the ordinary things of life—but then I think this is a kind of day-dream
and a 'cop-out' instead of an answer to anything. I think though
that the important new element in the situation is a sense of calm-
ness gradually sneaking over me, and a sense that, with the grace
of God, things will work out well, that the decisions will be the best
ones and that they will be right, if not easy. I know I need to trust
God and to trust myself—neither of which I have ever managed to
do in the past. I also know that I must begin to pray seriously, another thing I have not done much of. One of the mainstays in all this
has been the attitude of support and affection that these sisters and
many others at the college have shown to me. Thank God for them.

Hincmar [ed. my Spoodle] is doing splendidly –he seems to have
grown visibly in the past two weeks. He's taken to life here, of
course, but still has trouble with swimming—he doesn't like it yet.
But we're trying a bit at a time getting him into it. Made another
discovery—he gets car sick. Upchucked all over the back of the car
and all over Sister Nancy on the way up, and once since we've arrived. I hope this is something he will get over.

I'll write again in a week or so. I want to try to get a letter together
to the Vicar General with regard to options for the future to kind of
let him know what I'm thinking. I'll make a copy and send it along
if I ever get around to doing it.

I'm really very well and enjoying myself enormously. Thanks for
your patience, understanding and love. See you soon.

Bill

W.P. Shea
2563 St. Raymond's Avenue
Bronx 10461 NY
July 18, 1970

Dear Bill,

Glad you are enjoying yourself.

Mom and I read your letter more than once so that we can try to understand your train of thought. We are both puzzled about your failure up to now to set a fixed goal in life and strive for a worthwhile conclusion. I'm sure you realize better than we that you are thirty five years old and that you have about thirty years left to accomplish whatever you finally decide on. Most young men and women have made their decisions by age twenty five yet you still "fiddle" while "Rome burns."

Ten years ago you made a monumental decision and it was the happiest day of your life. So you said at that time and we believed it and we still believe it. We still hope you will recall that day and dwell on it for a while. Perhaps the inspiration of that day will rekindle the fire of dedication and love for others. Today even more than ten years ago the human race is crying out for knowledge and leadership, both of which you are capable of imparting. I am fully aware of this long period of preparation for the future and the need for it. I can also appreciate your indecision and puzzlement at times. But I cannot see or understand your lack of faith in yourself. You seem to take life as a tool or a toy to play with—to pick the best apples off the tree—to indulge too much in self-analysis and occasionally in self-pity.

May I say now as your father that you have more right now than most people—a good brain, a good physique, good health—mental and physical stability—priceless knowledge—and best of all you have God on your side, if you will only take a good look—a long look.

Use all the resources God has given you—and you have plenty—to good advantage. Help others who have much less than you. I believe that is what you are preparing yourself for. Share the apples! You know, too many can give you a bellyache (Parent-Child Manual).

Ask yourself, am I happier now than I was ten years ago—after all the 'goodies'? If I have more will my personal life be better? Will the frivolities of life make things more bearable? I suppose that, though, is a form of paganism. But I can't help philosophizing occasionally. There is not one day of complete happiness in this life, and I've had over sixty years of them. Forgive an old man for remembering and rambling on like this. But I must remind you that you and Tim are the only compensation God gave us for the hell of this life. And we can't help but being concerned about your compensation. What is it going to be? What hell do you have to go through for your reward? Is the choice wholly yours or do you look for inspiration? If so where do you look? You have many blessings, much more than others. Be thankful. You have many faults, much less than others. Still be thankful. We are thankful for you and Tim and how! The hell was worth it.

Think of your immediate problem only right now. And stick with it. Don't try to outguess God about the future. There are too many intangibles.

Love,
Mom and Dad

W.M. Shea
Vinalhaven Maine
July 24, 1970.

Dear Dad,

Thank you for your excellent letter and for your words of admonishment and encouragement. You take your responsibilities seriously and I'm glad that you do. And it is good, too, to know that I can count on you for an honest and direct response.

I'm really not all that sure how to respond to what you have said. Some of it (the remarks on self-analysis, self-pity, etc.) you've said before. The suggestion that I'm reaching for 'apples' is new in form but not in content. I think I suspected that you thought that I haven't been taking my responsibilities seriously enough—that I've been treating life as a toy—that I haven't been serving others as I should. Of course these are hard judgments to face. I'm sure that they are hard for you to make and that you are sad that such should be the case with me. I won't agree or disagree here with any of them. There would be no point in doing so. They are the kinds of questions that have plagued me all along, at every step of this path that has caused you and Mom such concern. I guess to a certain extent your remarks are justified and to a certain extent not. But there is little that can be accomplished in a letter on these issues.

One question I would like to raise. That is your suggestion that life is hell. I used to think that that is true, purely and simply with no qualifications. In those days (seminary, Yonkers, Pelham Manor) just staying where I was and functioning (walking, talking, doing some work of some sort—sometimes a great deal of work) was incredibly hard—it was hell. It was duty, it was God's will, etc. But it was a life lived in and because of fear and anxiety. Now, you may think life is supposed to be lived in fear and anxiety; you may think that life IS that way. I don't. I simply cannot believe that my life should be joyless, blind, anxious, and fearful.

Now, what I ask myself is this: how come my life is this way? Is there anything that could and should be done about it? What I'm doing right now is trying to answer those two questions in my living—not in thinking or speculation but in living. If, in fact, I can't live differently than I have lived for the first thirty years of my conscious life, then I don't want to live the second thirty. In other words, if life is hell (the hell having nothing to do with physical pain or hunger, etc.] then I don't even want to live. I don't think, honestly, that the priesthood has anything to do with my PAST unhappiness. That unhappiness springs from myself and not from the priesthood.

So, as I said in my letter, leaving the priesthood is not going to solve anything. I'm fully aware of that. If I thought it would solve anything I would have left already. If I think that leaving the priesthood makes sense I shall leave it. At present, it makes no sense at all. So I won't leave it—at present. What I will not do, in the priesthood or out of it, is live like a dumb animal. I will not live in blind, life-long pain without reason, and I will not live in sin. I will try to live a life that is purposeful, decent and full. And I want to do this because I think that life should be this way. Even pain, even hell should have some reason to it. I simply will not live any longer without reason.

You suggest that I analyze too much. I take that to mean (I may be wrong) that I shouldn't be wasting my time asking questions about myself and my past; that that questioning and turning within are debilitating and pulling me away from others. It appears to be another form of egoism. You may be right. I am a selfish man—I have been in the past and I probably will go on being selfish in the future in various ways. But because I am or have been selfish, should I put the questions aside? Should I not try to figure out what has caused me to be an unhappy man, what caused me to be depressed and miserable, what causes me to be afraid, what causes me to run away from people, what causes me to sin? And, above all, should I not try to change those things about myself that have brought me to where I am? I'm not shirking responsibility for myself. I am trying to take responsibility for myself for the first time in some conscious way, with deliberation.

I know that this is a gamble. Maybe the way is the wrong way. Perhaps I should have stayed in my parish slugging it out. Maybe I should just forget the questions and go on "doing things" for people. I know I may be wrong. I know I may be wasting time and my life. I know it's a risk. But I've tried the other thing for a long time and it didn't work. I'm trying this in the hope that it will work. It shows signs of success. I will press it for more success. I will abandon it if it doesn't work, and not one minute earlier.

Above all, I am sorry that all this has been a source of concern to you and Mom. Things have not worked out for and with me as happily as you might have wished, and I'm sorry that they haven't. For whatever pain I may have contributed to your already difficult lives I am sorry. But you will have to be patient for some time to come, perhaps for a long time to come. You will have to concentrate a bit more on living your own lives and a bit less on watching and worrying about mine. One of the things that I am angry and frustrated about is that I know how difficult for you all this is—and how helpless you are in it. All I can say for sure is that things are better with me than they ever have been, and appear to be getting better, and that there is little likelihood that a miracle will occur. So I expect to go on haltingly and with mistakes and with very slow progress for the next few years. In the meantime I intend to go on working with and for people who need whatever help I can give. It is precious little perhaps, but I shall try to give it.

The second thing I regret and that I am sorry about is the fact that we don't talk about us. I avoid it. I fear getting upset and causing you difficulty. What will happen if we don't change this situation is what happened before—you will be presented with a situation that creeps up on you without your being aware of it. I will go on treating you as less than human beings, treating you like people who are to be humored and kept happy and who are not to be told the truth. I will go on entertaining and acting the fool and socializing with you. More dinners, more drinks. More evasion. More verbal game playing. And you will not tell me what you really think about yourselves and about me. I sometimes think we will all die without having said some really important things to one another. Well, we must try, mustn't we?

Your letter upset me as mine did you, but that's not a bad thing. We should be upset. There's a lot to be upset about, and it's not all on my end.

So, the vacation goes well. Work continues. See you on August fourth or so.

Bill

Appendix 4

Homily at the Funeral Liturgy for William Patrick Shea—May 1977

The prophet Ezechiel spoke his word among a broken and enslaved people. So low had they been brought by Babylon's armies that he could liken them only to a valley of dry bones where death reigned as king. But there is another king, he told them—Yahweh, the giver of life. Ezechiel promised them, in the midst of their desolation, the breath of a new life. Be still as bones, he urged them, for the wind of God will blow. And you will live again!

Saint Paul taught the church in Corinth that an astounding thing had happened. Because God appeared in the life and work of a poor Galilean carpenter, the wisdom and power of the world was now foolishness and weakness. The ones who thought they held salvation by right, by special knowledge, by membership in a caste or clan or class, were deluded. Salvation belongs to the simple, the trusting, the outlanders, the ones who cling to the name and teaching of Jesus—Jesus who is God's foolishness, the foolishness that turns out to be wisdom. Who had ever thought that dying brings life—or that poverty is really wealth.

"Choose," Jesus said, "Choose." Which is it to be? Will you make your own way, or will you allow your Father to make a way for you? Will you cling to Him and seek His justice? Or will you snatch and grab at all the things that will finally betray you? Will you trust the one who can be trusted? Or will you trust yourself, the least trustworthy of all?

There are, then, three teachings here:

- You cannot get life; God alone gives it.
- There is no special secret to salvation; it is found in the ordinary lives of ordinary people, in their living and trusting and loving and dying.
- The only way with the Father of Jesus is the whole way.

You either give yourself to Him or you make a huge mess of your existence.

My father knew these three things, not because he read the New Testament but because he did them. He was not a theologian; he was a good Christian who spoke with God his Father and was taught by God his Father.

My father gave me only one piece of advice about how to be a priest. He listened to priests for fifty years before I was ordained. He said priests sounded like they knew what death and life were about, but they didn't know anymore than anyone else. So he told me not to talk down to people, because I didn't know anymore about being born and dying than they did—or he did—or you do. Well, he was right. On such matters he was rarely wrong.

He was a tough man. He had to be. Life was tough and he met it on its own terms. He was tough and proud and stubborn. He was a loyal man. He did not turn his back on people and he was loyal to his word. He was a loving man. The loving was fierce and demanding and final. He didn't just say he loved people—he did it with his heart and head and body. He was a truth teller. He sometimes made people uncomfortable with his truth—but it was his truth, the best he had to give, and he gave it, come hell or high water. He was an honest man. He worked for fifty years with other people's money and never took a penny of it. He could have taken it but he didn't.

He loved learning, always, from the hours he spent as a young immigrant in the public library in Brooklyn to his last four years seeking a college degree. He wanted to understand. It was an overwhelming passion. He wanted to understand what his life and my life and your lives are for. He looked for clues in anthropology, sociology, psychiatry, literature, and even theology. He was not terribly impressed with what he found.

Even the theologians didn't explain much to him. He once asked me if a book by the Protestant theologian John Macquarrie was any good. He was reading it at the time. I said it was. My father asked me to read a paragraph in the book. I stumbled through it, trying to make sense of the professional theological jargon. He asked me if I knew what metaphysics was, and I said I thought I did. He asked me to take another look at the paragraph. Macquarrie had used the word metaphysics in three different senses in that one paragraph.

He then said to me: "Do you write stuff like that?" My father was not only a very truthful man; he was a smart man.

But best and clearest of all about him, beyond even his loyalty and unending demand to understand was his trust in God. The thing that amazed me most about all this was that the God he trusted in at age sixty-seven was the same God he had learned about from his parents in Ireland. No priest ever taught him more than his parents had. The God he trusted in was the one who brought him through—through the loss of his homeland, through the voyage, through a lonely landing on an empty pier, through two-dozen depression-time jobs, through sickness and poverty. There were only two loves that touched his deep loneliness—his love of God and his love of my mother. Trusting God was the central fact of his life. Marrying my mother was the smartest and best thing this very smart and good man ever did.

He prayed like a child. I remember him in church. I would watch him when I was a child. His face was the face of a child, trusting in a Father he couldn't understand. And, wonder of wonders, God brought him through. Till today.

I couldn't do anymore and you can't do anymore for him today than to trust, to entrust him, to turn him over to his God. We might even twist the mocking words of the enemies of Jesus into a prayer. They looked up at Him as Jesus died and screeched out their mocking wisdom: "He trusted in God, let God deliver him." So be it. My father trusted in God. May God deliver him.

Appendix 5

Some Thoughts on Liturgy Preliminary to a Conversation

The following was prepared for a discussion with four or so friends while I was a resident scholar at Harvard Divinity School in 1976-77. My father had died a month before this was composed. I had been engaged over the previous ten months in weekly consultation with William Connolly, S.J. on my practice of the priesthood and Christian life.

June 22, 1977
William M. Shea
St. Jerome's Parish
Arlington MA

The relation between liturgy and my life is the first question. I shall try to sketch some of the elements of an answer to that [question] in historical form. I am quite sure that I became a priest in order to celebrate Mass. The only two seminary studies I took with full seriousness were [courses in] scripture and [the] history and theology of liturgy. I considered my ministry from the beginning to be liturgical and homiletic. I can't say that I liked very much the other aspects of the priesthood. Vatican II liturgical reform was welcomed and, in fact, had been anticipated by some four years [1961-65] of celebrating Mass.

All along, I expected and hoped that being a liturgical minister would mean "salvation" for me and that my celebration would bring salvation to others. I put enormous psychic energy over twenty-five years, and physical and intellectual energy over twelve years into liturgy. I was disappointed. It didn't "save" me or anyone else so far as I can tell. It's very important, sometimes very nice, but not quite what the theologians of the last couple of decades have cracked it up to be, even at its best.

I suspect that a good deal of the false expectations and later disappointment has to do with my spiritual sensibilities. They are decidedly pre-Vatican II sensibilities in a post-Vatican II age. I have no lack of sympathy for priests who still have and will continue to have trouble adjusting to new demands in ministry. I am shot through in the feeling side with individualistic and un-communal feeling tones in an age when ministers and liturgy are expected to "build community." I cannot quite place myself in a community, never mind build one up or serve one with ease. Liturgy, when I let myself "be" is to me precisely what it was when I was fifteen (1950). I have intellectually pushed well beyond that point but have not moved very much with regard to sensibilities. A second feeling connected with this is that I often experience liturgy as a judgment on my failure to live as a Christian—without any complementary release or transformation and no actual change in the way I live.

The result of the clash between knowledge, feeling and the present context of [Catholic] Christian worship is very painful for me and has been so for some ten years. I am at a loss on how to solve it and do not believe I ever will. Although there are times (the past year at St. Jerome's Church in Arlington MA, for example] when I can celebrate the liturgy somewhat unselfconsciously and without inner conflict, the conflict in the past has been very difficult and even these somewhat better days are threaded with and colored by wounded and conflicted feelings. My experience of the liturgy for the past decade has been largely an experience of conflict, guilt and self-doubt. It is no wonder, then, that I get somewhat nervous when I hear liturgical experts saying that persons should not be ordained when they show limited ability or interest in or happiness with liturgy. I wouldn't have been ordained myself under any such conditions.

However, it is clear to me that I love liturgy very much. The question is *what* I love. I wish it were for me what it seems to be for others. At [its] best it is two things: (a) a deep sense of the presence of God to me (whether I attend or officiate seems to make little difference here) which occurs in private prayer as well, and (b) sometimes a sense of belonging to a people and benefitting a community, and *occasional* joy at my being able to do this thing. But the community, in fact, often enough gets in the way of the consciousness of God for me. I *feel* the liturgy as attention to God and *feel* the actual attention to an actual community in worship is a distraction.

On the other hand, I am made furious and almost physically sick by the banalization of the liturgy when it is manipulated to create what I suspect is a shallow feeling of Christian community with very little moral and theological substance to it. I hate to see the liturgy used to fill the ego needs of the celebrant and to touch the feeling needs of the congregation when what is actually being offered is empty of gospel value. I am far better able to take mumbled, and even inattentive liturgy than I can stand such use of the liturgy even when in form it is quite well carried out.

The best I can manage with liturgy now is to do it prayerfully and seriously, including preaching which I take quite seriously. I am unable now to get into planning and working on liturgy as I once did. Such activities either bore me or upset me. By doing it as carefully and seriously as possible I mean to minimize any mockery of God such as mentioned in the last paragraph. I try to tell people what I think about the gospel as simply, directly and forcefully as I can.

I celebrate the liturgy when I am asked to do so. I never, or very rarely, offer to do so. I know and am convinced that liturgy is important to handing on, interpreting and making clear the gospel message and can allow a profound sense of God's presence. But the dimension of "celebration" and "community" can be focused in other ways. Celebration and community building are almost entirely absent from my consciousness when I offer Mass.

The liturgy allows me to focus attention on God. Occasionally, in either the scripture reading or homily I see something about life and God that I didn't quite see before, and I love those moments and they make all the rest of it worthwhile. But those moments are rare and seem not to make very much difference to the way I live. Sometimes, when liturgy is very well done, I am aesthetically pleased by it. It need not be done in the classical mold (although I like it better that way) to please me; occasionally contemporary music and forms seem to do. But the liturgy rarely helps my connection with other Christians—except to remind me that they are there. This might not be an entirely empty service when I think of it.

Most of all the liturgy provides me with a situation in which I can pray or better, be present to God. My sense of God's presence is often better focused in liturgy than elsewhere, but that sense is always with me and can be focused in other ways. What I like to do very much is attend Mass in the church I was baptized in and brought up near and still go to Mass when at home. I haven't celebrated Mass there in years [recently my father's funeral liturgy] and don't really want to. My sense of belonging to a family and a parish and a people and a tradition is sharpened at such moments. And this is also what happens to me at liturgy elsewhere without the special poignancy of the home church. But I often question all this "sense of tradition" since I am singularly uninterested in the people with whom I worship.[189]

It is, then, hard to answer the second question: what should one bring to the liturgy to make it a "good" liturgy. Liturgy is good when it makes possible an affirmation of one's own and the world's existence, when one can say because of this or that liturgy that life and the world are worthwhile. What one must bring is a heart open to that possibility that life is a gift rather than a curse, and some conviction regarding the connection between Jesus and that gift. One would hope, though it may often not be true, that the priest and the congregation want God and are willing to pay for Him (the cross). Like the clergy, when liturgy is good, it is very, very good; and when it is bad it is horrid. In the case of both my advice would be that of the psalmist: put your trust in the Lord, not in the liturgy. Or in the clergy. Or, for that matter, in the community. Or the church.

Which liturgical experience would I carry with me into the future? If that means which liturgical celebrations meant enough to me to be remembered I would list: my first Eucharist as a priest, one Eucharist I celebrated in an Italian parish in Yonkers; two final profession masses for Ursuline nuns; and my father's funeral liturgy [He died two months ago]. The rest, as liturgy as distinct from various kinds of happiness surrounding them, I could well leave behind. The only liturgy I look forward to [anticipate?] is my mother's funeral liturgy.[190]

---

189   This is either hyperbole or flatly untrue. I can't imagine now why I wrote it.

190   The essay as a whole, especially its peculiar take on liturgical celebration, seems to me now the words of a confused and lonely man.

Appendix 6

The Last Homily

I was intensely conscious of the fact that I would never preside the Eucharist again, ending what had been up to this point my chief vocational concern and chief element in my self-understanding. Celebrating at St. Rose and with its wonderful people had brought me out of my long liturgical funk. The tension of decades had faded. When Mass was over I left the parish relieved and happy. The decision had been made and was now going into effect.

St. Rose Parish
Gaithersburg MD
December 18, 1979
Third Sunday in Advent

It was not long after I began to preach some eighteen years ago that I realized that preaching did as much or more for me as it did for those who listened. Simply put, the task of preaching demanded that I attempt to step outside the morass and confusion of my own life and attempt, for the sake of others, to meet the Word of God on its own terms. This is not easy. The mood of the preacher has a great deal to so with the content and tone of his preaching—that is, his life shapes his preaching if his preaching is to be of value to others. And there is nothing wrong with this. Quite the contrary: if the preacher's own life does not appear in his preaching, he is not preaching at all. He is merely reciting. Ralph Waldo Emerson said in his Address at the Harvard Divinity School 150 years ago that preaching should be life passed through the fires of thought. And so it should be for every preacher worth his keep. And the listener after a while will know the difference between the preacher who recites or entertains, and the preacher whose own experience of life and death shapes his words.

But for every preacher there is more at stake than his own mood or experience. We Christians not only believe that God pours out his Spirit in our hearts, in our life's experience, in our own joy and suffering; we also believe that God has spoken in the heart, mind, life and death of one special man, Jesus of Nazareth. The scriptures are the church's memory of his words and deeds, and so the memory of God's words and deeds in our collective history. In the act of preaching, personal and collective histories meet. In preaching is found the Word of God uttered in the life of the preacher and the Word of God uttered in Christ Jesus. And so the mood and insight of the preacher are corrected, expanded, and even contradicted by the Word uttered in Christ.

This is, from my point of view, the great benefit and joy of preaching for the preacher: he is not alone, he does not speak his word alone, it is not his experience and suffering and joy alone that is spoken. No, if he even in the tiniest way allows his life to be touched by the Word of God in Christ, then he reaches beyond himself to his congregation with the Word of God pouring forth from his otherwise poor mouth. The greatness of the act of preaching is this, that it is not the act of a man, that it is not the act of speaking what has been spoken before as in a recitation, but the greatness of preaching is that the words are, sometimes at least, also the words of God, for the preacher himself and even for the congregation. I might be inclined to go along with the judgment of [the very Protestant] Emerson that the great gift of Christianity to the Western world is the institution of preaching. In the one act, when it is done thoughtfully and prayerfully, when it is honest and simple, when it is faithful to the words and deeds of Jesus, in this one act the mind and heart of one poor man, the minds and hearts of the congregation, meet in the mind and heart of God himself. The result is a Word that has not been spoken before and never will be again. Preaching is an act of love, and every act of love, of true love, is irreplaceable and unrepeatable.

I have a word for you today that I hope is not merely a repetition. But it is familiar. It follows from the word of the prophet Zephaniah who spoke to his people in the time of their troubles. It is a word that both you and I need to hear, a word of encouragement. God knows, we all need that. Listen to it and let it touch your heart.

Fear not, O Zion, be not discouraged:
The Lord, your God, is in your midst,

a mighty savior.
He will rejoice over you with gladness,
and renew you in his love.
He will sing joyfully because of you
as one sings at festivals.

Now I was startled by this Word when I read it, and for two reasons. First, I was very tired and discouraged, and this Word corrected me. Throw off your discouragement, the Word says, for your discouragement is born of lack of faith. Your discouragement is a lie, a lie you tell yourself. There is reason for confidence and hope no matter how you may feel, no matter what the circumstances of your life. The reason for courage is clear: God loves you and wishes to renew you in his love.

I find it difficult to climb out toward this Word. But the Word comes to meet me and forces me out to itself. The Word of encouragement will not leave me in my mood. It touches the deepest corner of my heart wherein there always lurks that desire for God, that need of God, that sense of wonder that God has bothered with me at all. And the Word shocks that mood of despair and drives it out with joy. Here He is again, says the Word, here is God again calling you to speak, to hope, to rejoice, to trust. God is a savior—and the savior will not leave you to yourself any more than he left Israel of old to itself.

The second reason for my being startled by this Word is the image in the last verse: He will sing joyfully because of us as one sings joyfully at a festival. Get the picture: God sings!! God sings over me!! When he renews me in his love, God himself bursts into song. Maybe he even dances as one would at a wedding. This great, eternal, inscrutable, mysterious, all-powerful God turns out to be like a lover who sings and dances over his beloved. And the beloved is me! And you. And every time I or you climb out of discouragement, despair, fear, self-concern, anger, resentment, any of the moods and feelings that destroy us and those around us, the great God leaps and sings for joy. What a wonderful image, what a saving Word!

There follows the Word of the psalm, which speaks for us in response to the word of the prophet:

God indeed is my savior; I am confident and unafraid;
My strength and my courage are in the Lord, and He has
been my savior.

Or, as Paul says, "Rejoice... dismiss all anxiety from your minds...
Then God's own peace will stand guard over your minds and
hearts."

My dear brothers and sisters, we are all often discouraged, often
frightened, often lonely, often burdened, often suffering. But every
week we come together to do this strange thing, to listen to ancient words, to do an ancient and distant thing, to pray to a God we
never see, to offer him bread and wine, to speak over the bread and
wine ancient words. Though we come here with our burdens and
sorrows, what shall happen to us? We should lay them down here
on the table, hold them up with the bread and wine, speak over
the bread and wine the very words of Jesus: "this is my body." We
must let them go again, these burdens and sorrows, let them flow
into his burdens and sorrows, and speak a word of renewed love
and joy and praise. God himself is waiting to speak over us. Let him
sing before him.

William M. Shea
Last Mass as a Catholic priest
Last Sermon as a Catholic priest

Appendix 7

Letter to Pope John Paul II

*This letter is part of the petition for a release from celibacy, a let-
ter required of every man resigning the priesthood who wishes the
pope's permission to do so. The priest is given no form, nor is he
told what to include beyond asking for dispensation and giving
reasons for it. It was difficult to write as I did. Many resigning
priests have refused to do so*

December 22, 1980

Your Holiness:

My name is William Michael Shea. I was born in New York City on
November 11, 1935. My father, William Patrick Shea was born in
Ireland on May 1, 1910 and came to the United States in 1927. My
mother, Sarah Margaret Power, was born in New York City in 1904.
They were married in St. Raymond's Church in the Bronx in 1934.
They lived in that parish throughout their married life. They educated my younger brother, John Timothy and me to love the church
and live faithful Christian lives. My brother and I were educated
entirely in Catholic schools, both of us in St. Raymond's parish
school and in Cardinal Hayes High School, I in Cathedral College
and St. Joseph's Seminary and my bother in the College of the Holy
Cross and Fordham Law School. My bother is now a successful
lawyer, devoted to his wife and three children.

My father died in May 1977. My mother now lives alone in the parish in which she was baptized and married, well provided for and
healthy, and has the attention and concern of both my brother and
myself. I loved my father and respected him profoundly. He was a
sober, serious, hardworking, intelligent and deeply religious man.
He is unquestionably the single most important factor in the shaping of my mind, heart, life and faith in God.

When I was ten years old, I was badly burned one morning while trying to cook breakfast for my family. My father saved my life. The top half of my body, from waist to my face, was badly injured, and my chest, neck and arms still bear the scars; so, too, does my spirit I fear. The event had much influence on in the formation of my character, for good as well as ill. From that moment on, as I discovered in the past few years, I felt ordinary life to be empty of security and meaning, and God to be untrustworthy and even dangerous. My parents told me years later of their shock at my profanity while I was in pain, and of my cursing God, doctors and nurses. All this I blocked from memory. What remained on the surface was the memory of terrible suffering and the conscious suspicion of and reticence toward life itself. My vocation from its inception has had something to do with this suspicion and reticence.

At thirteen years old, I decided to enter the Brothers of the Christian Schools. As I remember it, this was connected with the anti-Communist fear rampant in American politics and religion at the time (1949), and I conceived this dedication of my life to be an answer to the menace that was being scored in the pulpit and classroom. My father, after serious consideration, refused his permission and, after much argument, excluded the Brothers from our home and forbade me to talk of the matter again.

In my eighteenth year I decided to become a diocesan priest. This quite explicitly had to do in my mind with the senselessness of much of the life I saw around me in the world and with what I took to be the unhappiness and hardships of married life, as well as with my conviction that the priesthood was the best form of service to others and my love of the liturgy. I had throughout my high school years attended mass daily. My father and mother were both pleased and honored by my decision. I applied to Cathedral College and was accepted in 1953 immediately after finishing high school. After entering I chose as spiritual director Msgr. Joseph Quinn of the Marriage Tribunal who held residence in the parish. One of the problems that occupied us was my continuing problem with chastity, a problem that ceased when I entered the major seminary in 1955, and did not recur until after ordination.

My seminary years remain something of a mystery to me. I still do not understand my complex reaction to seminary life and its effect on me. I had no intellectual difficulties with studies. I got along well with my fellows and with most of the faculty. I was well liked and made a few friendships which have lasted over these twenty-five years. But I did not care for most of my fellows and had little respect intellectually and spiritually for most of the faculty.

Although I liked being in the seminary better than I liked being at home with my parents whose life together confused and upset me — it struck me as being sad — still the seminary experience was for me an unhappy one. In both cases, I had an oppressive sense of the power of authority in my life, in the one case of my father and in the other of the rector and the faculty. This sense was reinforced when in my first year, my mother grew deathly ill and I was allowed to visit her in hospital only once and then refused permission to leave the seminary again although she was still in danger. My anger and resentment at this was towering.

In the first two years, 1955-57, I had recurrent bouts of depression, some lasting as long as two weeks, during which I felt a loss of energy, purposelessness, fear and isolation. I remember going to the chapel late at night to pray. I would weep profusely asking God what was wrong, what He wanted of me, and why this was happening to me. My spiritual director was at a loss to explain this, and in my second year sent me to a priest-psychiatrist at St. Vincent's Hospital. I do not know what the psychiatrist reported; I remember being told by the spiritual director that my experience was not out of the ordinary. I do remember agreeing with the director to think over my vocation during the summer months.

I did so and decided not to return to the seminary. I felt relief and began planning to enter law school. When I spoke to my father about my decision to leave the seminary he told me that it would be cowardly for me to resign while at home and urged me to return and resign from there. I took his advice, returned, and never resigned. The conversation was crucial. My mother still remembers it and for years has wondered whether she should have opposed my father and that advice.

The first two years of theology passed quietly and without large event. Before ordination to the diaconate I had a serious conflict with the librarian, Msgr, John Harrington, over library journal policy and it was reported to me that he intended to ask for my dismissal on the basis of a letter I had sent charging him with censorship of the journal and that this dismissal would happen unless I retracted and apologized to him. I remember well my anger and chagrin that I had to lie in order to be ordained; I was deeply ashamed that I did not have the courage to tell the truth and lose orders. It was years before I forgave the man, and still cannot forgive myself for needing Orders more than I respected truth.

In the final few months before ordination to the priesthood in 1961 I lost twenty-five pounds, from my usual 200 pounds to 175. I cannot account for the loss except as a result of tension. I remember the time not as one of joy but as one of momentousness and seriousness, which had to be borne with courage. Tension prevailed through preparation, through ordination and afterward. One of the chief reasons for being relieved at ordination was that I would leave the seminary. But as I discovered, my difficulty with authority did not fade, nor did my tendency to depression.

Between 1961 and 1967 I had three parish appointments. The first, Our Lady of Mt. Carmel in Yonkers, was largely composed of Italian immigrants and their offspring and was staffed by Italian priests. I worked hard and successfully under trying circumstances for two and a half years. The pastor was very happy with my efforts—and this was true invariably of the men with whom I worked—but I experienced depression again, a high degree of tension, exhaustion and much unhappiness. Although I had and retain even now affection for the pastor, he was an ineffective leader and placed far too much responsibility on my shoulders. I experienced there my first serious problem with celibacy, and this within a year of ordination and through my second year in the parish. I asked to be transferred.

My second parish was filled with wealthy people. Our Lady of Perpetual Help in Pelham was firmly run by an effective but very authoritarian pastor who constantly confused and frightened me. After a brief period of relief at my escape from my problem in Yonkers I found that I had even greater problems in Pelham: a pastor who was smarter and tougher than I, who used me and had no respect for me, who lied and mislead me, and who had recourse to power whenever reason failed. I found myself utterly unable to cope with him, again depressed and now with bouts of digestive difficulty that required medical attention. I also found myself distrustful of wealthy parishioners and unable to work with them easily.

It was here in Pelham that it dawned on me for the first time that I did not enjoy most of the work of the priesthood. I did not like working with groups of young people; counseling couples and families frightened and confused me, and hospital work depressed me and called forth not only compassion and pity but an overwhelming sense of hopelessness and helplessness. Here I began to consult with a psychiatrist, ostensibly for direction in helping families but in the end for my own personal problems.

Again, after three years of well-received ministry, I sought a transfer and was sent to a small and lovely parish in the country, St. Patrick's in Bedford. I had a short stay there recovering from my previous assignment. There was a great deal of strife in the Bedford parish over the Viet Nam war and I spent most of the year trying to patch together the pieces of a torn parish and trying to put my own problems behind me. One morning in the Spring of 1967 I awoke and heard myself say: "I do not want to live as a parish priest for the rest of my life—I want to get out." I arranged that day to see Archbishop John Maguire, asked him for a release, and made plans to attend summer school at Harvard University and, in the Fall, to do graduate work at Columbia University School of Philosophy. I left Bedford a few weeks later with the reluctant permission of the archbishop and totally without any archdiocesan support. But at least I had, for the first time, declared myself as one who had a wish, who had some hope, and who would take responsibility for both. As an indication of my success in divorcing my action from deeper feelings, in all three cases the pastors of the parishes were visibly upset at my transfer and expressed the opinion that I was an excellent assistant.

From 1967 to 1971 I studied at Columbia University and resided at the College of New Rochelle, an Ursuline college for women. The studying progressed quite well. I finished in 1973 with a doctoral dissertation on American Aristotelian philosophers. The residence at the college was another matter. The three years were filled with increasing difficulties with celibacy and with inner conflict over the celebration of the Eucharist, and with some important growth under psychiatric care in my understanding of my family and the genesis of my difficulties with authority. Although I assisted the chaplain of the college and regularly celebrated the Eucharist and preached, I avoided contact with the women students as much as I could and avoided celebration of the Eucharist when possible.

Both evasions were brought about by guilt at my now frequent violations of celibacy. I was by then seriously considering leaving the priesthood, although the prospect frightened me even more than the prospect of staying. I remember well my discussing with my parents during those three years the former chaplain of the college who had recently married, gingerly approaching the question of my own possible leave. My father brought his fist down on the table in a restaurant and said: "If you go out that back door, you will go out with my foot up your ass!" I asked him what he thought I would do when he was no longer around, and he said he hoped he would live forever to keep me from leaving the priesthood. My own resolution at the time was that I would not leave in the flood of men then leaving, and would do so only after the most serious and prayerful consideration.

Because of an unfortunate conflict between the chaplain and the sister president I left the college in February 1971 and took up residence at a parish in Beacon, New York while I wrote my dissertation. In this parish I continued with the psychiatrist and fought to overcome my problem with celibacy, lived quite happily with the two priests there, did very little parochial work and worked hard on my thesis. It was the calmest, clearest and happiest living situation I had ever experienced. I remember it with gratitude.

In 1972, with Cardinal Cooke's permission, I took a position as assistant professor at the Catholic University where I taught courses in philosophical method and the history of American thought. I loved teaching and the university life, and intensely disliked the common living with the clergy. In my first year I was near emotional collapse as several of my relationships with women were strained by my move to Washington. I feel again into depression, but this time my response was a serious and sustained effort at prayer. For the first time I experienced what I had never experienced before, the closeness of God in Christ. This sustained me through seven years of turmoil and continued to sharpen and grow. I also attached myself to a parish in the suburbs of Washington—I was one of the very few university priests to do so—and offered mass and preached there for seven years. This was a great grace, for over that seven years, my inner conflict with celebration gradually subsided.

My happiness with my work and faithfulness in prayer did not bring an end to my difficulties with celibacy, however. In 1973, 1974, and 1976 there were serious incidents. Realizing that the situation must be met spiritually I arranged a research leave and a fellowship at Harvard where a Jesuit spiritual director with whom I had made several retreats would be available to me. I saw him every week from October 1976 to August 1977. My father died that Spring, on May 9, 1977. I had, a few months before, arrived at a decision to leave the priesthood and had intended to convey this to my father in June. But his death created a new situation.

I returned to Catholic University in the fall (1977) without mentioning my resolve to my mother who had suffered greatly over my father's death. I was promoted to associate professor in 1978 and tenured in 1979. In those two years I did my best work as a teacher and scholar, at the very time when I was making my first attempt to find another teaching position. I made every effort to care for my mother, took her to California with me for a summer while I taught at the University of San Diego summer session, and had her with me in Washington as often as I could. She began to revive from the shock of my father's death, and now seems well, is independent and secure, and is still the object of my deep concern.

I do not wish to turn this letter into a sexual autobiography but I should say something at least in outline about my troubles with celibacy over the past twenty years and about my attempts to solve the problem. Perhaps I can be brief with a painful subject. In my first assignment and within a year of ordination I became emotionally attached to an older single woman in the Yonkers parish and, although we never slept with one another, the situation, which lasted over a year, frightened me terribly. I obtained the counsel of my classmate and close friend, Father John Haggerty, and the counsel of a noted diocesan spiritual director, Msgr. Daniel Dougherty. The situation became more dangerous with time, and I finally asked Bishop Cooke, then Vicar-General, for a transfer.

In Pelham (1963-1966), although there was no trouble with celibacy, I did have enough trouble with the pastor to require both medical and psychiatric attention. The latter was my first contact with Dr. Thomas Fogarty who helped so much then and with my later trouble with celibacy. At this time I began to learn from him the connection between my problems and my family. In 1968-1970 I had my second and third sexual relationships, and several less physical but still emotionally dangerous attachments. I was distraught, returned to Dr. Fogarty, and continued in therapy with him for almost two years on a biweekly basis, now learning in detail the psychic shape of my dealings with women, my dissatisfaction with my ministry, and my trouble maintaining stable relationships. Dr. Fogarty forced me to concentrate on family rather than on overt sexual problems alone. This was wise. With his help I managed to end the affairs and came much closer to my father and mother and began to overcome my fear of authority and women.

At Catholic University (1972-1976) I became involved seriously with two more women, and almost married the elder of these. The other woman was a recent graduate of CUA college. During these years, while trying to find a way of changing my behavior and find a so-lution to the overwhelming problem, I made several retreats with William Connolly, S.J., director of the Center for Religious Devel-opment in Cambridge Massachusetts. In 1976, when at Harvard, I began with him an intensive program of direction and prayer that lasted through that year and through another year of telephone con-ferences between Washington and Boston on a weekly or biweekly basis. Father Connolly is an expert spiritual director. He taught me to pray, to face both my fear of and love for my father and God, my own enervating sense of worthlessness and my despair, my anger and loneliness, and even my unbelief and resentment of God.

I had decided in Spring of 1977 to seek laicization. When my fa-ther died, I put it aside while my mother needed me. I continued with spiritual direction, now by telephone. In Spring 1979 I began biweekly spiritual direction with Sister Mary Kay Liston, C.S.J., a member of the campus ministry team at Georgetown University and the only person in the Washington area trained by Fr. Connolly at his Center. At this point, I had had the benefit of direction for three years. This last year was a time for inner settling, for psychic and religious healing, and for dealing with such unanswered prob-lems such as marriage and employment.

When I consulted with Cardinal Cooke in October 1979 and with Father Benedict Groeshel in November, I had already been blessed by God with time for understanding with expert help and with good advice from devoted friends. Throughout these many and difficult years I had the grace of supportive friendships with Father Joseph Komonchak and Sister Mary Alice Gallin, O.S.U., the direc-tor of the American Association of Catholic Colleges and Univer-sities, both of whom were fully acquainted with my struggle and who gave me advice and support at every turn.

My present understanding of this long and difficult journey is this:

- The first two decades, 1950-1970, were unhappy years of increasing confusion and flight from fam-ily, God and self.
- The third decade, 1970-1980, although showing an increase in overt difficulty, also saw at last a grow-ing sense of purpose, clarity, self-understanding, and a reversal of the pattern of flight and evasion.

I conclude now, with regard to my ordination to the priesthood in 1961, that, although I was sane and responsible, my knowledge of and consent to the priesthood was notional and abstract rather than real and concrete; my knowledge of celibacy *for me* and my knowledge of myself were severely limited. This lack of a truly realized self-knowledge is evident in my sinfulness but especially in the lack of a devoted prayer life. The confusion has two sides to it, each of which hindered my effectiveness as a priest and brought me, and others, unhappiness. First, my relationship with my father and mother was never sufficiently clarified. To put it bluntly, I never grew up as a son and, as a result, was unable to live with authority and responsibility in ministry, and even with the authority of God. Second, my fear of psychic and physical intimacy, of tenderness and warmth, of pain and death, and my loneliness and need of fellowship, all wrecked havoc with my relationships with priests, with laity, and especially with women. In several important ways, I think I was unfit for both the celibate priesthood and for marriage.

As I tried with help from God and other Christians to meet these problems over the past decade I have discovered that I am, for all my genuine love for the Eucharist and preaching, a teacher rather than a priest or a pastor, and that I have no great and unifying desire for the reality of the priest's life. I doubt, quite frankly, if I would wish to practice the priesthood even if celibacy would not be required. My mind and heart have been at peace since I went on leave over a year ago. I do have a great need for a companion, for family, for children, for ordinary Christian fellowship, for ordinary work. I knew about the priesthood and about celibacy in 1961, but not about myself.

When I decided to leave the priesthood, I set out to do so with a minimum of trouble and embarrassment to all concerned, to my family, friends, my church and bishop, and my university. I was resolved to slight no one, to injure no one, and to heal as far as I could every threatened breach of relationship and Christian comradeship. I left Catholic University quietly. In all these efforts, I had the kind support of Cardinal Cooke.

I took leave of the priesthood on 1 January 1980. I celebrated Mass for the last time on the first Sunday of Advent 1979 in St. Rose Parish in Gaithersburg, Maryland. It was a happier and more peaceful celebration than my first Mass in 1961. I left Washington and on February 22, 1980, I married Helene Anne Lutz in Connecticut civilly, with only our parents present. Helene is a Catholic, with deep dedication to God and church. I have known her since 1970 when she was a student at the College of New Rochelle. Over these years, our friendship grew very gradually. When it became apparent that our friendship might end in marriage she entered spiritual direction and continued under it in order that she not avoid God's will. She has supported my efforts to do no injury to family, friends and church. After now a full year of marriage, we find our decision confirmed and our love for one another blessed by God's comforting grace. We look forward to a family as soon as God allows, and deeply want full communion with the church for our children and ourselves. We are Catholic in belief, in affection and in intellect. And we need the sacraments of the church to live well in Christ.

I have taken a job in the College of Arts and Sciences of the University of South Florida, a state institution, where I teach courses in modern culture and the history of American thought. We live in the diocese of Tampa-St. Petersburg. I will apply for tenure here in 1981 and we hope to remain in the area and raise a family here. We want to build a life of Christian love on the foundations of suffering and love already laid down over the past two years. We need the church's blessing on our marriage and our hope for the future.

I know how serious is the decision I have made, and in conscience I have made it for serious reasons and carried it through with maturity and decency. I have made every effort, taken every step to discover God's will for me. My frailty is great, my capacity for self-deception great. Yet God has spoken to me through friends and counselors and to my own heart. I have tried to avoid injury and scandal. I hope in Christ that Your Holiness will grant me the right to live as a Catholic layperson, to receive the sacraments of the church, and to participate fully in the life of the church.

Respectfully,

William M. Shea

Appendix 8

A Deposition before the New York Archdiocesan Tribunal

Also enclosed in the petition to Rome is testimony given under oath and recorded in a formal procedure at the archdiocesan judicial office. It is composed of questions formulated by a canon lawyer on the basis of the petition to the pope, and forwarded with it to the Congregation for the Doctrine of the Faith.

METROPOLITAN TRIBUNAL
Archdiocese of New York
1011 First Avenue
New York, NY.Y. 10022

N-80/7 Sec.
December 27, 1080
TESTIMONY OF WILLIAM M. SHEA

The Petitioner William M. Shea, testified as follows:

1. What is your name? William Shea
2. What is your address? 229 Sunnyside Rd., Temple Terrace, Florida 33617.
3. When and where were you born? Bronx, New York; November 11, 1935.
4. What are your parents' names? William M. Shea and Sarah Margaret Power.
5. When and where were you ordained? I was ordained in St. Patrick's Cathedral in New York City in 1961—May 27, I think.
6. Do you recognize this as an authentic copy of the petition that you have submitted? Yes.
7. Do you swear to the truth of its contents? Yes.
8. Would you very briefly describe your family background, keeping in mind that we have your petition?

Yes. My father was an Irish born immigrant American citizen who came here at age seventeen years old and worked as a retail manager for forty-five years in New York City and on Long Island. My mother was a housewife who worked for many years when I was young because of need of money. Both were practicing and very serious Catholics.

9. Did you find that you were particularly close to either parent more so than the other or was it equally close to both?

Well I would say that I was emotionally closer to my mother but I was personally psychologically engaged with my father.

10. Did your father tend to be a stern disciplinarian?

He was a stern disciplinarian and he was a very strong authoritative personality who was, I think, very powerfully dominant in my life.

11. Do you have any brothers or sisters?

I have one younger brother who is four years younger than I am.

12. Was that a close relationship?

Yes, it was a good relationship and it has become closer in the last decade. I would say that even when we were younger it was a good relationship.

13. Growing up did you experience any physical or emotional difficulties?

Well, I would say physical difficulties were that I was burned when I was a child of ten years old.

14. You mentioned in your petition that this had quite a profound effect on you both at the time and personality wise. As a matter of fact you mention that it kind of created in you a general suspicion toward life in general. Could you elaborate on that just briefly?

I think that the effect of that burning was an almost unconscious feeling that life was under a threat almost all the time and that ordinary experience and processes of life had no great value, that they could be destroyed at any moment just the way my own body could be destroyed at any moment.

15. Did that tend to leave you an insecure person?

Well, it left me tense and suspicious, I think, suspicious of the value of relationship, suspicious of positive, warm and close feelings toward other people. It really, I think, left me afraid of decisions, afraid of stands and afraid of commitments.

16. Growing up through grammar school and high school, did you have a normal social life, athletics, friends, etc.?

Yes, I think I had a fairly normal life. I played a good deal of baseball and in high school I dated girls. However, the ten year old burn experience did make me feel even when I was engaging in heterosexual activity and in sports, it did make me feel as if there was nothing to be won. All that stuff was almost like a charade of some sort that masked like a pain.

17. Would this have had any effect on your practice of religion at that time during early adolescence and was that just [going] through the motions, too, or did that have some genuine feelings.

No, no, no! Religious feelings were very strong. In fact they remained. I would say the strongest fact in my life now is still religious. A funny thing is that it hasn't changed very much from the time I was a teenager. I go to Mass in St. Raymond's when I am home regularly, that was my parish. I was baptized there. I go to Mass there and I am every bit as happy going to Mass there and praying as I was as a teenager. It is a funny thing but that remains almost like a thread of strength and decency in my life. The way I felt about life aside from religion, though, is very curious I think.

18. You mention that you had an idea of entering the Brothers of the Christian Schools but your father forbade this. Why is this introduced as significant in the biography of your life?

It is significant as one instance which is sort of a symbol of the relationship between my father and myself and I really think very much the same pattern is very much in evidence later in my dealings with people in authority, the seminary people who were in authority over me in the priesthood and that it, that I really wanted to make my own way in my own life but I always wanted approval and support where I would try to make my own way, and someone like my father who had such enormous emotional importance to me withdrew his support—his disagreement with what I wanted to do. It was almost as if my inner life would collapse. Up until the time I was almost thirty-three or thirty-four, those forays that I would occasionally make to establish my own world collapsed regularly.

19. How would your father and authority figures withdraw their approval?

    Well, they would say "no," or simply disagree very strongly and then tell me in effect, "You are going to be wrong. You will fail. You will make a mistake and if you do tough luck. Our esteem and respect are withdrawn if you go in this direction." Honestly, I think that was a very powerful motivating force in so many critical points of my life, the inability to stand up to the withdrawal of affection, particularly the affection of those whom I needed and feared such as my father and the seminary faculty and later on pastors.

20. How then did the idea of a vocation to the priesthood develop in you?

    Well, I think it happened because I went to Mass every day when I was in high school, and the Mass and the priests who said Mass became very important to me because they seemed to be doing the really important thing that could be done. Like my father's work in life seemed to be empty and unimportant. The work that priests did seemed to me to be terribly important. It was almost as if the real business of human life went on inside the Sanctuary and outside the Sanctuary there wasn't any real business going on at all.

21. Did your parents and friends and maybe the faculty of high school encourage you in this pursuit?

Well, actually I never talked to anybody in high school about it until I had made up my mind and was ready to take the test at Cathedral. I never talked to my parents about it until I had pretty well had made my mind up, but once I did speak to them I got a great deal of support and approval.

22. How did you do in Cathedral College the first two years you were there?

With respect to how I just feel about Cathedral College?

23. How did you do academically and [in] relationship to the faculty?

I would say I did modestly academically, something like a B average maybe. I had trouble with Greek. I got along pretty well with the faculty. I didn't like going to Cathedral College. I mean Dave Rea and Joe Moody were really something in the classroom and I liked them but I found going to Cathedral College [...] always strange and in many ways the same kind of strangeness I felt in the first two years of the [Major] Seminary. Not an adversary relationship. I enjoyed arguing with the faculty and they enjoyed me because I did argue and could argue. There was some lack of communication with other students, lack of emotional ease with other students, I think a lack of ease with the idea of being a seminarian, going from my home every day down there when everybody else was going to college, going away to college or going to college in the city. I always felt a little strange about going to Cathedral College and I was never really fully at ease even in the school itself for some reason.

24. During that period you mentioned that you had a confessor and spiritual director. You mentioned also in your petition that there were some problems in the area of sexuality at that time. Was that a cause of anyone counseling you to desist from the idea of going on or was that relegated to merely adolescent activity?

I think it was relegated to the kind of moral problem that every young man or many young men would have to deal with. I was not at all discouraged by my confessor at that time [from going] to the Seminary over that. I was told it would solve itself in time.

25. Then you went to the Major Seminary for six years. Would you describe what you experienced there in relation to the present discussion?

Yes. Well, I was quite distinctly unhappy for the first two years in the Seminary, in the philosophy year. In the theology years, I was not quite at ease with the whole thing. Not terribly well adjusted to it, I think, but I had an easier time with the theology years than with philosophy. The difference being, I think, that I got over some of the fear of the first two years and I got intellectually engaged for the first time and the only time in the Seminary with the Scripture courses that were being given.

26. In the first two years when you were unhappy did you have any authority problems with either your father or with the faculty?

Well, I would say two main problems that I remember, one in the first year there when Charles O'Connor Sloane was rector, temporarily rector while Msgr. Fearns was on a trip. My mother was very seriously ill and was really expected to die. She had a terrible hemorrhaging ulcer and he allowed me to go visit her once. I think actually [that] when I went to him I was so distraught that he could hardly say no. I think he might have said no if I had been more rational about the thing. But I went and visited her in the hospital with his permission. She was still very sick and [for] quite a while was in danger of death after the operation even. I asked to go back a second time and he refused and upset me terribly. I was very angry but I said nothing and did nothing whatsoever to indicate to him that this was the case.

27. You also mention that during this period there were bouts with depression.

Yes.

28. Were you able to put a cause to that?

Yes. I think it was about fear, kind of repressed fear of not being master of my own life and being angry at so many other people who seemed to have more control over my life than I did. It was almost like a kind of sinking feeling that I was not the captain of the ship at all and I just didn't understand where the ship was going or why the ship was going in the direction it was. It had to do not only with work in the Seminary that was terribly boring to me but also with the very vocation itself. When I prayed in the Seminary, I was praying asking God why I was doing this and why I had to do this and what was the point of this and I had very little sense of the point of it. Those claims of prayer were connected with the depression that was regular, periodically regular depression.

29. Well granting this unhappiness why did you stay, what factors led you to stay?

I think what led me to stay was a lot of very strong religious convictions that I had when I was a teenager carried through to the present time. That is I really believed that the priesthood was an important way of life and really the only important way of life.

30. Did you discuss these difficulties with your spiritual director?

Yes, I did.

31. What did he advise?

Well he really didn't know what the answer was to the problem, why I was there, why I was so depressed. He sent me to a psychiatrist. The psychiatrist interviewed me for fifty minutes. I think this was a big mistake by the way if you ask me. I think more should have been done at the time. It would have helped me if more had been done. He interviewed me for fifty minutes or an hour, made a report to the spiritual director. When we talked it over, as I remember it now, we were close to the summer vacation and we decided that I should think over whether or not to go back in the fall. I did think it over. My opinion at the time, my decision if you can call it that, was to take a leave of absence from the Seminary for a year.

32. Was this the end of the first year or the second?

This was the end of the second year. I went to my father to tell him this during the summer and told him I wanted to take a year off and he did not like that at all. He disapproved of that and said it would be cowardly if I left the Seminary from outside the Seminary, that I must go back and put in the time and make a decision there.

33. In your petition I think you went so far as to say you started thinking about plans to go to law school at that point.

Yes.

34. How concretized had those plans been? Did you write away for any literature?

No, I did not.

35. But you were definitely thinking of alternatives?

Oh yes. I was thinking of where I would go, what I could do for say working for a year before I could get into law school but I never got so far as to take any steps.

36. It was once again your father's decision that you should go back?

I think I would have left at that time had I received any sign of encouragement or even acceptance on his part of the decision.

37. For the next four years of theology was there any significant problem that you could point to that would help us to realize the development of your vocation and training?

Well I would say that in those four years, I did well and I learned how to handle the place intellectually, and to a certain extent I learned how to handle it emotionally. I found my way around the seminary. I learned how to deal with the faculty up to a point of enough ease to allow me to go through it without any serious day-to-day, week-to-week depression problems that I had in the first two years. However, I would mention that I had a fairly strong resentment against the faculty because it seemed to me that I had to win their approval to be ordained and I just didn't like having to answer to a group of men [whom,] by and large, I did not hold in the highest regard. I remember once that Msgr. Reh asked me when I was a deacon if I would keep an eye on the younger men on the corridor that I was living on to help steer them in the right direction and exercise authority over them. I was one of several deacons living on corridors that he asked to do this and I got very angry at that suggestion and I simply refused to do that.

38. "I didn't like being put in the position of a policeman." Is that the idea?

Yes, exactly. I didn't want to exercise over anyone the kind of authority that I felt would be exercised over me. I resented it when it was being exercised over me and I didn't want to exercise it over anyone.

39. Did you manifest your displeasure to the rector about that?

I did, yes. Now the rector liked me and we got along fairly well but I told him I simply would not have any part in the thing at all and he dropped it. He dropped the matter. He told me, by the way, the result when he made a short character report when we were called to Orders to the priesthood. He told me my large fault, according to the faculty, was that I had a big mouth and that I ought to learn to shut it.

40. You did mention in your biography an incident with the faculty member who was a librarian. Would you tell us what the significance of it was?

Well, I think it was the single most significant event in the entire six-year period in the Seminary because so much of my feeling particularly in the last four years that remained submerged here came to the surface. I was very, very annoyed that he was exercising the censorship over the library periodical that he did and when I protested that in written form and he told another faculty member that he would ask for my dismissal. I was furious that in effect I had to go to him to apologize for telling the truth. That summarized for me the whole mentality of the attempt to manipulate other peoples' ways of speaking and thinking that I felt at the time that was part of the Seminary system, and that man was to my way of thinking the epitome of the sort of uncaring exercising of authority that I experienced to a degree more or less with other members of the faculty as well. The size of my resentment of that was considerable and I was humiliated and angered and ashamed that I apologized there and really ashamed in a way of being ordained on that condition.

41. Did you have any doubts about pursuing the idea of the priesthood as you came closer to the date of ordination?

Yes, I did. I did.

42. Did you share these doubts with anyone?

Well, as I remember it, it was during my last retreat before I was ordained. I was quite upset during that last retreat and I sent for a priest whom I had known in the Bronx [my parish] to come up to talk with me while I was on retreat. He actually kind of calmed me down. I was quite disturbed. I didn't know at the time precisely why but it was almost as if a lot of the tension over that last year preparing for ordination kind of broke loose and I went to confession and talked to him about sexuality and talked about whether I would be a good priest and so on. I took it to be at the time kind of normal nervousness but I suspect now that it was more than a normal nervousness. It was the coming to the surface of a tension which I had suppressed at the time, and here in this immediate facing of the event I could not any longer suppress and [it] broke out, and as I said, he, [being] a very smart man, was able to calm me down and get through that last week before ordination.

43. Was he "smart" in the sense of trying to brush over the problems that existed?

Well, I think the same thing happened there that happened with the psychiatrist four years before that, and that there was a signal being sent up which I was incapable of understanding and interpreting, and the people to whom I was talking were also incapable of interpreting in any deep way but were capable of handling the situation in such a way that I could get through what I had to get through. They helped me to do what it seemed on the surface of things I should have done and what seemed on the surface of things to them to make a great deal of sense and they would interpret my experiences then as being quite normal when perhaps in effect I don't [now] think they were.

44. Looking back at it now from this point of view were these apprehensions that you had and doubts about going on for the priesthood within the range of what one would consider normal and relatively common, or in your case were they outside the border of that normalcy and did they really signal a problem?

Well, I'm convinced now that it was a problem. I talked to several classmates of mine over the years about those years while they were in the Seminary and I must say that I can't connect positively my emotional state or going through the Seminary with theirs. I.e., I don't think my reaction to the Seminary education was normal, if I can use other men as a standard of normalcy. I think I was sitting on a good deal of unexplored emotional and personal psychological response to a situation, and I simply went ahead and rode right over it and never came to grips with it. The kind of emotional and psychological experience that was underlying those doubts of mine quite frankly [are not] the normal experience of a person who is going through to be ordained.

45. Did you find that you were able to find help in pursuing this life because of the structure of the Seminary system without really having the emotions that reverberated with what was going on outside in the external order? Was there a resonance between inside, what you wanted to do, and externally, what was happening?

Yes. I have a very strong distaste for disorder, competition, for unstructured situations, and the Seminary was almost like a womb for one side of my personality, and I appreciated, really appreciated, the structure and order of the Seminary. I think after initially the first two years of getting used to it, once I got used to it and learned the ropes I did rather well with it and I did feel a good deal of safety there. That disappeared once I was ordained. I didn't have the structure and the order and the clarity. I had the same authority problem as the Seminary system presented me with but I didn't have the same safety factor that the Seminary system presented me with.

46. With the Seminary structure and given your personality, would it not have inhibited growth rather than contributed to it?

Oh, I think so! I would say now looking back on it that the periods in my life of which I am most proud and happiest about were the periods where I was forced to abandon safety and structures. I think the Seminary system kept me at a lower level of maturity than I would have achieved had I been outside doing the things ordinary people do.

47. Speaking specifically with regard to celibacy, were there any problem or doubts in your mind immediately before ordination?

Yes. I remember well discussing celibacy with classmates in the general [sort] of way that we were given to discussing it and making remarks about it. I remember even then celibacy made no religious sense to me at all. Celibacy to me was what I had to do in order to be a celebrant in the Eucharist. I know I received the usual instructions in the Seminary on the religious value of celibacy. At that time just before Vatican II in the Scriptural revival there was a great deal of stuff being done on the eschatological character of celibacy and I listened to that and recognized all that in the New Testament text but I could not and never have been able to make any connection between the religious significance which intellectually I could recognize and my own personal life.

48. At that particular time before ordination did it occur to you that if celibacy became too difficult that you would not abide by it, that you would be unfaithful to being a celibate?

Oh, no! I would be horrified in fact at stories of a few priests who left the priesthood even before 1961. I remember one or two names mentioned and I heard those names, and I got so upset that I lost sleep over it—the thought that anything like that would ever happen to me.

49. Did you accept Sacred Orders of your own free will?

Yes.

50. You were not pressured or forced into Sacred Orders?

No, I don't think I was pressured or forced in any way that would relieve me of responsibility for what I did.

51. Intellectually and emotionally, do you think that you knew what you were doing when you accepted the obligation to celibacy?

I think intellectually I knew what celibacy required of me. Emotionally, I think, I didn't understand celibacy religiously at all and that I didn't think it was of any personal value for anything that I personally appropriated myself at all. It was simply an institutional requirement that I couldn't make any religious sense of but would do.

52. Were you happy on ordination day?

I was tense, tired and I would say somewhat happy but the Ordination day and the First Mass were felt as a tremendous honor and I felt them as a great blessing. I also felt that I wanted to get through with it and get it over with as fast as I could because of the level of personal attention that I had with regard to any [...] public act involving a lot of people always upset me. The tension of the First Mass and the reception and being the focus of any kind of attention of that sort even for a couple of days always unnerved me and I was considerably tense about that at the time.

53. Did your father's approval of your ordination help you at that particular point?

Oh yes! I was very, very happy for them because they were obviously so happy. It was a major family event. [It was] probably the major family event in the entire history of the immediate family in this country.

54. In your report once again you explain in some detail your experiences in the three parish assignments you had after ordination. At what point can you say you were unhappy? How soon after the ordination can you say you were not happy in doing the ordinary things of a parish priest?

I would say I said it to myself about three to four years after ordination but I think there was recognition of something [wrong] that I felt from the first six months.

55. Was there any connection between this dissatisfaction that was somewhat six months after your ordination and your becoming involved to some extent with the opposite sex?

Oh, yes! I think so. I think the level of tension and unhappiness that existed was a major factor in my involvement with that woman in the first parish but that was so frightening to me that I pulled back [from] that and then spent like three to four years in almost a state of suspended animation in fear of involvement with women but it was I think the level of considerable unhappiness in the parish that activated my need for another person to with me.

56. From a human point of view, were you successful as a priest?

Well I will be very modest but yes, I think so.

57. People would compliment you and reinforce you?

Yes. I had absolutely no lack of positive feedback from parishioners. With a few major exceptions, usually incidents, I had a very positive feedback from the pastors I worked with and yet even with that amount of positive feedback there was a sort of drift and purposelessness.

58. To what do you attribute that if you were successful as a priest and getting positive feedback, why were you so unhappy and unfulfilled?

I didn't like doing this and still don't like doing it.

59. Have you discussed this with anybody?

Yes, yes I did. I would say soon after and during my second assignment, which was in Pelham [Manor] when I realized that I was bored and unhappy with most of the things that I had to do, I began to talk for the first time to friends, priest friends, about this unhappiness. Several of them I mentioned to you in that report. Over the years several people have known quite well that I did what I did well but that I didn't like what I had to do, was unhappy with it. They knew my difficulties with celibacy but I also think they knew of my dislike of the ordinary practice of the priesthood, a good deal of it at any rate.

60. Were you able to gain any insight as to why this was so? Was it that you weren't prepared for the priesthood?

No. I don't think it was a matter of education or lack of education in that sense, a lack of training. I don't think it was the fault of the Seminary. I think it was largely a factor of the makeup of my character and of a very deep and personal struggle that was going on about my own identity at the time. I have the greatest admiration for priests and what they do and I have great positive feelings about priests and what they do. I also know that even what I did in the priesthood [...] was important and valuable but there was some considerable struggle going on in myself that vitiated almost everything I did as a priest.

61. Would you attribute this to a psychological or emotional problem?

Yes, I think so. I think it was both psychological and emotional.'

62. Was this something that developed after ordination or would you say it was a continuity of what went before?

Oh, no. I think it is very much part of my character and personality. Often in conversation with my mother [and even with my father when he was still alive] she remarked on the fact that I could remember practically nothing that happened before I was burned at ten years old. I had very limited recollection of anything that occurred before I was ten. That was a traumatic thing. I could say that the problem that appeared after ordination was very much connected with the personal, psychological and emotional [...] complexion of my personality that developed, as far as I can remember, at ten years old.

63. You mentioned that within the first six months or so of ordination you became romantically involved with a woman. At what point did this involvement with the opposite sex become physical in the sense that there were sexual relations?

Oh, no. There were no sexual relations with that woman. The first time there were sexual relations with any woman was I would say seven years later, in 1968.

64. Did this cause any guilt reaction?

Oh, terrible, terrible. The [first] relationship I had was with a woman when I was at New Rochelle College... She was from a previous parish I served in. It was a physical, sexual relationship, which lasted two to three years, and I had tremendous upset and guilt through that. The physical relationships that I had with a few other women over say the last thirteen years, maybe half a dozen women, all of them have been friends. None of them have been casual. All of them were upsetting. None of them were brief. All of them were serious. Guilt was experienced in every one of the situations but in every one of the situations, I went ahead anyway.

65. You state in your report how after some years in three parish assignments then you began going into the academic world both studying and teaching. At what point did the

idea of leaving the priesthood enter your mind?

Well you know, the idea of leaving the priesthood shocked me but that entered my mind within one year of ordination. When I was emotionally involved with the woman in Yonkers I was already thinking of how I could possibly leave the priesthood and live and exist. The idea of leaving the priesthood has been in my mind since my first year of ordination, and it became an acute possibility for consideration after I left the parish ministry. While I was working at the College of New Rochelle and pursuing my degree and I was at that time having an affair with the woman in [   ] I was seriously thinking of leaving the priesthood. It was [so] from that time until last year.

66. Would you be able to estimate as to why you didn't leave before that particular time?

I think several factors entered into [it]. One was a lot of men were leaving the priesthood and I resolved to myself that I would not leave in a flood of other men leaving the priesthood. I would not leave until I was sure that God wanted me to leave and that there was no other way of dealing with my unhappiness. It would have to be plain to me religiously. I couldn't leave because I wanted to marry. I couldn't leave because I was unhappy. I needed to know that this was not a violation of God's will for me, in fact that it was God's will.

67. How did you come to know that?

I decided that I would pursue this matter in prayer and with spiritual direction. I also had a good deal of psychological counseling and I knew that wouldn't answer it either. I knew the matter was a spiritual matter and not a matter to be settled on other grounds. Although it took me a while to find a situation in which I could let the question of vocation come up to a spiritual state in prayer with help, it took four or five more years to find that. When I found it I went after it like a hound dog.

68. How much do you think that your father's death might have had a bearing on your making the ultimate decision to leave?

I decided two or three months before he died to leave and I even called him up. He was going to college at the time and he was going to graduate from college. He had retired at sixty-two and went to college and was going to graduate from college in early June of '77 and he died in May of '77. In March of '77 I knew that I was going to leave the priesthood and I tried to set up a situation in which I could be with him a long enough time to talk to him and fight it out with him because I knew it was going to be a very big battle. I arranged to see him for a week, and to go away with my mother and him for a week after he graduated in June but he died in May.

69. Apropos of what you mentioned before that your decision to leave the priesthood was only going to come after much prayer and thought, what was it then that brought you an answer, so to speak, to this vexing problem?

Well, I think that I found out that God put me in this world to be free, and what I had done for years and years and years was as if He was constraining me that I had to spend my life in a certain way if my life was to be valuable. It was almost as if I learned from my religion what really the value of me was, and once I found that out I couldn't do anything else. I didn't know that God put me here to love Him and to be free to do what comes naturally to my being and my heart. I felt for years that this God was ordering me in ways that ran counter to what I wanted and pulled me into a thing I didn't want and that I was afraid of but had to go. Then I found out through prayer that that isn't true at all and that what God most of all wants from me is a free loving of Him and a way of being that fits with the gifts I have.

70. Why could this not have continued in the priesthood?

I don't think I'm celibate. For one thing I don't think I am a celibate. For another thing, the ordinary kinds of work that priests do don't really interest me much at all. The kinds of work that I find myself doing as a professor are of great interest to me. The kinds of work I would do as a priest are not of great interest to me at all.

71. At any time or at the present time did you have any problems theologically with the Church's teaching?

No, I don't think so. I just don't have any problem with being a Catholic. I like being a Catholic. I love the Catholic Church.

72. Have you already civilly married?

Yes, I have.

73. What is the name of your wife?

Helene Anne Lutz.

74. Is she a Roman Catholic?

She is.

75. How long are you married?

I'm married now eleven months.

76. Are you well-adjusted into this marriage?

Oh yes.

77. From what you can observe is your wife well-adjusted into this marriage?

Yes. I think we both knew before we married that this was the right thing, and the experience of the last eleven months confirmed that.

78. Have her parents and family accepted her decision to marry you?

Oh, yes. Very much. There is no problem with her parents at all. One of her [four] uncles and aunts refused to come to the ceremony but that is the only part of the family that showed any disagreement. Her parents are wonderful people who have been most supportive and helpful.

79. What about your mother and brother and his family, and your lay friends. Have they come to accept your decision to marry?

They certainly have. I would say that my mother was very, very hurt about my leaving the priesthood. I don't think a seventy-six year old is able to fully understand how anyone could leave the priesthood but she does understand why I did. I don't think she is quite capable of making the full change of attitude toward it but basically I think she likes Helene very much and she has shown no animosity or difficulty towards me at all. My brother and sister-in-law are very happy about it. My priest friends have uniformly agreed that it was a good idea and my lay friends have accepted it as well.

80. In the environment where you presently teach is it generally known that you have left the active ministry of the priesthood?

I would say that there are no more than three or four people who know it.

81. Would the fact that you left the active ministry of the priesthood be a cause for criticism of the Catholic Church or scandal to anyone?

I can't think of anybody where I work or in fact anyone I know well from the past that has received any scandal from it.

82. Have you definitively decided to leave the active ministry?

Yes, I have.

83. What are your future plans?

My future plans are to work at the university and to be tenured there, and to live in Tampa and to raise a family.

84. What subjects do you currently teach?

I teach courses in contemporary philosophy and criticism of culture, and courses in the history of American thought. My specialty is the history of American philosophy.

85. Do you attend Catholic Church services at the present time?

Yes I do.

86. Is it generally known in Florida where you are living now that you have left the active ministry of the priesthood?

No, no one knows that. I have only been there four months and no one knows me in fact. No one in the parish I attend on Sundays knows me.

87. Do you have anything else to add that might have a bearing on this matter that we have not yet discussed?

I think the only things I would add is that my heart is very much at peace about what I have done. I think I am happier than I have ever been in my life. I think I am in the right place and I think God led me there through a great deal of trouble, trouble which I now appreciate but I am sure God's grace led me to where I am and I am happy with it.

88. Do you now swear to the truth of all the statements you have given to us?

Yes I do.

THE PETITIONER TOOK THE SUPPLEMENTARY OATH

Given at the Hall of the Tribunal,
1011 First Avenue, New York, New York
27th day of December 1980.
Signatures:
William M. Shea
Rev. Msgr. Desmond J. Vella, Delegate of the Ordinary

Appendix 9

The Rescript

The Rescript is the document from the Sacred Congregation of the Doctrine of the Faith granting the dispensation from celibacy. It is approved by the pope before being issued. It takes effect when the priest accepts it and is thereby formally laicized (i.e. "returned to the lay state"). The priest remains a priest but is forbidden any exercise of the priesthood except in cases of emergency, i.e. the imminent death of a Christian when no other priest is available, when he may hear the confession and perform the sacrament of the sick and dying.

Sacred Congregation for the Doctrine of the Faith

Prot. N. 222/81s

William M. Shea, priest of the archdiocese of New York, requested dispensation from sacerdotal celibacy.

His Holiness, Our Lord John Paul II, by divine providence pope, on October 29, 1982, informed of the case by the Sacred Congregation for the Doctrine of the Faith, gives his assent under the following conditions:

1. The rescript shall take effect once the competent ecclesiastical authority has notified the petitioner, and he accepts inseparably the dispensation from sacerdotal celibacy and simultaneous release from the clerical state. Never shall the petitioner separate the two elements, accepting the first and rejecting the latter. If the petitioner is a religious, the rescript contains a dispensation from vows; indeed, moreover, insofar as it may have happened, the rescript includes absolution from censures, even from excommunication incurred by attempted marriage of the parties, and the legitimation of offspring.

2. Notification of the dispensation is to be placed in the baptismal register of the petitioner's parish.

3. When the petitioner marries canonically the norms stated in the Code of Canon Law are to be applied. The Ordinary is to be very careful that the matter is conducted cautiously, without ostentation or evident splendor.

4. The ecclesiastical Authority to whom this rescript is sent should examine it with the petitioner and encourage him strenuously to participate in the life of the People of God in accord with his new state of life, giving good example and showing himself to be a most loving son of the Church. At the same time, however, he must take note of the following:

a) The dispensed priest has lost his clerical status and its obligations, ecclesiastical dignities and offices; as well as other obligations not connected fully to the clerical state.

b) He is excluded from the exercise of the sacred ministry with the exception of what is specified in Cannons 882, 892 #2, and so he is not to preach. Neither is he to act as an extraordinary minister of the Eucharist or hold any directive office in pastoral ministry.

c) He is not able to hold an office in a seminary or comparable institution. In other institutions of higher studies that in some way depend on ecclesiastical authority he is not to hold any leadership office or the office of teacher.

d) In these same sort of institutions of higher studies, even if not dependent on ecclesiastical Authority, he is not permitted to teach any properly theological discipline or any discipline intimately connected with it.

e) In institutions of the lower grades depending on ecclesiastical Authority, he may not hold any leadership office nor is he allowed to teach unless the Ordinary, exercising prudence and avoiding scandal, decides that he may teach. The same law binds the dispensed priest in teaching religion in institutions of the same kind not dependent on ecclesiastical Authority.

5. The dispensed priest (and, a fortiori, the married priest) ought to leave the places in which his prior state is known. However, the Ordinary of the place in which the petitioner settles, or the Ordinary of his incardination or his major religious superior is able to

dispense from this clause if the petitioner presents no current threat of scandal.

6. Finally, some work of piety or charity ought to be imposed. However, by the time this is referred to the Sacred Congregation for consideration and action, if scandal of the faithful should occur, prudent explanation should be provided.

Whatever to the contrary not withstanding,

From the offices of the Holy Congregation of the Doctrine of the Faith. 29 October 29, 1983.

Appendix 10

Letter to Joseph Komonchak at Catholic University

This was written to a friend during my stay in Florida. It took seven more years to find the job as chairman in the department of theological studies at Saint Louis University (1991). We had bought a very comfortable Florida bungalow in Tampa by that time, Christopher had emerged, and we had made many friends. I was quite happy in the work at University of South Florida and especially enjoyed the students. We moved for the money (about plus $20,000 a year), for the opportunity for Helene to get a Ph.D. in medical ethics and for the boys' chance for a free Jesuit college education.

1/21/84

Dear Joe,

We have not seen the sun for a month, maybe six weeks. This is only the slightest of overstatements, for it has appeared to us for a few minutes of an afternoon on occasion. But Florida has been reduced to an apparently unending Advent. The only (no exaggeration) thing more than bearable about Florida is the winter, December through March, when the days are cool and sometimes brisk, and the sun is bright, the sunrises and sunsets utterly lovely. The three previous Winters for me made the rest of the year bearable, for I could walk to school and back, and even though the human surroundings are either ugly or uninteresting, the sky was magnificent (nothing conduces to communication with the Deity better than a fine sky except maybe a fine woman). This year, Depressionville, USA. The natives are UPSET, not just because the Superbowl got good and screwed up, but because they cannot stand damp, cold weather of any sort for any length of time. I can't stand the grey sky day after day, with the constant threat of rain (can't walk to school). I want cold, clear, bright days. That's a simple enough need, isn't it?

I have spent a lot of time since the summer thinking and feeling my way around my future and that of Helene and the children. The questions have to do with wishes, I think, or priorities of wishes. Somewhere around the end of the summer, I decided I don't want to stay here any longer than I have to. As usual, such a decision for me appears on the surface to be a negative emotional reaction; to me it appears so at any rate. I think that I am not only slightly paranoid—I also need scapegoats for my decisions, so I paint the decision in dark and lurid colors for myself.

I started to get upset at the USF situation and my place in it—a few of the pages in the enclosed report will communicate some of that to you—and began my usual ranting and raving when I am not sure of myself and of what to do, the object being the administration, the state leadership, the local professors, etc. But in fact it's a decent job in a decent place, and my future and that of the family is well placed here.

The problem is two-fold: where and what. I don't want to work in the Deep South any longer; I want to work in the Middle Atlantic States between NC and Maine, and nowhere west of PA. Secondly I want to work in a RC place (more on that below) or a Protestant place, but even a secular place if that will help our geographical situation. I am even willing to take on an administration job to get myself out of here.

The situation here involves several factors urging me north, or at least elsewhere, factors beyond personal wish to live in a civilized state near a civilized city. I am blocked from any large jump in salary since the sixty-five year old chairman can and will continue in the chair until he is seventy and is forced to retire. His salary now is c. $55,000. If I were promoted to chair my salary (now 28,000 including summer) would jump to about $35,000. A full professorship would provide another significant increment—somewhere around 2-3,000 per year, and expanding. But as it is now it will be years before I hit the chair and several years before I will apply for full professorship. I am forty-eight. As much security and promise as the job holds, the money will not come fast enough or large enough to keep me here, and believe me that is all that will keep me here.

The second and larger problem is that Florida is no place for Helene and the children. I realized this summer in San Diego that I do not want my children to grow up here and be uneducated and uncivilized. The educational situation is a frightful mess and private education is very expensive (RC, Episcopal or secular). I want Helene to be in a place where she can work happily. I want the children in a place where they can be educated decently, and I'd like to work at an RC place that will educate them free.

The third problem is the social life here. Neither one of us is socially backward, but our progress in forming attachments is almost entirely linked to one family and one childless couple, neither one of which units is attached to the Great Mother of us all (the wife/mother of the family is RC but not exactly concerned with the true religion, or at least with religion's truth). We both want a pool of varied friends, with a large mixture of Catholics who have children, and have an active attachment to the Great Mother. Florida has been and continues to be a social dead end. We are uninterested in the university bunch socially, and we have no other contacts. We need a place with an active, settled, mixed, and heavily RC/Christian component. This is for ourselves as well as for the children.

One facet of the local mixture is important to point out. I mentioned it briefly on the phone. The four years here at USF have convinced me, if I ever needed it, of just how much a Catholic I am, and that in two ways. First, just the ordinary day to day working in a place which has no otherworldly point, and on whose walls there is no Cross, and whose academic life in fragmented by lack of a religious vision is enough to teach one the value of religious vision. But more: the academic world is simply anti-Catholic still. With more or less vigor and more of less bluntness, sometimes with good-natured humor and sometimes in direct insult, my peers, from secular humanists through liberal Protestants, think that the Great Mother of them all is abhorrent. They "reprehend it," as a local philosopher said in print. "No Catholic should be hired to teach philosophy," said another philosopher. [My] chairman's wife makes little jokes about the chair's Catholic childhood, but only at instances of a negative sort. The chairman himself is surprised why I would be still a Catholic. One can win some respect as an individual, but in spite of one's church. I am a bit tired of it, tired of being considered at best an exception and at worst a termite. I recognize now with some sorrow that, even if the money here were large and fast, I would not want to work in such an atmosphere any longer. Nor do I want to work with the people. Sorry, but resolved. *This* consideration would bring me to accept financial loss to leave—as long as the move held promise for Helene and the children.

But more important, at least for me personally, is the dawning of a clearer appreciation of the importance and the truthfulness of Christian belief and practice, esp. in its RC variety. I have my work criticized regularly by the Chairman and by Zylstra (he of the Calvinist-Barthian-Ogdenian admirations), and their criticisms of it—some of it revealing how deep is the conceptual and affectional crevice between us is—have shown me that I not only *like* my religious world; I think I think right about it, too. Their criticisms, while momentarily shaking me, have over the last two years driven me to see how attached my mind and spirit are to Catholic Christianity, and helped me better understand that belief is important and possible for me, and that it is right—even if sometimes I am not so sure the beliefs are correct. I realize now that I am a theologian! Now I intend to be that here, and I have taken some steps toward coming out of the closet as a theologian here (i.e., admitting that I am not just *describing* but have a stand in relation to God, church, etc.), and so I can survive with some integrity. But I'd rather work with theological types and with religious people, all else being equal. I am willing to regard my work here in a missionary spirit, and there is good reason to take it that way and good spiritual reasons indicating that that is not at all bad for me to do, but I think I'd like to work again where the Great Mother and one's theological persuasion are not two strikes toward being out of the game.

An added complication is the state of the church here—no relief. The one local priest with brains and sensitivity has just been transferred to his own parish on an island near Ft. Myers. We'll have to import him to baptize the new baby. Nowhere else to go!

Now I shall put an end to the moaning. I am trying to make it clear to you, and to myself, why it is that we need to move. Aside from that, there is plenty of reason to cheer. For one thing, even living in Florida does not dim my happiness in my marriage. The big mystery to me is how I managed to think for twenty-five years that I didn't want to be or didn't need to be married. Thank God, this deception did not last for life. And did I ever marry the right woman! She remains my chief evidence that there is Divine Providence. Grant you, she has her faults—occasionally, for example, she seems to hesitate before accepting my views as her guide and she expects me to share household duties and sometimes grows restive under the "liberal" leadership of JP II and our bishops—yet it would be hard to find anyone better put together to stand under and understand and oversee my life. It must have been all the training in the heavily male dominated Lutz family. We live well together. If it weren't just too kitsch, I'd say we are devoted to one another. And being in Florida, so far removed from our families and friends, we have become good friends. Having her with me puts all the other confusions and strains about job, work, even church, in the shadows. Lonely is not good. Lutz is good.

And the kid is a marvel. Right now, he's sleeping. He kept his mother up most of the night, and he got up the other morning at 5 AM to keep his father company while I read. I couldn't sleep, thought to read, and ended up playing with him for an hour and a half till 6:30 AM when he went back to sleep and I went to work. This morning I cleaned a bit of shit off his rear, an act of such intimacy that it can't be described. I have no adjectives—and I can't understand how he managed to catch my heart. He is so beautiful, so funny, so happy, so smart that I get aches watching him. Another mystery: how did I convince myself that I didn't want and wouldn't love children? The resources for self-deception in important matters stagger me. I know, through grace, that "nothing will ever separate me from the love of God..." But the closest thing to it would be the loss of Helene or Nathanael. The light would go out; the darkness of those many years would return with a vengeance.

We are well. We have managed to save some money while apartment living, we have been healthy, we have fought through little problems, had a baby and long for a second. I am too heavy but I am healthy and feel fine. Helene works out every few days. Nathanael goes to "school" twice a week for a day. We're about to start Lamaze classes again. I am spending the weekend reading New Catholic Encyclopedia articles on faith, doctrine, dogma, belief, knowledge, etc. and reading Kant's refutation of rationalist arguments. My teaching is going as well as it ever has, although I get few students since I teach upper level courses usually. I have the sense that I'm getting on top of my work and getting clear on my work's direction over the next few years (knock wood; I'll probably die this afternoon!) My values have been affirmed, and my affections engaged and purified. God has not been good; He's been very, very good! [Remember John Harrington on that one?]

Well, that's the report. Hope you've enjoyed it and that it makes you envious.

I miss you.

Bill

JUDAS WAS A BISHOP

Appendix 11.

Letters to Archbishops Laghi and Quinn

The following was sent to the Vatican's Pro-Nuntio to the United States, Archbishop Pio Laghi, on the occasion of his refusal to celebrate the Eucharist for or speak to the meeting of the Leadership Conference of Women Religious in 1985. He was joined in the protest by Archbishop John R. Quinn of San Francisco. The reason was the Sisters' invitation to Margaret Farley, S.M., to address them. Sister Farley is a professor of theology at the Yale Divinity School and was under investigation by a Roman congregation over the orthodoxy of her book, Just Love. She was later cleared (more or less) by the congregation.

September 18, 1985
Archbishop Pio Laghi
Apostolic Pro-Nuntio
3339 Massachusetts Avenue North West
Washington D.C. 20008-3687

Dear Archbishop Laghi:

Your refusal and that of Archbishop Quinn to speak to the national Leadership Conference of Women Religious brings to our attention once again the situation that exists between American religious women signers of the statement by Catholics for a Free Choice and your colleagues in Rome. I have already expressed my opinion of Cardinal Hamer's behavior and you have a copy of that letter. Within the next week of so the *National Catholic Reporter* will publish a statement of mine assessing the significance of the altercation for American Catholic theologians. I want here simply to express my shock, indeed my scandal, at your refusal to speak on a program with Sister Margaret Farley. I assume, not unjustly I hope, that you also wished to express your displeasure and that of your superiors about the fact that the conference leaders did not withdraw their invitation to Sister Margaret.

You know as well as I do, and perhaps better, what kind of woman Sister Margaret Farley is. Archbishop Quinn certainly does. She is a woman of deep faith, of courage, of dedication, of compassion, of profound and life-long love of the church. She is intelligent, well-educated, moderate in her opinions and doctrinally conservative in the best sense of that word. She talks of Jesus and the church with conviction. Her mind and soul belong to God and no other. You need not take my word for this. Ask those who have known her far longer than I. The leaders of the conference are women of the same sort. They are, one and all, adults, free human beings, Catholics and faithful religious.

Your refusal to speak with them and on the same platform with Sister Margaret is an insult to her and to them, gratuitous, calculated and cruel. In my fifty years as a Catholic and including twenty years in the clerical state I have never seen the like. You are a man with responsibilities of political sort, no doubt, and you answer to those who sent you. You would undoubtedly rush to break bread with politicians whose hands are bloody, with a Gorbachav, with a Reagan, with the leaders of the Argentine junta. Yet you would not speak to nuns on the same platform with a nun. My dear archbishop, I am ashamed for you. The act is close to being unforgivable.

Since I became president of the College Theology Society a year ago I have had to focus my attention on the politics of the church in a way that I had managed to avoid throughout my life. I am a quiet man who deeply dislikes argument, confrontation, political maneuvering. But the past year and a half has convinced me that we, you and I, belong to different churches, so profoundly do we disagree over the simplest meanings of the gospel. I would like to speak with you, to see whether there is any communion whatever between us, but I despair even of a conversation and fear its results. I am deeply and increasingly pained at what you and your superiors are doing to the church of Christ.

I ask myself: could it be that he and they still think that the Catholic Church belongs only to them? Could they actually want to crush and eliminate opposition and dissent? Do they treat people so that they have a dignity to preserve from stain of association with those who will not obey them? Could it mean that they still think that

they speak for God and Jesus and Truth, and that those who disagree with them speak for Satan and unfaith? For a week I have
asked myself what could be behind such an action? What kind of a
church is it whose leaders humiliate religious women? It seems to
me that these rhetorical questions have a point that needs explicit
communication.

There is, and there is growing a gap between ordinary Catholics
like myself and our leaders, especially those who are connected to
Rome. I wish, my dear brother, that you would understand and
bring your superiors to understand that the Church you wish to
rule no longer exists, at least to a large extent in the United States
and in many other places. Something has happened and will continue to happen which will give you less and less to rule. This
process is visible in a thousand ways, as you well know, and you
cannot stop it. You can only try to understand it and guide it grace-
fully. You will be able to control less and less by arrogant commend
and medieval gestures. The Catholic Church no longer belongs to
the bishop of Rome, and certainly not to you as his representative.
The Catholic Church belongs to Catholics of all sorts, Margaret Farley and I among them.

My dear archbishop, please take counsel and council your superiors in turn; the path that you and Cardinal Hamer and the Pope are
taking will do damage and not good. We need to respect one another, support one another, pray with and for one another, and be
willing to embrace in our differences even over matters of the most
serious sort. I hope that you will find the courage to seek Sister Farley out and apologize to her. She deserves better of you and your
superiors. You may disagree, as I do, with the position announced
in the document she signed but she deserves your respect in both
public and private.

I confess that I am tired of these displays of *hauteur*. What we need
in our church are servants, mediators, genuine leaders, not *poseurs*,
hacks of outworn ideas, strutting ideologists out to bring children
to heel. You may have much in your service of the church to be
proud of while I have very little. Yet you dishonored us both last
week in New Orleans. My dear archbishop, I will continue to pray,
as I have since I was a child, for you and the Pope and the whole
church. I do so with a heart sadder and far less hopeful than it has
ever been.

Cordially,

William M. Shea
cc. Archbishop John R. Quinn, San Francisco CA.

Letter to Archbishop John R. Quinn

Archbishop Quinn led the archdiocese of San Francisco from 1977 to 1985. From 1977 to 1980 he was the elected president of the United States Conference of Catholic Bishops. He joined in Archbishop Laghi's boycott of the Leadership Conference of Women Religious in 1985. Archbishop Laghi did not answer my letter, a copy of which I sent to Quinn. Quinn did answer and, apparently thinking I was a priest at the time, rebuked me for my intemperate letter to Laghi. This is a belated response to Quinn. Quinn did not answer it. I am not surprised. The surprise was that he answered the letter above.

The Most Reverend John R. Quinn
Archdiocese of San Francisco
Chancery Office
445 Church Street
San Francisco CA 94114

Dear Archbishop Quinn,

I apologize for not responding to your letter of a year ago. It was kind of you to answer mine at a time when you were preparing for the meeting of bishops. I appreciate your directness and honesty. We need more of that, both formal and informal, in the dealings of bishops and theologians.

I did not answer you then because, in the first place, I misplaced your letter and kept hoping it would turn up. My best guess is that my three-year old son, Nathanael, got his hands on it and stuffed it somewhere. It may yet turn up. In the second place, I got myself busy with the ordinary and the extraordinary matters of the year, including the College Theology Society's annual convention and the Curran case. Thirdly, I was not at all sure there was a point to carrying the matter further since we clearly disagree.

But now that I have finished my term as president of the CTS and before I take up a year's fellowship at the Woodrow Wilson Center at the Smithsonian, I thought I might write. Sr. Dolores Greeley of

St. Louis University is the new president and she will be carrying on business with your successor, the archbishop of Savannah.

You said, if I remember correctly, that my language to the Nuntio is "intemperate." I have read the letter of several times during the year and, although I recognize that I am sometimes given to rhetorical overkill, I must say that I think the letter well represents my reaction to what you and he did in New Orleans. I think that what you did was not merely a mistake; it was outrageous. I think it falls in line with the even more objectionable behavior of Cardinal Hamer. I hope the like does not happen again, although my hope is dim.

Secondly, I wonder still about the possibility of conversation when moral perceptions differ so radically. I *hope* that the difference doesn't mean that we do (metaphorically, figuratively, not literally) belong to different churches. But it means at least that the abyss is great, and from occurrences of the past two years, I conclude that it is getting greater. I refer not merely to my own admittedly volatile emotions, but to the real and deepening static between many of America's theologians and the hierarchy.

To give you an example, precisely because of my own deeply felt opposition to abortion, I find it very difficult to speak about it with Dan and Marjorie Maguire. That is a problem the price for which the Maguires, the American theologians and the American church will go on paying. The same is true between theologians and bishops, perhaps. In effect, who among the bishops is talking to Dan and Marjorie? To whom do they speak? I don't think there is a conversation going on, nor in many other cases and questions that affect the life of the church. I don't think we are doing an important part of our job. You people are not doing any better than we are, and our responsibility for it may even be less than yours.

I wrote to the *Nuntio* as I did because I thought he probably rarely gets spoken to directly and with some feeling and conviction about the way he and Rome behave. I did communicate my views to Cardinal Hamer in the same vein, and thought it responsible to give the Nuntio a dose of the upset and anger he aroused in some of us. Politically my judgment might better have been kept to myself and silence maintained. Or I might have sent a more diplomatic letter, masking my reaction. But I did what I thought best to achieve what I thought needed achieving, that is, informing him that I think he has well exceeded the minimal bounds of public charity expected of a bishop and that he would do well to think about that.

Finally, I enclose a copy of my presidential address to the 200 theologians who met at Xavier University in May. You will not agree with it, I am sure, but you know what some of us think and feel about Rome's views and policies. It expresses the convictions of only one person, to be sure, and you should not take it to represent most theologians. But I do hope you will take it as seriously as it is meant, and I do hope the American bishops will address the problem constructively and soon.

Cordially,

William M. Shea
The University of South Florida

Appendix 12.

St. Margaret of Scotland Parish Council Letter to Justin Rigali, the Archbishop of St. Louis

Dear Archbishop Rigali,

As members of Saint Margaret of Scotland Parish Council, we have discussed and considered the recent scandal involving priests abusing minors. Whether such behavior occurs in Saint Louis, Boston, Kansas City, or in other nations, the Body of Christ is wounded. Those wounds were magnified at times by the Church hierarchy's reluctance to respond to those crimes in an effective way. Now, revelations have forced the bishops of the Church to examine the situation, create new policies and review old ones, in an attempt to rectify the past wrongs. This is a good first step, and we applaud the bishops.

Now we are writing to ask you to consider some further changes, some of which are within your authority as our Ordinary of this diocese, and some of which we know must be decided by the larger Church.

- We would like your assurance that the new policies set forth in our Archdiocese will no longer allow a priest accused of a crime to be cloaked in secrecy—especially if the crime is the sexual abuse of a minor. Secrecy in these matters not only adds to shame but, more importantly, perpetuates future abuse. No priest should ever again be allowed to hide behind the Church's decision to handle these wrongdoings within the church system
- We urge you to allow the police and others who are trained investigators handle these matters in a professional manner. This step of using legal processes and standards to judge criminal offenses would be a meaningful first step to protect our children.

- Further, we urge you to request any other priests with abusive background to step forward so that the Church and community can settle this issue in a timely fashion.
- Moreover, we request that the Archdiocese examine celibacy for all priests, not just those few whose illness manifests itself in pedophilia. We urge you to support healthy relationships for its priests and for their mental health and to effectively respond to the many questions that face the priesthood. Some of these questions are:
    - How can celibacy be lived out in a healthy way and what are the signs when it is not? Who is there to spot a priest in need?
    - Are our priests required to have a spiritual director, therapist, or peer support group?
- Thus, we urge you to find ongoing ways to minister to our ministers. Some possible suggestions could include a review by experts, especially lay experts, of the educational process, standards, and selection of priests. Bishops need to listen to sociologists and psychologists and experts in human relations and sexuality.
- We also hope that the archdiocese can recognize the gifts of lay ministers and regard them as complementary to, not in competition with, our ordained ministers. While the laity have often been seen as a way to serve in the marketplace and in the world, it is now also time to recognize the contributions that trained lay ministers can offer within the Church. Our country currently has over 30,000 lay ministers as professional members of parish pastoral teams. Another 30,000 people are currently in lay ministry formation programs. We are called and gifted and wish to broaden the ways in which we can serve our Church
- We request that you consider providing more programs to train and support lay ministers. To that end, the archdiocese should invest more funds, personnel, and other resources into training and supporting ecclesial lay ministers.
- On a national basis, we request that when the U.S. Conference of Catholic Bishops meets this summer there will be willingness to utilize the studies regarding the priesthood and pedophilia. The bishops must take positive actions from these findings to deal with systemic causes of pedophilia in priests on a national, as well as local basis.
- We urge that the U. S. Bishops' Conference also create

standards used to determine the fitness of our seminarians. Rigorous standards of judgment of suitability and equally intense attempts at cultivating sexual maturity must be applied if we are to understand and prevent continuing incidents of abuse.

We believe that, as individuals, it is in times when we are most wounded, and aware of our need for God, that we are most able to listen to the Holy Spirit. We pray that this will be true for our Church (bishops, priests, religious, and laity) as well. It is time to come forward to confront the public in a way that would inspire confidence that the Church's leadership has the concern of its people and its priests at heart.

Sincerely,

William M. Shea, Chair
St. Margaret of Scotland Parish Council
[list names, officer title, and signatures]

Appendix 13.

A Report to St. Margaret's Parish Council on the Meeting with Archbishop Rigali, June 13, 2002

June 8, 2002. 7PM, Our Lady of the Cedars Auditorium, Archbishop Rigali appeared with a phalanx of archdiocesan personnel: Bishop Timothy Dolan, the director of communications, a child psychologist, a clinical social worker, a psychologist attached to Kenrick Seminary, the archdiocese's lawyer, and two other clergy diocesan administrators. About 300 lay Catholics from across the diocese, parish council members and church workers attended. The coffee was not up to Starbuck's standards and the cookies were an ordinary commercial variety. The presentations lasted about an hour. The question period lasted for two hours. About 30 questions were posed from the audience. The theme of the archbishop's opening address was "drawing life from death—the renewal of the church." What follows is a summary:

Rigali: A new policy has been formulated and implemented in the diocese and a policy will be so for the nation's dioceses by the bishops in Dallas. The money paid out to victims is not from diocesan budget but is from the church's investments, etc. The diocesan initiatives include the establishment of the Child Welfare and Safety Committee, education on the prevention of abuse diocese wide, and the complete extirpation of this evil. We must guard against false accusations. There must be a "radical recommitment" but not change in the church (*radical* recommitment would mean change in the church!)

Auxiliary Bishop Timothy Dolan: Keep some truths in mind. (1) The tremendous suffering of victims; (2) there is real anger at the bishops; (3) Contrition and regrets at our mistakes and we can't apologize too much for them; (3) there must be transparency—no more business as usual; (4) full cooperation with the civil law; (5) the clergy must rely on lay people—no more closed circle of the clergy. But there are falsehoods that must be refuted: (1) child abuse is NOT a Catholic issue, it's a societal issue; (2) the problem is NOT due to celibacy—other members of other professions and parents are also pedophiles; (3) bishops were not negligent or malicious—they acted on the best advice they had and the best evidence up to that time; (4) there was NO cover-up in the confidential agreements; (5) the vast majority of priests were faithful to celibacy; (6) this won't destroy the church—it will cleanse and purify it. The bishops' strategy is to keep doing what we do—nobody has taken better care of children; and get very pointed and precise in what must be changed. Finally, the church is "resilient."

Huber the lawyer: "Payments were made to meet needs detailed by the victims, generally for therapy, not to keep people quiet. Keeping people quiet was never the issue." But the signed agreement means no lawsuit (as is usual in such agreements), and so an agreement on confidentiality (not always if the other party doesn't want one).

Bishop Dolan: The charge of extensive homosexuality in seminaries is wildly exaggerated. The problem of homosexuality has not been ignored. Rigali distinguished between homosexual orientation and gay active life-style. The second is never to be tolerated.

Question from A School Sister of Notre Dame: language creates reality—clericalism is rooted in the language of vocation, in the formulation of prayers for it, and in the refusal to grant women equality. The narcissism and sense of entitlement of seminary life must go. There is homophobia in the seminaries. The priest perpetrator is himself a victim—how about hearing the story of the priests themselves? (a couple of people expressed reservations about dumping the perpetrators on the public)

A former SNAP member who himself was victim of abuse by a priest: saddened that the bishops will not meet with SNAP reps in Dallas. Now is the time for dialogue. Have we given the church over to lawyers? You may win legally but lose the soul of the church. Rigali responded that individual victims will be heard, but not those groups engaged in the SNAP lawsuit.

Question answered by Dr. Nancy Brown: When did we know that pedophilia is incurable? Beginning in 1995 in journals. The state then sought to set up a facility for permanent incarceration of pedophiles. Up to that time we didn't know that it doesn't stop with one victim, and even now we don't know if there will or won't be repeats.

Other attendees said the issue is power rather than sex, that the dialogue between bishops and people must continue, that they appreciate the presence of Rigali and Dolan. [It is clear from this group that Catholics are not cowed by bishops.]

My comment to the meeting and to the bishops: (1) be careful about false charges and injury done to innocent priests; (2) don't go on an anti-homosexual witch-hunt in the seminaries; (3) Cardinals Law and Eagan and the bishops who behaved irresponsibly in this matter of reassignment of abusers must resign or be retired.

Appendix 14.

Letters to a Saint Louis Bishop

William M. Shea
Professor of American Religion
Humanities Building
Saint Louis University
St. Louis, Missouri 63108

Numquam oblivisci

Bishop Michael Sheridan
The Catholic Center
4445 Lindell Blvd.
St. Louis, MO 63108

Dear Bishop Sheridan:

I gathered at the meeting between the Archbishop and the theologians concerning the mandate that you are representing the Archbishop in this matter, and so I forward to you a copy of a statement on the mandate that I posted for my colleagues on the College Theology Society list-serve and distributed to my colleagues here at SLU as well as to the president and the provost of the university. I hope you will pass it to on the Archbishop if that is appropriate.

This is not an easy matter for us, though I gathered from listening to you and from reading statements by other bishops that we should not take it to be so difficult. You will see from my statement that it is difficult indeed, and nothing that has been said or done has made it any less difficult. Granted that the bishops were put on the spot by Rome, the buck has been passed to us and we are now on the spot and must over the next few months figure out how we should respond to that spot. You will likely be receiving a good number of varied responses, some quite different from my own. I hope that we do not add one straw to the load you must already carry for the church.

I thought the meeting with the archbishop was educationally very profitable and I deeply appreciate his hospitality and am as always impressed by his strength of mind and soul. I hope that you will make further opportunities for such discussions. I am personally convinced that the connection and communication between the theologians and the local church are in very bad repair and need a lot of attention, not to say the relationship of the university and the church. Nothing could do that relationship more good than more personal contact with yourself and the archbishop. I look forward to meeting with you at any time on this or any other matter.

Cordially,

William M. Shea
Saint Louis University
Department of Theological Studies

William M. Shea
Professor of American Religion
Humanities Building
Saint Louis University
St. Louis, Missouri 63108

Numquam oblivisci

August 7, 2002

Michael J. Sheridan, Vicar General
4445 Lindell Boulevard
St. Louis MO 63108-2497

Dear Bishop Sheridan:

Thank you for your response to my note and short essay.

In response to your statement, "Nevertheless, this stance remains a mystery to me. I suspect I will never fully comprehend how a

Catholic teacher of Catholic theology at a Catholic university can be indifferent to the Church's *magisterium*," may I add the following:

1. The mystery may be deepened by the fact that theologians in universities and bishops are on two distinct, though interrelated, vocational tracks with remarkably different experiences on the way. Many things about bishops remain mysterious to others. We do have to get used to that distance and respect each other's knowledge and conscience, as I am sure you do.

2. I do not know any Catholic theologians who are indifferent to the *magisterium*. I don't think I wrote that anywhere, and I certainly do not think that theologians could or should be indifferent. Over all they have shown themselves to be the opposite of indifferent.

3. You should not take my statement and its reasoning to be common among theologians, here or elsewhere. As my essay points out, I do not consider myself a theologian though I do teach in a theology department. The fact that I therefore do not think the proposed mandate applies to me and even the fact that I think theologians should not have anything to do with it, does not mean I am indifferent to the *magisterium*. In my judgment the mandate is a mistaken policy decision on the part of the curia and will not help and may hinder solving the serious issue before us: the Catholic identity of the universities.

4. I do think that you and the archbishop have and should exercise a pastoral concern with the state of Catholicism among the university faculty and administration. I hope and pray that you will take that up, and not merely with theologians. I think you could begin with an information gathering and sharing discussion with interested faculty. I would certainly be interested in such a discussion. If you need any help in that regard, I offer my services.

Please give my best to Archbishop Rigali. Tell him again how much the people of St. Margaret of Scotland love Fr. Brown and pray for him. We are sad for his suffering yet proud to have such a splendid Christian as our priest.

Cordially,

William M. Shea

There was no response to this, and no meeting with the archbishop or other diocesan leaders ever took place. This is understandable given the fact that the theology faculty had told the archbishop in the meeting that Rome made a mistake in enforcing the Mandate and its procedure. Upon reflection, I doubt that either the archbishop or the bishop had any interest in what theologians had to say about the Mandate.

Appendix 15.

Two Responses on the Mandate

Copies of the following statement were sent to the president of Saint Louis University, Lawrence Biondi, S.J., and to Bishop Sheridan, Archbishop Rigali's delegate in charge of the Mandate, and was published in the theology department's on-line journal The Heithaus Forum.

From William M. Shea
To: Members of the College Theology Society
Re: the *Mandatum*

I want to communicate to you my view of the *Mandatum* to be offered by the bishops. I begin with a distinction that is important to me. It arises from my forty-year experience in theology and religion departments, and from my ongoing attempt to understand what I am and do.

There are several different kinds of Catholics working in theology and religion departments.

(A) There are "ecclesial" theologians who regard themselves as teaching and believing in "full communion" with the episcopal and papal *Magisterium*. Avery Dulles, S.J., is one fine example. Typically they would find disagreement with the teaching authority of the church to be an irresponsible act on their part.

(B) There are academic or critical theologians whose self-understanding is deeply conditioned by work in universities and colleges which have passed through the traumatic move to ecclesiastical independence of the late sixties and some of whom regard the Roman *Magisterium* as important but not absolutely and universally determinative of their belief, research and thinking. They find disagreement with the episcopal and papal *Magisterium* conceivable for adequate reasons. Most of my theologian friends are of this sort, whether they work in Catholic or other sorts of colleges and universities.

(C) There are what I call Catholic intellectuals, whether in theology departments or elsewhere in the university, who attempt to teach *about* the Catholic religion as it appears in various cultural forms (film, novel, documents of Vatican II, ritual, its history, etc.), who do not take responsibility for transmitting anything other than a sympathetic and accurate understanding of it, and who neither teach doctrine nor evangelize students. For their work agreement and disagreement with the episcopal and papal *Magisterium* is irrelevant. These are often characterized by a full *sacramental* communion with the church as a whole, and usually by communion in belief.

(D) A fourth group are those academic students of religion whose academic specialty is Catholicism or the Catholic Church as one religion among many, or languages or other cultures and religions, for whom communion with the church and the practice of religion is not a necessary underpinning of their academic work or responsibility in any sense. There are likely to be few of this sort, perhaps only in large doctoral departments where specialization to a high degree is a prime requisite.

I am in the third group, and it seems to me that no room for me and for those like me has been made in the now years' long discussion of *Ex corde ecclesiae* and of the *Mandatum*. There may be, and probably is, good reason why this is so, but until the problem presented by the third option is discussed explicitly and directly, we will not know. Although I am not pushing for a discussion of it now, it is well for readers to know that I regard myself not as a theologian but as a Catholic intellectual. I can then proceed to discuss the mandate, counting on this background to preclude at least some confusion. The issues that are important to me are as follows:

1. I think that Theresa Moser (*Horizons*, 27/2) is correct on the proper reaction to the *Mandatum* by academic theologians: don't ask, and send it back respectfully if a bishop sends it. Canonical reception is the key. In no way should this bad law and procedure be allowed to become practice in universities. By accepting the mandate theologians gain nothing for their work in the university, and they stand to lose by it. Nor do the universities gain by it. Only if theology is understood the way many bishops and Cardinal Ratzinger understand it: as a faithful participation in the bishops' tasks of

evangelization and catechesis does the mandate make any *theologi-cal* or *religious* sense. Even then it adds nothing to anyone's practice of theology in the American university. Mandate or no, we will do what we have been doing. At the same time, the mandate received raises the question of the standing of theology as a discipline in the university, and the standing of the Catholic university in the current and common sense of the term.

2. The bishops maintain direct control over clerical and indirect control over male and female religious theologians whether there is a mandate or not. These classes of Catholics are already "juridically" linked to the bishops. They can be reprimanded and corrected, and even removed, at the discretion of their bishop or their religious superior. As an example, I recall that one Jesuit moral theologian was removed from our faculty four years ago by the local provincial with no reason given to him or to the department, and with no consultation whatever. As a department chairman, a colleague and a friend, I was deeply impressed by this event and am unlikely to forget it and its implications. But lay theologians (the growing class of theologians) and former priests and religious (a class of theologians now declining and soon to pass from the scene) are not under episcopal direction, and these are the people, perhaps, over whom the mandate is meant to gain a new juridical control and to whom the bishops wish to give or refuse approbation. But many of them will not accept either juridical control or approbation (whereas they might very well accept a proffered pastoral relationship and collaboration), and so in addition to the distinctions between clergy and laity in theology, and between those with personal tendencies to liberalism or conservatism in their theology and church life, the bishops will have added another distinction that is bound to have its effect in the departments: those who are publicly approved by their bishops and those who are not. The distinction will become increasingly important as time goes by, if in fact the mandate is received by even a sizable minority of academic theologians. Sooner or later the non-mandated will be excluded or driven out or allowed to die by attrition (the latter, if prudence wins out). Not only will some departments be split into two groups, but, depending on whether the mandate is made a condition for employment, so will universities and colleges. I do not think either the bishops or the universities will gain, and the universities will surely lose. The theologians have plenty of reason, theological as well as moral, to avoid the mandate trap and I hope they do so, not only for their own sake and for their institutions, but also for the bishops who appear to be pushed into something that many of them know by

instinct is a mistake. I believe that many of them still favor a strictly pastoral solution to the issue rather than a juridical one.

3. The bishops and the pope are correct: the problem faced by Catholic universities, and not the hierarchy alone, is the Catholic identity of the institutions. It is a thorny problem, providentially highlighted by the Holy Father, that has taken at least three decades to develop and will take decades of clear-headed action to resolve. The mandate doesn't appreciably help to solve this problem. The genuine resolution involves presidents and boards and administrations and faculties and bishops, all of whose eyes needed focusing on this question. While *Ex corde ecclesiae* addresses the real problem, and calls for a real solution, the canon and the mandate process address a minuscule part of it and do so badly. The Roman curia and the Pope had plenty of good advice in good time on the perils of issuing mandates to American university theologians, and chose to ignore it. The only more egregious example of hearing but not understanding in my memory is the CDF's miserable and foolish treatment of certain theologians.

4. The university in fact is made up of people who do not practice theology in any ecclesiastical sense, and they are untouched by the legislation, even those who, like me, work in theology departments but are not theologians *a la Ratzinger*. I, and the hundreds of faculty, staff and administrators at my university are effectively excluded from the small (less than twenty theologians), charmed circle of those whom the bishops and the Curia apparently see as the actors in the drama of saving Catholic higher education from its present peril of secularization.

For the last decade, our ecclesiastical leaders seem obsessed with theologians. When and how do they intend to address me and the rest of the university? Many of us are vitally interested in enhancing the Catholic identity of the university, and we, from faculty members to presidents, not the theologians alone, will determine the outcome. How can we help and how can we be helped? I hope that *Ex corde* is not their last word, their last call. The public silence of the bishops and the presidents on the question of their responsibility in strengthening Catholic identity is deafening. I hope the newly constituted Bishops and Presidents Committee works well and quickly, and even that is only one small step.

5. So, though I do not want or need a mandate, I and my sort, those Catholic intellectuals among faculty, staff and administrators, are

the key to the future. For good or ill I am neither an ecclesial (Avery Dulles) nor an academic (David Tracy) theologian. In 1964, when I decided to study at Columbia University rather than at Fordham, and philosophy of religion rather than theology, I removed myself from that lofty pursuit without being fully aware of what I was doing. When I arrived at Catholic University (1972) I soon recognized that the theologians were doing one thing and I another, though I was teaching in theology programs. Working comfortably at a state university for a decade (1980-91) helped clarify that difference. Though I teach as a Catholic, I do not teach *sacra doctrina* as St. Thomas called it. I teach about it often enough, but as a philosopher would, or an intellectual who claims no religious charism or mandate or share in the Magisterium. Although some of what I teach overlaps with what ecclesial and academic theologians teach, and so I might at times be mistaken for one, and while in the university I sometimes teach about Catholicism, I am in fact a Catholic who lives by his mouth and his pen, and even his slow wits, an intellectual who rejoices in his Catholicism but who wants as little as possible to do with the responsibilities of bishops, preachers, evangelists, ecclesial theologians et al. Some of my best friends are theologians. I like theologians and admire bishops and what they do, and I recognize the burden and glory in which they share, but it is not mine. I love teaching, I love students, I delight in my office with its northern exposure, my new Dell, and my books, and I find the pain of thinking and writing in the light of a good class dialogue or a published essay. I cherish the church and my participation in it. I want to go on doing my work until I can work no longer. I don't need or want a mandate. My academic responsibilities are more than enough for me. I will cling to God's gift to me, to my own vocation, and stay away from full communion. The mandate is no gift of God to me, His Holiness and Cardinal Ratzinger and the American bishops notwithstanding.

The bishops' statement to the effect that the acceptance of a mandate means only that I do not teach as Catholic doctrine what is not, and teach correctly what is Catholic doctrine when in fact I teach it. Of course. What responsible professor would not? This is an excessively modest meaning for a weighty term such as "full communion." For myself, I do believe that bishops think that people who teach in theology departments *must* teach Catholic truth as true to people who *should* believe it. My job, as I understand it, is to teach undergraduates about religion and about Catholicism in particular, and thus to serve the university and the community.

I am, in other words, in full communion with the commonly received understanding of what a university professor in the American setting is to do. I do all of this to the best of my ability, and, according to some, I do it well. To all of this the mandate, and the approval and disapproval of the bishops and the Holy See are entirely adventitious. To me the Christian *kerygma* and *didache* are data to be understood, not judgments to be preached or inculcated. I do cherish the church and my archbishop. I think he is a fine bishop. But as an academic person, I take him to be another piece of the Grand Puzzle of Catholicism. I believe he values what I and other academics do, and takes it for granted; I certainly value what he does and take it for granted as a vital religious and social good. I even understand his desire to have me share in his mission, but I must respectfully decline. I do not think that the university is or should be part of the catechetical mission of church. I know I should not.

7. Finally, I very much appreciate the contributions of my colleagues and friends across the country to our CTS list-serve. I have often paid them the compliment of downloading. I do hope we can continue our exchange without the sarcasm and occasional snippiness I have come across in the past few months. If even a *discussion* of the mandate cheapens us, imagine what may happen when it goes into effect. I hope nothing I have written here lacks respect for the bishops and my own bishop, for all of whom I have due religious and intellectual regard, but at the same time I hope that the ways of dealing with one another that in the past have done our relationship damage will not haunt us. The hope I have for both the university and the church is that we can follow the words of Jesus about the exercise of authority among the Gentiles (Mt 20:25ff).

Letter from Professor Francis W. Nichols to the Archbishop of St. Louis, Regarding the Mandatum.

A colleague at SLU explains to the Archbishop why he rejected the invitation to apply for a Mandatum.

January 30, 2003

Archbishop Justin Rigali
4445 Lindell Boulevard
St. Louis, MO 63108-2497

Dear Archbishop Rigali,

Thank you for your kind invitation to request a formal *mandatum* as a Catholic teacher of theology here at Saint Louis University. I and the rest of the theology faculty here support your concern and that of the Holy See, along with that of all the other American bishops and Catholic theologians, for the preservation and promotion of the Catholic character of this and all the other American Catholic colleges and universities. However, as you of course understand, the administrations and theological faculties of many American Catholic colleges and universities have, and have had for many years, very serious worries about the canonical implementation of *Ex corde ecclesiae* in the United States. Since I share these concerns, I am sorry to have to tell you that I do not feel it would be prudent for me to formally request this *mandatum*. Since this response might disappoint you, and, as it might be open to unfortunate misunderstandings, please permit me to express my reasons briefly.

First, I and others are concerned that this procedure might lead to troubling legal entanglements for the archdiocese, the university, and individual Catholic theologians. Some legal authorities discount these problems; others disagree. In a litigious environment, it does not seem difficult to imagine situations where individuals or groups unhappy with the Catholic Church, with Saint Louis University, or with a particular theologian might make an issue of this.

The American bishops insist that a *mandatum* implies no "appointment, authorization, delegation, or approbation." Doesn't that come close to claiming that a *mandatum* means nothing? Doesn't "formal acknowledgement" that a theologian teaches "within the full communion of the Catholic Church" imply some sort of guarantee? It is, after all a formal legal requirement in Church law. Doesn't it have a legal effect?

Second, the phrase "teaching in full communion with the Church" seems threatening and obscure. Though your letter and comments of other bishops have been very generous and understanding about the legitimate freedom and creative space granted to Catholic theologians, I am not so sure that the lawgiver and other interpreters of the law are likely to be so accommodating. The Sacred Congregation for the Doctrine of the Faith has in recent years enunciated a novel theory: that there is a category of magisterial teaching which is not formally defined as part of the deposit of faith but which is to be "firmly held." That is, there are non-infallible teachings that are not to be questioned, not even to be further discussed. Many Catholic theologians find these claims difficult to understand. Not a few questions that come up in courses I teach seem to touch on these areas.

Third, the promise to teach "authentic Catholic doctrine and to refrain from putting forth as *Catholic teaching* anything contrary to the magisterium" is puzzling. It would clearly be gross incompetence for any theologian, Catholic or not, to violate that expectation. When a Catholic professor of theology proposes interpretations of, or difficulties involved with, or alternative formulations or understandings of received Catholic doctrines, a responsible teacher would also be careful to accurately explain the present position of the Roman magisterium. Why would a Catholic theologian be asked to promise not to be a bad teacher? I myself am always careful to alert students about tensions between authentic magisterial teachings and differing theological opinions.

Fourth, I feel that the imposition of this *mandatum* on American Catholic college and university theologians will sow seeds of discord within our own theological faculty and among American Catholic theologians generally. I fear this discord will also spread to the Catholic community at large. I am thinking of the antinomies introduced between those eligible for a *mandatum* and those who are not, between those who request one and those who feel they should not, between those who receive one and those who do not.

I also think it is naïve to imagine that there will not be persons and organizations who will rate Catholic colleges and universities according to the quantity of *mandatum*-bearing theologians they employ. They will be inclined to assert that some obviously Catholic colleges and universities are not actually Catholic. In fact, it is hard to understand how the implementation of this public law of the Church would not have public consequences. Indeed, one would suppose that the *mandatum* has been imposed precisely to ensure a public effect.

Fifth, the history of the Church and my own personal experience seem to caution against attempting to ensure doctrinal fidelity by means of oaths and legal promises like this. I have been a student of the history of Jansenism for some years now. Part of the noxious consequences for the Church in that centuries-long dispute seem [sic] to stem from a misguided imposition of oaths and promises that mutated into endless and futile legal and theological machinations. In addition, my personal experience has been that I myself, though never a cleric, have been asked to take the old Anti-Modernist oath twice in connection with the reception of ecclesiastical theological degrees. This oath, as theological development unfolded in the course of the twentieth century, became increasingly problematic. It seemed to insist on theses that had become almost impossible to reconcile with contemporary understandings of scripture and tradition. Indeed, they seemed to be in conflict with what my own Lateran University teachers taught. Still, these teachers renewed this oath each year, kneeling in the basilica of St. John Lateran before the rector of the university. I signed this oath with serious misgivings. I don't feel that I should repeat that behavior.

Though I am not asking for this *mandatum* for these and similar reasons, I would still like to assure you, Archbishop Rigali, that I do in fact teach Catholic theology in a very Catholic way. I know no other. I began teaching religion in Catholic high schools in 1952. Except for five years away for graduate theological studies, I have been teaching theology in Catholic institutions ever since. This is my thirty-fifth year here at Saint Louis University. Every course I teach, no matter what the formal topic, is an exercise in Catholic apologetics: giving a reason for the faith in which I live. Furthermore, I believe that the goal of *Ex corde ecclesiae* of preserving and promoting the Catholic character of Catholic universities is something that not only I but all the members of our theology department support in ways appropriate to their several academic specialties and their own specific religious affiliations. If I and others have misgivings about this *mandatum* policy, it is not a disagreement about goals but only about means.

Thank you for your expression of appreciation and prayers for Saint Louis University. Be assured of our own support and prayers for the continued success of your apostolic ministry here in St. Louis. We continue to trust that our own work contributes to that ministry as well.

Sincerely in Christ,

Francis W. Nichols, Th.D.
Associate Professor
Saint Louis University

Bibliography

of some books that helped form my mind

Robert Bellah. *Religion in Human Evolution: From the Paleolithic to the Axial Age.* Harvard University Press, 2011.

Christopher Bellitto. *Renewing Christianity: A History of Church Reform from Day One to Vatican II.* Paulist Press, 2001.

Jason Berry. *Lead Us Not Into Temptation: Catholic Priests and the Sexual Abuse of Children.* New York: Doubleday, 1992.

_____. *Vows of Silence: The Abuse of Power in the Papacy of John Paul II.* NY: Free Press, 2004.

_____. *Render unto Rome: The Secret Life of Money in the Catholic Church.* NY: Crown Publishers, 2011.

Boston Globe Investigative Staff. *Betrayal. The Crisis in the Catholic Church.* Boston: Little, Brown & Co., 2003.

Jimmy Breslin. *The Church that Forgot Christ.* NY: Free Press, 2004.

Michael D'Antonio. *Mortal Sins: Sex, Crime and the Era of Catholic Scandal.* NY: St. Martin's Press, 2013.

Andrew Greeley. *Priests: A Calling in Crisis.* Chicago: University of Chicago Press, 2004.

Geoffrey Gros, Eamon McManus and Ann Riggs, *Introduction to Ecumenism.* NY: Paulist Press, 1998.

Dean Hoge, et al. *Young Adult Catholics: Religion in the Culture of Choice.* Notre Dame IN: University of Notre Dame Press, 2001.

_____. *The First Five years of the Priesthood: A Study of Newly Ordained Catholic Priests.* Collegeville MN: Liturgical Press, 2002.

Anthony Kemp. *The Estrangement of the Past.* New York: Oxford University Press, 1990.

Diarmaid MacCulloch. *Christianity: The First Three Thousand Years.* New York: Penguin Books, 2009.

John O'Malley, S.J. *What Happened at Vatican II?* Cambridge MA: Harvard University Press, 2008.

Jacob Neusner. *A Rabbi Talks with Jesus.* Kingston Ontario: McGill-Queens University Press, 2000. 2nd ed.

Mark Noll and Carolyn Nuystrom. *Is the Reformation Over? An Evangelical Assessment of Contemporary Roman Catholicism.* Grand Rapids: Baker Academic, 2008.

Michael Papesh. *Clerical Culture: Contradiction and Transformation.*

Collegeville MN: Liturgical Press, 2004.

Rodney Stark. *The Triumph of Christianity.* NY: Harper One, 2011.

Francis A. Sullivan, S.J. *Teaching Authority in the Catholic Church.* NY: Paulist Press, 1983.

_____. *From Apostles to Bishops: The Development of the Episcopacy in the Early Church.* NY: Newman Press, 2001.

Garry Wills. *Papal Sins: Structures of Deceit in the Papacy.* NY: Doubleday, 2000.

_____. *Why I am a Catholic.* NY: Houghton Mifflin Co., 2003

_____. *Why Priests? A Failed Tradition.* NY: Penguin, 2013.

OTHER ANAPHORA LITERARY PRESS TITLES

Film Theory and Modern Art
Editor: Anna Faktorovich

Interview with Larry Niven
Editor: Anna Faktorovich

Dragonflies in the Cowburbs
Donelle Dreese

Domestic Subversive
Roberta Salper

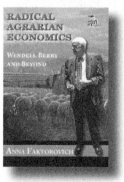

Radical Agrarian Economics
Anna Faktorovich

Fajitas and Beer Convention
Roger Rodriguez

Spirit of Tabasco
Richard Diedrichs

Skating in Concord
Jean LeBlanc

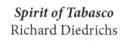

CPSIA information can be obtained at www.ICGtesting.com
Printed in the USA
BVOW08s1917270716

457091BV00001B/36/P